# RSKY BZNS

# *RSKY BZNS*

## PAUL ILLIDGE

Published by New English Review Press
a subsidiary of World Encounter Institute
PO Box 158397
Nashville, Tennessee 37215
&
27 Old Gloucester Street
London, England, WC1N 3AX


Cover Art and Design by Kendra Mallock


ISBN: 978-1-943003-61-7

First Edition

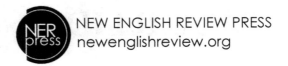

NEW ENGLISH REVIEW PRESS
newenglishreview.org

*To my father John Milton Illidge (1923 – 1994), a quiet, gentle man who took me to the library with him as a boy and taught me to love books.*

*The fraudulence paradox was that the more time and effort you put into trying to appear impressive or attractive to other people, the less impressive or attractive you felt inside.*

—David Foster Wallace, *Oblivion*

# Contents

# OPEN HOUSE

JOHN WAS UP EARLY. In the best of moods, he had shaved, showered and dressed by 6:30. Karen came out of the bathroom in her white terry robe after her shower as he was leaving the room. Stepping over, he leaned down, gave her a lingering kiss. She pressed her body into his. "—Uh-uh," he said, backing away. "The suit!" They laughed, he gave her bottom a pat and went out.

Entering the kitchen, the fluorescents flickering to life, he noticed the business envelope with his name on it on the counter beside the portable phone. Karen had put it there before going to bed, reminding him not to forget it in the morning. He wouldn't, but he'd wait for her to give it to him. That always worked best.

He switched the coffeemaker on, Kenya AA beans, dark roasted, Karen's favourite brew. He sliced honeydew melon, bananas, oranges and strawberries then poured a bowl of granola for each of them. The radio on, soft rock, he left the kitchen to go to the front door and pick up the morning editions of the *Toronto Star* and the *National Post*, which Karen took with her to work. John would buy the *Globe and Mail* at some point in the day, read the business section and the *Financial Post*, and Tuesday through Friday the *New York Times* and the *Wall Street Journal*.

They talked while they ate, about an anniversary documentary they'd watched last night on the sinking of the Titanic one hundred years ago. John kidded Karen about their relationship having avoided the icebergs that sink so many. And speaking of anniversaries, he added that it was exactly six months since the Valentine's dating site meeting of RSKY BZNS and BLYTHE SPIRIT9 had taken place.

A headlong romance neither thought possible at this stage of their lives (they were both fifty-six), Karen had thrown her usual caution to the wind and let herself fall for this tall, dark, self-assured and charming man who had just enough of the bad-boy about him to suit her comfort level. His moving into her house after they'd been seeing each other for three months had seemed like the natural thing to do.

Her friends were instant fans of John's; her family was too. He was handsome, humorous, hard-working and happy-go-lucky. To their minds, he was the best thing that had happened to Karen since her divorce eleven years ago. He had brought joy back into her life again.

As they were getting ready to leave, John asked if she wanted to do something special that night to celebrate their six months. Karen hesitated, ruminating as if something of great weight was on her mind.

— "Of course we should!" she blurted suddenly. It was a great idea. She could use cheering up, what with the various crises at work that had been getting her down. She apologized that she'd been so preoccupied by them. She honestly hadn't remembered that it had been six months since they met. John waited for her to finish putting her coat on then slipped an arm around her shoulder, gave her a hug and said not to worry. He was happy to do the remembering for both of them.

Karen was senior planner for the town of Milton, the fastest-growing municipality in Canada, a demanding, high-stress job that paid her $225,000 a year but which saw her bringing work home every night and on many a weekend.

Everything was so new at work these days, so fluid, moving so fast, but decisions had to be made in spite of the fact that the planning department was badly under-staffed, severely under-funded, and generally under-appreciated by her fellow bureaucrats, by politicians and by developers champing at the bit to start building.

John coming into her life changed all that. Right off the bat, he called her on what he termed her work-a-holicism, saying if she wanted a real relationship with him, either the weekend and weeknight work had to go, or he did; she couldn't have it both ways. He told her to make up her mind. She was living to work, rather than working to live. What was it going to be?

The decision turned out to be an easy one. Even with all she had on her hands at work, this was the most fulfilled Karen had ever felt in her life. Sometimes she had to pinch herself to prove it was really happening. With John she fully believed she'd found the love of her life, the soul mate that everyone talked about finding in a partner. Of course, his personal wealth, his homes in Miami, the Bahamas, London and New York didn't hurt, but even without that, his larger-than-life personality, his patience, humour and easy-going manner made him a significant catch, a fact that left her friends more jealous of Karen than they were willing to admit.

They came outside, Karen locking the front door, hurrying over to her silver Mercedes C 300 4Matic, a briefcase in each hand. (She'd had to break down and bring home some papers the night before.) John opened the passenger door for her, closed it then walked around the front of the car, a real estate sign on the front lawn of a house ten doors down catching his eye. Open House Today, 1:00 – 3:00.

With the car started, his seatbelt on, John shifted into reverse, was glancing in the rear-view mirror to begin backing out of the drive, when Karen held out to him the envelope that had been beside the phone. He'd forgotten it.

John took it, thanked her, leaned over and kissed her. "Let's make some money together, Blythe Spirit!" he said, tucking the certified check made out to Conquest Capital for $200,000 into the inside pocket of his suit jacket. "Come here," he said, a gentle hand behind her head, pulling her toward him. "There's nothing to worry about, okay?" He kissed her. She looked into his eyes. "You promise?" "Hope to die," he said, crossing his heart.

Driving west on the 401, rush-hour traffic moving east into Toronto, it was just twenty minutes to the municipal offices in Milton where Karen worked, twenty-five this morning since they'd stopped at a Starbucks drive-through so Karen, who'd left her thermos of Kenyan AA on the kitchen counter, could pick up her all-important second cup of coffee.

As he did every day, John let her off at the entrance to her building, telling her he'd think of something they could do that night. He'd surprise her.

He watched her go up the steps, waited till she turned and waved, waved back— he'd pick her up here at five— then drove out of the complex back to the Starbucks where he parked, took a screwdriver from the glove compartment, removed both license plates and, opening the trunk, put them in one plastic grocery bag before taking another set from a second grocery bag. After closing the trunk, he screwed the new plates on, picked up a coffee for the road and headed back to the highway in the Mercedes with its RSKY BZNS plates now attached for the thirty-minute drive to Toronto.

The branch of the bank where John kept his holding company accounts was on King Street, just east of Yonge at Toronto Street, adjacent to the King Edward Hotel. He deposited Karen's check into Conquest

Capital, then transferred the funds into his Medallion Capital account, and finally into J.J. (for John James) Holdings, the account into which he "squirreled away" funds for times when he had to "take to the mattresses," a phrase from *The Godfather*, his favourite movie, meaning when people are looking for you. He had a word with Giselle, the bank manager, the seventh he'd dealt with over his twenty-eight years at the bank, a small, unprepossessing branch, yet the fortunes of some of Toronto's wealthiest families were said to be kept there.

After a trim at the barber shop in the basement of the King Edward, he went upstairs to the news kiosk, bought his newspapers and read them while having a light breakfast in the cafe. He made some phone calls while having his coffee, checking some of the irons he had in the investment fire as he phrased it. Things had been slow to recover after the meltdown of 2008. The Madoff bust hadn't helped. More and more, deals that did come through, in some cases, weren't worth the effort that went into getting them. The situation wasn't desperate yet; Karen's check would keep the wolf from the door for several months, but in the meantime, he was going to have to work harder stirring up business. It was as simple as that. The beast had to be fed.

He drove up River Street, took the Bayview Extension north to Lawrence Avenue and turned off at the Granite Club, one of the city's more exclusive private social clubs, where John had been a member for eighteen years. The sports cafe on the second floor overlooking the outdoor tennis courts served as his ad hoc office several days a week. He had his own table in a corner by the window that faced the door, the way he preferred it for security purposes. Not that he had anything to worry about on that score right now, but old habits die hard.

He phoned Pfaff Motors in Newmarket to confirm that his new black Porsche 911 Turbo would be ready tomorrow as promised. The owner, Chris Pfaff, who had been personally looking after John's custom automotive needs for twenty-five years, assured him that it would. He could come in any time that was convenient.

Graham Wishart arrived for lunch at noon. Graham had been the pilot in the executive air service John operated out of the Toronto Island and Buttonville airports in the 1990s and early 2000s. Flying executives, celebrities and the wealthy up to their estate properties and cottages in the Muskokas and up and down the Georgian Bay shore. John was in a position now where he could buy a pair of used Cessnas and bring Aviation Capital Holdings to life again, maybe this coming summer if Graham didn't have anything else on. Graham didn't. And even if he had, he would have dropped it out of loyalty if not devotion to John, who had been the only one to give him a break and hire him after he'd done his two years less a day for sexually assaulting several dozen boys when he was head of music at Oakwood Collegiate Institute in west Toronto. John didn't care that Graham had a criminal record and was a registered sex offender. He'd done the time for his crime. He was a good pilot. When you were flying famous multimillionaires with high-powered lawyers around, that's all that mattered to John.

Graham pulled up the listings on his phone of Cessna 206s current-ly for sale in southern Ontario. There were three that Graham felt John wouldn't be wasting his time to take a look at. He agreed with John that the clientele was still there, and, in fact, had grown substantially with traf-fic congestion to the north, during the summer months, becoming such a nightmare. *Fifty-minutes instead of four hours and you're sitting on the dock having a cool drink* was still a hard-to-beat selling feature for the vacationing rich and famous.

After Graham left, John checked his laptop for messages on the var-ious dating sites he subscribed to. There were numerous new emails for RSKY BZNS. He didn't bother reading them. He did go to his LinkedIn page, however, and added Aviation Capital Holdings to his resume. John had found that LinkedIn was the first place women on dating sites went, when they learned your real name. To see what your job credentials were, and, even more important, what your financial status was likely to be.

John prided himself on a business pedigree that women seemed drawn to but that anyone with the least knowledge of the securities and investment business would recognize in a second that his numerous inter-national investment CEO and board of director profile was no more than cut-and-paste nonsense, one hundred percent ersatz: as fake as you could get. The irony for John was that the more unbelievably accomplished he made himself sound on his LinkedIn page, the more intensely certain kinds of women found themselves attracted to him: a man warning them in advance that he was risky business.

He left the Granite Club a little after one. The early afternoon west-bound traffic still light, it was coming on one forty-five when he reached Mississauga. He turned down Karen's street, went on past her house and, reaching the one with the for sale sign on the lawn having the open house, turned in the driveway.

The door opened as he walked up, the agent, a woman named Melanie Roberts stepping out, welcoming him to the open house with effusive mock formality, letting John precede her inside where she quickly shut the door and locked it—John with his lips on hers before she had fully turned around, the two of them undressing on the way upstairs to the master bedroom for some Open House sex.

This had started during the second open house. John had popped in during the first one six weeks earlier. It wasn't well attended. John stayed around to keep Melanie company. They hit it off. Went to dinner (Karen was away at a conference), and after a second dinner and a night of wild sex, they started seeing one another, evenings when Karen was tied up with work, and at open houses during the day. It was John who suggested Open House Sex. Add a little risk and adventure to the sexual occasion, the thrill of being caught *in flagrante delicto* made for what they both agreed were explosive results. They hadn't been caught yet, at least not quite. One time, a man came in the back door, which Melanie had forgotten was unlocked. John got dressed first, went downstairs and said the agent would be right down. He raved about the house, waited till Melanie arrived, thanked her for the tour, and said he'd be in touch about putting in an offer.

They were enjoying some post-climax cuddling when the doorbell rang. It took a moment to register, and when it did, they both started laughing. Melanie, throwing on her clothes, felt she should be the one to go. He could leave by the back door—the bell rang again. A last smooch amid laughter, she'd call him later, she went downstairs. John finished putting on his suit.

Melanie had no idea when she opened the door who Karen was. "Sorry to bother you," Karen said with a confused look, "but is that your black Mercedes in the driveway with the RSKY BZNS plates on it?"

# CHAPTER ONE

# FIFTY SHADES OF JOHN

S ATURDAY, SEPTEMBER 3RD. My forty-fifth birthday. I'm awaken-
ed by a phone call from my mother. No hearty felicitations on
my natal day, instead she tells me in a shaky voice that my father has died
during the night, complications from pneumonia. Apparently, many Alz-
heimer's patients die this way. She wonders if I can come over, my brother
John is. To help with *arrangements*.

No word on whether my other brother Peter and kid sister Judith
are heading over, I contact John and we drive to St. Catharines at a mean
speed of eighty-five miles per hour in his newest vehicle, a black BMW
E90 (his cars were always black), the new-car smell still fresh on the leather
upholstery, soft rock on the stereo, tinted windows. After the usual conversation about "the kiddies," as he always refers to my three children, he
updates me on his three daughters, whom he refers to as "Les Girls," adding somewhat incidentally that his wife Ellen had passed her latest cancer
screening *with flying colors*, at which point he segues into business mode and
reports, as if it was to be expected, that things at Credifinance Securities,
where he's been a registered representative and company director for three
years, are booming. The bigger news, though, is that he's been shifting
some of his work away from the trading desk and more into mergers and
acquisitions, leveraged buyouts, that sort of thing, where he says the real
money is.

"The profit margin on some of these deals is practically criminal."

"Mergers and acquisitions. Isn't that where you buy a company, fire a
bunch of employees in the paring down of expenses before you sell it at
twice what you paid for it?"

"No laws get broken if that's what you mean."

"There was a guilty tinge when you said *practically criminal.*"

"Figure of speech."

We drive in silence for a few minutes.

The Beatles' "A Day in the Life" builds toward its explosive final crescendo. John lowers the volume, changes the channel and the subject.

"You know how much I'm worth right now?"

I pause to make him think I'm actually calculating. Our father has just died and all he can talk about is his net worth—

"Five-million," I take a wild guess.

"*Five?*" He's insulted. "Try four times that."

"Twenty-million?"

"Twenty-two. But who's counting."

"Beats my pair of jacks."

"What?"

"I made sixty-five thousand dollars teaching high school last year, before tax. I'll never reach the million-dollar bracket in my lifetime. I'm happy with that."

"I'm just saying."

"I know what you're saying. You're rich, or at least richer than I'll ever be, and you want to crow about it. I get that. It doesn't make any difference to me one way or another.

"You're good at making money, John. You always have been. I'm happy for your success. Just as long as you're being honest in what you're doing. It's a long road. Things can catch up with you."

No reaction, eyes on the road, the Eagles starting "Hotel California" on the radio, he reaches for the dial, turns up the volume. *On a dark desert highway, cool wind in my hair . . .*

Once business is taken care of at the funeral home—my father to be cremated, his ashes deposited in the columbarium at the church he and my mother attended, where in a few weeks we'll hold a memorial service.

We go to lunch at *Glendennings*, the restaurant where my dad in late-Alzheimer's confusion took the linen tablecloth a year ago and blew his nose into it. A strange memory, it perks my mother up, the three of us laugh thinking about it, then talk about other inimitable moments we'd had with him in his pre-Alzheimer years, some of which I'll include in the eulogy I'll deliver at his funeral.

My mother's voice is strained, the rasp drier than usual. Along with the tremor in her hands and the anxious licking of lips, it's a sign she hasn't taken her medication today, or perhaps for a few days.

After dessert, while we're having coffee, she brings out a small Tiffany

Blue jewellery box, opens it and takes out the two halves of a gold wedding ring I recognize as my father's. She explains that the hospital staff had to cut it to get it off his finger. With a quiet reverence she says she thought we might like to have them. She passes each of us our half, closes the jewellery box and puts it back in her purse.

When John drops me off back in Toronto, he asks if I want his half of the ring. If I don't, he's going to throw it out.

I tell him I'll take it. That if he decides he wants it back later on, he'll know where to find it. We laugh.

"I don't think we have to worry about that," he says, dropping his half into my palm.

Over the next three years, he sells his third house and moves Ellen and the girls into their fourth, a 5,500 square-foot home off Yonge Boulevard overlooking the picturesque Don River valley. Only two years old, it had been custom built for a doctor who was relocating to Vancouver. John apparently heard the news from a neighbour, the new house being only two blocks from his current one. The property was one of several in upscale North Toronto that he'd been "keeping his eye on." He got in touch with Rosie his real estate agent, had her find out what the asking price was likely to be when the house went up for sale. She arranged for him to meet the owner two days later, the doctor only too happy to accept John's lower offer because, besides sparing him the disruptive real estate process (he too had three children and a working wife), John had made a point of slipping him fifty thousand dollars in cash as a deposit.

After they'd moved in, Ellen joked about the irony of him wanting a house so badly when he was so seldom home, run off his feet, stirring up new business for Credifinance Securities in Montreal, New York, London, Dubai. Bigger and better stock deals, more mergers, more acquisitions, more leveraged buyouts, according to him, the few times I was able to reach him to update him on my mother's situation. Whenever he was home in Toronto, he was out schmoozing with prospective clients most nights of the week, staying over at downtown hotels as far as anyone knew, shaving and showering at the Cambridge Club in the morning, going into the office just before the market opened. He'd attend family birthdays and special occasions, but otherwise he was a phantom on the home and family front. There was no more socializing with old friends. He lived almost exclusively in the *World of John*, a world to which no one else had access.

He bought Ellen's father's cottage, one that he'd owned since the 1940s with three old friends from university who agreed to the sale since the cottage would be staying within the group of friends. After one summer, he sold it for more than he'd paid for it, and bought a bigger cottage on a "better lake" that was closer to Toronto. A thunderstorm hit the area Labour Day night a year later. Lightning struck the boathouse and it burnt down. Taking it as an omen (I was sure it was, having stayed in the apartment above the boathouse the night before), John took the insurance money, sold the place and bought a bigger cottage on Lake of Bays in prestigious North Muskoka for more than what most people at the time were paying for a house.

My mother called me in November on what would have been my father's seventy-second birthday. It was Sunday; she'd been to church and, clearly having a manic episode, wanted me to know that the sermon that morning had been about fidelity—faithfulness—in all areas of life, one of Reverend McKinley's quotations on the topic from the Book of Proverbs: *Drink waters out of thine own cistern.* She paused for me to let the significance sink in. It didn't, and I told her she'd have to explain.

"So, you don't know?"

"Know what?"

"John is *running around* on Ellen, and has been for several years."

I made a point of sounding suitably shocked so as not to ruin the scoop (she liked being the first to break a story), but I had guessed as much long before. Not meaning to excuse it, just making my mother aware of business world realities, I said that I'd heard a lot of that went on with the high pressures in the investment industry. I asked her how she had come to know— if it was from a reliable source. *Very* reliable apparently: Ellen had confided in her cleaning lady, Victoria, one day when Victoria asked why she wasn't seeing Mr. John around much anymore. Victoria also cleaned for my mother's good friend Eunice Bennett, who passed on the news that set my mother off, bothered more by word spreading among her friends than by the philandering itself and his neglect of Ellen and the girls.

Not long after, Ellen confronted him. He confessed that he was having an early mid-life crisis. He'd gone from school right into marriage, to a career-path job, to having three kids, the responsibilities, the expectations, the daily grind—basically living to work rather than working to live. He couldn't be home every night for dinner with the kids as Ellen wanted. (They'd argued about that regularly.) He told Ellen straight out that he just wasn't that person anymore, now that he was a company director and the job required him to bring in new business. He brought in a lot and was making the money necessary to keep up the lifestyle to which she and the girls had become accustomed. He needed to work pretty much all the time. It was getting to him, and he was burning out. He needed some space, some freedom, some time to do a few of the things he hadn't done before getting married. *Get a handle on what he was making of his life.* Ellen would just have to adjust her expectations, whatever they were. Like he said, he wasn't a nine-to-five kind of father or husband. Divorce? He didn't necessarily think so. He just needed time to figure some things out. He'd pop in here and there to pick up his mail, the monthly bills and some clothes. Be available on weekends and social occasions as much as possible, but otherwise, he'd be doing his own thing, and Ellen and the girls could do theirs. It would be good for everybody for him to *get things out of his system and move on*—which Ellen naturally took to mean *on from her and the girls*.

The hurtful tirade was about as defensive, demeaning and manipulative as you could get, but all Ellen could think was, "Get what things out of his system? Weren't there things she wanted to get out of her system too? What was she supposed to do, release him from his obligations and responsibilities as a husband and father so he could live the salad days she never knew he wanted to have? And worse, what choice did she have?" Telling her off the bat that this is what he intended to do was as much as saying there was nothing she could do or say to stop him, so she shouldn't bother trying.

He took up mixed beach volleyball on summer nights in front of the Balmy Beach Club, the club where he'd paddled and played beach volleyball when he was a teenager. At forty-three, he was about ten years older than most of the other players, but he was there for the same reasons as most: to meet people. Plus, there was windsurfing further west at Ashbridge's Bay, which John decided to take up, a catch for those women (he said there was no shortage of them) doing much the same thing as he was: windsurfing skills were incidental to the attraction.

There was a succession of girlfriends, shopping excursions with the luckier ones to New York, Miami and London, women responsive to what we'd come to call the *Fifty Shades of Grey* aura that John exuded: the wealthy bad boy with all the right lines and a take-a-walk-on-the-wild-side swagger that was hard for women to resist if he was coming on to them. Whether it was doing any good at helping him to find himself was hard to say. He certainly revelled in being single again or, as his detractors maintained (and there was no shortage of them among his and Ellen's friends), entering second childhood. Shirts custom made in Hong Kong, shoes by Bonafè, suits by Giorgio Armani or bespoke Gieves & Hawkes at No. 1 Savile Row in London, luxury European cars bought or leased from Pfaff Motors, a high-end auto dealership just north of Toronto. At one point, I counted six different high-end vehicles he was driving, all black, all foreign-made, his vanity license plate reserved for the latest Porsche, a 911 Turbo he called *RSKY BZNS*. With five hundred and eighty horsepower, John liked to boast it could go from zero to sixty miles per hour in just two point nine seconds. When I asked him if he'd ever done that, he said, "No, but I've come close." Was it the speed or the power that he liked most? I once asked him. Neither: it was the freedom.

The same freedom that led him to obtain his pilot's license, buy two small Cessna 206 airplanes and create Aviation Capital Holdings, an executive air service for rich people and celebrities, flying them north from Toronto to and from their Muskoka cottages, vacations, business meetings, romantic getaways. If I wanted, he could put copies of my screenplays on the seats of the planes for Hollywood types to read during the flight. Some of the celebrity names included Tom Hanks, Cindy Crawford, Martin Short, Steven Spielberg.

"You never know where possibility lies," he told me in reference to this latest venture, inveterately optimistic as always, not a doubt in his mind but that the aviation business would be a roaring success. In no time, his pilot and he were flying stars to Muskoka vacationland, or so he said. The business was literally taking off, he joked. He never did ask for any of my screenplays. Once when I asked him how much he charged Spielberg for the two-hour ride to his Muskoka mansion, John answered vaguely: "It varies," and then changed the topic of conversation.

In February 1996, at my mother's request, I went downtown to see him. She hadn't heard from John in a while, nearly nine months, and she was anxious to find out why. She worried that something might be amiss with her money; that his company Credifinance might have been in trouble, her investment nest egg lost.

I hadn't heard from him in a while myself, which was unusual. I couldn't be sure that I'd get much information from him; John was hard to read about such things, holding his cards close to his chest always. I didn't want to push it, to seem like I was sticking my nose in business that wasn't mine. It was really a matter between him and my mother; he'd take my involvement as interference and it would only make the situation worse. He would clam right up thinking I was accusing him of not being above board with Bev. From the time my mother took power of attorney away from me and gave it to John, because he knew more about investment, he had always harboured suspicions that I resented him having access to her money. The truth was, I didn't; I knew the day my mother told me of her decision that she would never see her money again.

I met him at Credifinance at five o'clock, in someone else's office several down from his own, which was filled with packed and taped boxes, nothing on the walls, the desk bare except for a landline telephone. The trading day was over but he was rushed. There weren't too many people around. He cut me off as I was explaining the reason for my visit. He assured me Bev's portfolio was just fine, that she'd be receiving a check once he got up and rolling with his new brokerage. *New brokerage? That's right.* St. James Securities. He hoped to have it up and running in about six weeks. The office was on King Street, he'd hired his people, he'd raised the capital, and was now going to be making the big money, but on his own terms this time round. He wasn't able to do that at Credifinance, since it had come to light that someone was *taking money out the back door.* Profits had fallen. John was bailing out while he could. Besides, it was time to move on. He'd worked at Credifinance for five years; what he needed was to be his own boss at this point in his career. Spread his wings, fly higher than he'd been able to in the environment at Credifinance, which he was finding completely stifling.

It took longer than six weeks, of course, but at the end of May, St. James Securities Inc. (James was John's middle name) opened for business. John was chief executive officer, a director, and the major shareholder of St. James Holdings, the parent company of St. James Securities.

Forty-three and running his own brokerage, now he was ready to make some real money.

# CHAPTER TWO

# CAVEAT EMPTOR

O NE MORNING IN EARLY JUNE, three years after starting St. James Securities Inc., Danny Dietrich, a friend of mine from university, a jack of all trades when it came to finance and investment (a chartered accountant as well as a securities lawyer), called me up and asked if we could get together that afternoon for a drink. He had some news about John. Sort of urgent. A friend of ours named McLanahan, who worked in legal affairs at the Securities Commission and was familiar with John's growing reputation as a lone wolf, rogue trader, possible Ponzi schemer—as in Bernie Madoff, Jordan Belfort *Wolf of Wall Street* Ponzi scheming—had offered to find out if John's behaviour had reached a level where the Securities Commission would become involved.

At two-thirty, I met him at *Brown's*, a midtown bistro just off Yonge Street south of St. Clair, well away from the downtown financial district. Most of the lunch crowd had left since the restaurant closed at three—not a problem according to Danny, since what he had to show me was due back at McLanahan's office by four o'clock.

We took a table by the window that overlooked Woodlawn Avenue, ordered drinks, waited for them to arrive, at which point Danny handed our server fifty dollars, saying he hoped it was all right if we stayed a little after three to finish up some business. (A wide smile as she took the money, our server said it was just fine.)

He took an interoffice Kraft envelope marked *Confidential* from his attaché, undid the string and withdrew a document that looked to be ten or twelve pages. "McLanahan got wind of this report by the Investment Dealers Association for the Securities Commission legal department and felt this was something we might want to look over."

24

"Have you?"

"Haven't had time." He scanned the first page. "It's an investigation report from the Investment Dealers Association. They've been reviewing John's industry conduct from 1990 until now in response to client complaints of unauthorized activity in their accounts. Looks as if they're considering penalties in connection with his personal trading."

"Unauthorized activity meaning what exactly?"

"Making trades with investor accounts where he's required to have the client's permission before buying or selling. It contravenes the Association's by-laws to act on his own. They call it in the report 'actions unbecoming and detrimental to the public interest.' His present behaviour is, quote, 'Being evaluated in light of a previous penalty on record with the Commission: there had been a disciplinary hearing in August 1996 with respect to breaches of I.D.A. by-laws while John was working at Credifinance Securities.' Did you know anything about that?"

"How would I know about it? It's not like he'd call me to let me know he was being investigated for wrongdoing. It is wrongdoing, isn't it?"

"A little more than that." He read: "Failing to give client accounts priority over accounts in which he had a personal interest. Instructing staff to change bond prices held in client accounts, which caused the margin requirements for client accounts to be understated." A brokerage, he explained, has to have the cash or assets on hand to back up trades that it makes through loans from the company. "There's nothing criminal here per se, at least not yet. Some brokerages exceed margin requirements unintentionally on occasion. Those that do so on a regular basis get noticed, caught and disciplined by the Investment Dealers Association, or in more serious cases, the Securities Commission."

"But he's in fraud territory . . ."

"Well in. Changing bond or stock prices in client accounts. Lying about asset margin in client accounts. They're serious fraud because they were done with intent."

"Meaning?"

"They were deliberate. Not accidents, not oversights. The reason fraud is seldom if ever prosecuted is because you have to prove there was a clear intent to commit fraud. Hard evidence. A paper trail. Facts that can be adduced—produced as evidence—at trial. The first instruction in the *How-To-Be-A-Fraud* handbook is don't leave a paper trail."

"Will he be prosecuted?"

"That's the thing. The investment industry is self-policing. If the I.D.A. or the Securities Commission find somebody playing loose with the agreed-upon rules, the trader can only be disciplined. Compliance is the goal, not punishment. It's bad for business."

He took a sip of his drink then turned back to the report: "The disciplinary action as a partner and company director at Credifinance," he read, "was to take the form of a $30,000 fine; John was to agree to the statement of facts, agree to rewrite the Securities Institute's Partners, Directors and Senior Officers Qualifying Examination, and he was to be prohibited from being approved by the I.D.A. as a partner, director or officer of a securities company until he passed the re-qualifying exam; if he did, the prohibition would remain in place for six months afterwards."

"A slap on the wrist. No real enforcement."

"Now he's being investigated for operating the same way at St. James Securities for the last two years as he did at Credifinance. This time, however, the 'contraventions' are considerably more serious in that, he quoted—'John Illidge has again failed to properly designate his own accounts as separate from his clients' accounts, thus obscuring the line between his personal trading activity and St. James client activity.'" Danny read ahead quickly. "'Further, in client account documentation, Illidge repeatedly indicated his own personal address as being the client's address. He conducted transactions in various client and personal accounts without benefit to those clients or to St. James. For at least four securities, he fixed prices that didn't represent fair market price for those securities, securities which John was cross-trading between client, non-client and St. James Securities accounts. Three of these securities were sometimes held in large volumes in various St. James Securities accounts. The effect of these contrived prices was, at times, to overstate St. James's capital position and unduly favour him in the cross-trades.' Does any of this make sense?"

"Perfect sense. He's ripping off his clients and his own company. The clients I can understand, but why rob from your own company?"

"Brokerages operate using other people's money. Client funds are effectively the company."

"He talked about someone *taking money out the back door* at Credifinance."

"That's the phrase they use."

The ice had melted in my Scotch and soda. I took a sip. I noticed Danny was only about halfway through the report.

"There's more?"

"He's been trading," Danny went on, "in what we call registered debentures—unsecured bonds, sold on credit rather than collateral assets, meaning they weren't eligible to be traded. They call it '*acting outside the bounds of good business.*'" Danny continued reading, "'Illidge had made transactions between St. James's own accounts and the accounts of numerous companies he controlled, unduly prejudicing St. James's capital position—i.e., leaving it with insufficient company cash to back up its trades. For several months, he made trades in one company client account before the company had been legally incorporated. He purchased securities for many cash accounts in which there were no funds; and for prolonged periods of time, he traded in many accounts without sufficient or with zero margin. Besides failing to obtain and complete necessary legal documents for many of the company's client accounts, he also failed to question documents purportedly signed by clients that appeared, on the face of it, to be forgeries.'"

"It's quite a litany. And all this falls under the I.D.A. category of *conduct unbecoming an investment dealer?* When he's stolen people's money and won't give it back to them, and maybe never have to?"

"Now, now," he kidded. "Nobody said anything about stealing. What seems to have triggered this new investigation has to do with a St. James client known as B.S., a client of John's since the early 1990s, when he was with Credifinance Securities. She was introduced to him by a mutual friend. He persuaded her to move her investment accounts to Credifinance to be personally handled by him. Initially B.S., who was in her mid-seventies at the time, provided John with approximately $500,000 for investment purposes, which represented a fair portion of her available liquid assets. When John transferred to St. James Securities in 1996, B.S.'s investment accounts were transferred to St. James as well. From 1997 to this past March, there were more and more transactions in B.S.'s accounts, where John exercised his personal discretion without her written authorization, and without the accounts having been approved as discretionary. The Investment Dealers Association seemed to have got wind of what he was doing and felt it warranted an investigation."

He turned to a new page and continued reading.

"'Pursuant to which, investigators determined that in February 1998, Illidge went further and opened fake corporate client accounts in the name of an estate trust called Provident United that had been terminated, listing particular individuals as clients. It turned out that neither those individuals, nor any corporation controlled by those individuals, had ever opened accounts at St. James Securities. These accounts from an estate trust that had ceased to exist he used regularly for his own personal trading.

"'In June of 1998 Illidge learned that another estate trust, of which he was the registered representative, was being terminated. Rather than clos-

ing Saints Trust accounts, however, Illidge continued using the accounts
for his own personal trading. In regard to the trusts, correspondence for
Provident United and Saints Trust was regularly directed by Illidge to be
sent to either a house at 62 Alvin Avenue (Provident United) or one at 42
Tranby Avenue (Saints Trust), high-end brownstones in mid-Toronto that
he apparently owned as of 1998. However, correspondence sent to him
at both Alvin and Tranby was always returned as 'Address Unknown.'"

"Addressee unknown?"

"No. *Address unknown*," said Danny.

"So did he own the houses?"

"He claimed he did."

We sat quietly for a few moments, Danny letting me absorb the news.
I joked. "So is he going to the slammer?"

"Not quite. The way it works is he agrees to the facts as presented to
him, signs off on them, agreeing to comply with their disciplinary measures, and by doing so, avoids anything being used against him later in
a criminal prosecution. The paper trail showing his intention to defraud
clients disappears"

"So what happens with the clients' lost money?"

"What money?" he mugged. "The I.D.A.'s not a legal body. All they
can do is discipline members for by-law infractions. As I say, they present
the facts of their investigation, have you accept them, agree to whatever
non-negotiable penalty they impose, plus costs, the matter disappears and
it's back to business."

"So John can never be criminally prosecuted because the industry is
self-policing."

"That's the idea. Built-in invulnerability all round. The securities and
investment industry is a *caveat emptor* business, my boy." He waved to our
server, requesting the bill. He wondered, incidentally, if I knew anything
about the houses on Alvin and Tranby Avenue referred to in the report—
both of them million-dollar properties in an exclusive part of the city.

I told him I knew about them insofar as I'd been to both addresses.

"What's the score?"

"After ringing the bell at Alvin Avenue, barking from a large, and
from the sounds of it, ferocious dog erupted in the kitchen and the thing
charged down the hall, vaulted at the glass window in the door, claws
scratching, Rottweiler was my guess. At Tranby an old, plumpish cat sat
quietly on the veranda ignoring me. I rang the bell several times. No one
came. I didn't bother looking in the windows at Alvin, not with the Rottweiler baring his teeth at me. I tried to look in at Tranby, but the California

shutters in the living-room window were closed. There was nothing in either mailbox, no cars in either drive. Impossible to tell what might have been going on."

Only half kidding, Danny asked as we left *Browne's* if I happened to know whether John had been making any other big-ticket purchases lately. Other houses, cottages, cars. Boats, electronics, jewellery. Purchases people make when they're trying to launder money.

"Come to think of it," I said as we walked to the subway, "At a recent family gathering, he boasted of a house he'd bought at the Palm Beach Polo & Country Club in West Palm Beach about an hour north of Miami. The pro golfer Fred Couples' ex-wife, who had got the house in their divorce settlement—plus $58,000 a month in alimony—lived across the street, apparently, the kind of impressive detail John likes to add to his stories to let everyone know the circles he travels in. He didn't reveal what he had paid for his house, no doubt assuming that the size of the ex-Mrs. Couples' alimony payment alone would suggest it was not to be sneezed at. He'd bought the place, so he explained, because he was doing a lot of business out of Miami. Much less expensive than staying at hotels when he was in town—"

Danny jumped on that. "Doing business *out of* Miami?"

"That's how he put it."

"The Bahamas? Cayman Islands?"

At mention of the Caymans, I clued in. "Offshore banking . . ."

"Certainly a possibility."

"He's mentioned it several times in passing. I never took it seriously."

"Maybe you'd better. Anything else?"

"There's a 750-acre farm south of Collingwood that he bought a little over a year ago."

Danny looked astounded.

"A client whose money he handled died, leaving the farm to a former lover who lived in Spain and had no use for property in southern Ontario, so he sold it to John. It's apparently quite a place, has an estate house, a farm manager, groundskeeper, gardener."

"Incredible," said Danny shaking his head as we arrived at the subway. We paid our fare, but lingered a moment before heading down to the trains.

"And there're the motorboats," I said. "I forgot about them. Two mahogany classic inboards which he keeps in the boathouse at his cottage on Lake of Bays in north Muskoka. I've seen them. One is from the late 1920s, the other from the 1930s. He told me he paid $168,000 for the

1930s model, the other one $195,000, a 1927 Ditchburn, a famous name in antique boat-making. He bragged about the provenance of *BLACKIE II* (the Ditchburn). It had belonged to the former lieutenant-governor of Ontario, John Black Aird. Plus, he's driving what looks like a new European luxury car every time I see him. At one point, he said that in addition to the three family vehicles, he owned three others himself. All black. I asked him where he kept them. 'Around' was all he said."

"I'll mention that to McLanahan." He looked at his watch. He had to run.

I thanked him for the update, told him not to worry, my lips were sealed. And asked him to thank McLanahan. Difficult as the information was to hear, none of it was entirely unexpected.

"Will you tell your mother?"

"No. She'd go into cardiac arrest."

"It's a dicey situation. If you suggest he return the money to your mother's account, tell him that she's requesting it only for her peace of mind—"

"What are the odds there's any money *in* the account, Danny?"

"Fair enough."

"If I confront him about the I.D.A. investigation, she'll be sure never to see it again."

He gave me a sympathetic look. "In any case, I wouldn't wait too long. St. James will probably be on the rocks soon at the rate he's going."

"Somebody taking money out the back door . . ." I quipped.

Laughing, we shook hands. Our trains came. I headed home.

I knew that Danny was right. Confronting John and alerting him that my mother wanted her portfolio back at the value of her last account statement would tell him something was up. We were onto him. He'd go into avoidance mode. And that's the last she would hear of her $700,000, the account balance, if the last statement from St. James—the first one she'd had in eighteen months—proved accurate. If the money had disappeared, which to my mind was the case, my mother's only option would be to fire him as her power of attorney, something he likely wanted all along. Let Judith take his place. Let her try to get blood out of a stone, the analogy I'd heard him employ often enough, regarding other people's futile efforts to, as he phrased it, *hit him up for money.*

On the walk home from the subway, I realized there couldn't be any beating about the bush. In memory of my father, who for his whole career put money aside whenever he could to build a blue-chip "nest egg" portfolio for my mother and him after he retired, I had to confront him soon, and ask straight out for the money to be returned. If he monkeyed around, went manipulative on me and started playing games, I'd inform him that I knew all about the I.D.A. investigation and would let my mother know, in full detail, about their report, as well as her accountant, her lawyer and Revenue Canada. One way or another, I couldn't see what we'd have to lose.

It occurred to me that John might think it was more than a coincidence that I happened to be asking him to refund my mother's money, when he was aware (according to Danny) that the I.D.A. were investigating him. If he caught a whiff of anything suggesting that he might have to cough up any amount of money, he'd close right down, that was John's way. It was an article of faith with him that the last thing you ever did was give people back their money when there was more to be made, by him, of course, not by the client.

He'd make himself impossible to reach—he had three different cell phone numbers that always went to voicemail. There was no point asking Ellen. She was in the same boat as my mother. The mental harassment would begin in earnest.

John would get my mother on the phone early in the morning before she'd taken her medication. He'd talk fast, demanding to know what was going on, who she'd been talking with, why she was in a panic to close her account and have her money back when everything was in perfect order. Give her his rant that the investment industry didn't work that way if you wanted to make money. Didn't she want him to make money for her? He would make her feel guilty and ashamed for not trusting him. He'd bully her with the made-up, sorry for himself spiel he gave all his clients: that he was too good to everybody, and so they took advantage of him. He always acted in the best interest of his clients, and here was his own mother suspecting him of being a thief?

My mother would end up confused, frightened, ashamed, all of which John would make sure she felt to an extreme—laying it on even thicker by telling her that she was paranoid and taking her fears out on him, getting herself all worked up to the point she was going to give herself another breakdown and end up in the psychiatric unit at St. Catharines General Hospital. Why couldn't she just accept the fact that her money was in good hands, the balance rising higher every day? There was no need for her to have it back, sitting in a bank earning 2% interest, when with him she would be getting 25 to 30 percent. "*Wait till you see the numbers on your next statement!*" he would jubilantly sign off. "*And the size of the check I include,*" the promise of imminent cash that clients simply couldn't resist.

## CHAPTER THREE

# THE POSTMAN ALWAYS
# RINGS TWICE

I T TOOK UNTIL the end of July to penetrate John's voicemail firewalls and let him know there had been a crisis in St. Catharines that we needed to talk about. This was no ruse; my mother had almost killed several people. As her power of attorney, he was to be notified.

John phoned back a day later, no time for details, brusquely suggesting I meet him at *Centro's*, an upscale restaurant on Yonge Street just north of Eglinton, where I'd met him several times before. A tony clientele, known as much for its celebrity sightings as for its *cucina moderna* Italian cuisine, it was John's favourite restaurant.

Arriving at five-thirty, the agreed upon time, as the restaurant didn't open for dinner until six-thirty, I rang the bell on the wall beside the front door, waited for someone to open up. That night it was the owner, Adriano, whom I'd met several times before.

He beamed me a jovial smile, put out his hand and vigorously shook mine. "*Buonasera*, Paulo."

"*Buonasera*, Adriano."

We walked inside, Adriano stopping me as we passed the lectern with the reservations book on it. "All these years and his nibs tells me tonight you're not the younger brother after all, he is. Why didn't you let me know?"

"I guess I was flattered that you couldn't tell."

A wink, a smile, a gentle elbow in the ribs. "You got the brains, right?"

"And the good looks," I quipped.

Adriano roared, slapped me convivially on the back and pointed to the far corner of the high-ceilinged main room, John at his usual table, a clear view of the entrance, a quick walk to the hall leading to the rest rooms and the restaurant's back door. I wondered sometimes whether the habit stemmed from actual worry that someone he didn't want to see would come in looking for him, or whether he'd just watched his beloved *Godfather* movies too many times and it was a persona that he liked to put on about himself: that he was connected, a wise guy, not to be messed with.

The waiters were receiving a briefing on the evening menu from Marcellus the manager. One of them spotted me heading over to John's table, got up and was there to meet me when I arrived. John was talking on his cell. He put up a finger for me to hold on. The waiter took my drink order, a dry martini with two olives, no ice, stirred. He looked to John, who pointed to his nearly empty glass of white wine. Chardonnay, the only alcohol he touched. There was a plate of grilled garlic bread with diced tomato on top of a round slice of bocconcini cheese on the table in front of him. He pointed to it, pulling the phone away from his ear, hand over the speaker. "You have to try this. Can't beat it. To die for. Best in the city." He went back on the phone—"Talk to me, Henry!"

*Can't beat it. Best in the city. To die for.* John loved his superlatives, conferring them freely on things that, like his garlic bread with bruschetta and a small slice of soft cheese on top, most people wouldn't have felt warranted such hyperbole.

"So how are the kiddies?" he asked—then went briefly back to the phone—"I'm tied up at the moment, Henry. Call me later." The waiter brought our drinks.

I talked about my twelve-, ten- and seven-year old *kiddies* briefly, he filled me in on his girls, who were older, then gave me a capsule update on Ellen's mastectomy, which had taken place in early June. She was close to a full recovery, John said. She would continue on leave from her teaching job until January. Overall, her prognosis looked good—

His phone rang. He glanced at the number, held up his index finger again then took the call, obviously a personal one since he stood up and stepped away from the table to talk.

I sipped my martini, glanced around the empty restaurant waiting for him to return. His back to me, I couldn't make out the words, but from his general tone, the conversation seemed to be a difficult one: an argument, a dispute. John was actually wrought up in a way I'd never seen.

In light of this, and since he didn't bring up the topic of the crisis in St. Catharines when he finished the call and returned to the table (his uncharacteristically wary look turning to a smile), I decided to abandon my head-on approach to money matters and let them go for the time being.

Several glasses of Chardonnay while we ate loosened him up (I joined him with a glass of red), though as he usually did, John led the conversation: asking about different people we had known long ago, from roughly the same social circles. (We were only two years apart, his friends had brothers and sisters who were friends of mine.) His reminiscence that night was of the twins Charlie and Gordie Mitchell, with whom we'd played hockey at the local arena when we were boys. Their father Charlie Sr.—our coach, a bit of a boozer but a wonderful guy, their older brother Bill, who was still a floor trader at the stock exchange, whom John bumped into every so often, and of course their big sister Linda with the Playboy boobs. He wondered if I remembered them. "*Va-va-va voom,*" I humoured him.

It was a routine, almost a ritual that John had engaged in for years whenever just the two of us got together: what Carl Jung called *distancing* and Freud *avoidance*—defence mechanisms that we adopt to deflect and prevent the personal from being exposed. After some safe small talk about superficialities to begin with, he might move to a current event from politics or business, or shift to gossip and speculation about relatives, friends, or people we'd known (like the Mitchell family) as far back as high school or even boyhood, John's two favourite periods to reminisce about. I asked him once if he thought the people we talked about ever sat around reminiscing about us.

"*What kind of question is that?*" he asked. I remember thinking from the perturbed look he gave me that I'd offended him somehow. John liked a conversation to go where he wanted it to. If it didn't, watch out.

"When I called you in July," I said, when it looked like he'd run out of topics to use as distractions and was fully applying himself to his dinner. "Bev had just come home from a four-day stint in the psych ward at St. Catharines General, her fifth stay in the last three months. 'Grieving widow syndrome meets bi-polar disorder,' as her social worker, Lyn, describes it—as wicked a mental health combo as you can get, according to her. 'How do you separate grief from depression? They're one and the same, aren't they?'"

It was Lyn's rhetorical question, but John gave me a defensive look as if I expected him to answer it.

To his relief, the finer aspects of manic depression having always eluded him, I got to the point. "Judith was visiting last week on her day off from work. She stayed the night, woke up early the next morning to find Bev lying on the floor of her bedroom closet in her nightgown in the fetal position, fists tucked under her chin, whimpering through tears that she'd been a *bad girl, a bad, bad girl.* Judith called me, left to go back to camp when

I got there. I got her out of the closet and calmed her down enough to get her to the hospital, they admitted her to the psych ward. She promised me she would be a good girl and behave herself, and that I wasn't to worry.

"I hadn't spoken to her since, so I figured she was stable, otherwise I would have heard something, but then Reverend Michael McKinley phoned after church two Sundays ago, highly distressed because Bev had pulled out of the line waiting to exit the parking lot after the ten-thirty service. She roared across the lawn, wasn't watching where she was going and clipped two elderly women and a gentleman who couldn't jump out of the way in time. Reverend McKinley didn't want to involve the police if at all possible, but he said something has to be done with her. There have been other incidents. He hated to say it, but she was a menace. *'People are frightened, Paul,'* he said."

John laughed. "I'll bet they are." Always a fast eater, he had finished his dinner. Waving our waiter over, he asked me if I wanted some dessert, maybe a sambuca. I thanked him, but declined. "Cheesecake and a sambuca for me," he said to our waiter, "the same for my friend. So?" he said, sitting back in his chair, "What should we do?"

"We?"

"Very funny."

"You're the power of attorney."

"You know what I mean."

"I've told her she can kiss her hopes goodbye of getting into a seniors' residence if there's any more breakdowns and psych ward stays. With her mental history, she's already in jeopardy. Either she cleans up her act and behaves herself, or we tell her we're washing our hands of her. I told her you'd be over to take away her car keys, that we were giving the Buick to Peter."

He winced. "Can't you do it? I really don't have the time."

"I don't think it's too much to ask after all the heavy lifting I've done recently."

"Why not send Pete? He's getting the car."

"No, you have to do it, John. And read her the riot act on staying out of the psych ward. I've played bad cop long enough. It's your turn."

"She won't listen to me."

"She will if you tell her you'll quit as power of attorney and nobody will take your place. She'll be on her own. Living in a house with no car. See how she likes that."

The relief in his face when his phone rang was palpable. He picked up and took the call without checking the number.

He listened for a moment. "*I owe you?*" He laughed. "Come on, Robert. I thought we could play ball, make some money together. Now you're telling me we can't? Well, that's what it sounds like. . . listen to me . . . relax, Robert. Trust me . . . it's all working out—"

He hung up, checked his watch, the waiter brought the bill along with the cheesecakes and sambucas. "You really can't do it?" he pleaded, getting back to the topic.

"I really can't."

"We're trying to close a big deal at Hucamp right now. I don't know when I'll be able to get over there."

"What's Hucamp?"

"Hucamp Mines. I thought I told you. I bought it three years ago for six million."

"What kind of mines?"

"Gold, diamond, silver, copper. Plus, I'm working on winding down St. James by November and taking over as CEO of Rampart Securities, a division of my holding company, Rampart Mercantile."

"Mercantile? What does that mean?"

"Commercial trading. Corporate accounts."

I kidded him. "What will that do to your net worth?"

"Will you get off that?"

"I'm serious. You told me after dad died it was $22 million."

"It's forty-six now," he said without hesitation. "Give or take."

"You've doubled your money in five years. That's pretty impressive."

"It'll be over fifty by Christmas."

"How's that?" I said, holding back the urge to ask if it was because someone was taking money out the back door.

But no more shop talk, no more discussion of taking away her car, he finished his cheesecake in silence then polished off the Sambuca in one go, adding apropos of nothing: "St. James didn't offer the growth potential that Rampart will. I'm bringing most of my trading team with me too," following up with half a dozen names that meant nothing to me then, though they would later on.

Taking three one hundred-dollar bills from his wallet, he handed them with the check to Adriano, who had come over and was most appreciative. He walked us to the door, kidding John about staying out of trouble.

John laughed. "You know me, Adriano."

Adriano with a teasing wink to me, "Good to see your *older* brother again." Laughing, we shook hands, the amiable Adriano patting me on the back as we came outside.

Nearing six-thirty, the restaurant's parking valets on duty now, one was holding the door of a glossy black Porsche open for John, the car shimmering under the street lights which had just come on. The engine idling noisily, passersby on the sidewalk slowing down for a possible celebrity sighting, John threw Adriano and me a wave, shouting over the sound of the engine that he'd *Let me know how things went in St. Catharines—fingers crossed—by next week. And everyone's invited up to the farm for Thanksgiving weekend! I'll talk to you about it!*

Handing the valet a twenty, he slipped into the car, the door was closed, he revved the engine high for several loud crackling seconds, let it settle, shifted into gear and pulled out, waiting as the valet walked to the middle of the street, waving traffic to a stop in both directions, at which point John honked to him, made a quick U turn, down-shifted as he came out of it and accelerated *RSKY BZNS*—he called the car after his vanity license plate—north on Yonge Street, the high-pitched throb of the turbo engine rattling the evening air.

"Home to the wife and kids?" Adriano speculated aloud when the performance was over, a tone in his voice suggesting he wanted me to think so.

*No wife and kids, Adriano,* I could have told him. He doesn't live there anymore. But I had a feeling Adriano already knew that about Mr. John.

We shook hands again, exchanged *buona nottes,* he went back inside and I headed down Yonge Street to the subway . . .

Ellen had called me in late May, five weeks after her mastectomy, with a story about an experience she'd had half an hour earlier that she thought I'd get a kick out of hearing. "I've told you how fast John's mail accumulates, haven't I?"

She had, adding that there was such volume coming in each day it overflowed from the multiple shoeboxes and grocery bags she was using to store it. Since he was living elsewhere so much of the time now, he was supposed to stop by the house and pick it up once a week, but of course he never did. Ellen called him the Elvis of Mail he received so much. Real estate catalogues, architecture, car and boat, art, clothing, business magazines, investment magazines, annual reports, correspondence for his various holding companies, legal and financial mail, junk mail. Drawing the line, Ellen had told him enough was enough. From now on she would only hang onto his mail for ten days, at which time it would be shredded. She was fed up deciding what was important to him and what wasn't.

"So," she continued, "today was day ten, postal pickup. I was having a cup of tea after lunch, double-checking each piece before putting it through the shredder, feeling a little on the weak side since I've been having problems sleeping and was contemplating a nap. However, I was having so much fun I thought I'd put it off until I got the shredding out of my system.

"I was dropping pretty well everything into the machine, I'd gone through it once already after all. But the teacher in me always forces me to check my work. I spotted a piece of business mail that had got mixed in with some grocery store flyers, plucked it out and pitched the flyers into the shredder. It was a letter from our insurance company, home and auto. I guess I'd put it in the shredding pile originally because we were up to date on our insurance payments. Wondering what it was about, I opened it.

"Proof of insurance slips for a new white BMW 525i Sport Coupe, the ownership made out to John Illidge at 357 Golfdale Road. Three blocks down on the other side of Yonge Street. Maybe a ten-minute walk. The girls have friends on Golfdale. The house wasn't really a surprise. I know he has others, but the white BMW Sports Coupe?"

I saw her point.

"I wasn't feeling the greatest, as I say. But I thought *fuck him*. I spruced myself up, put on a suit and heels, grabbed a realtor presentation folder from the dozens I was about to shred, got in my car and drove over to 357 Golfdale Road, about as far from Yonge Street on the east side as we are here on the west. One of those Teddington Park almost Georgian places, older and slightly smaller than ours but nice—as was the spanking white Sport Coupe sitting in the drive.

"I parked in front of the house, tucked the realtor folder under my arm, went up the front walk, pressed the doorbell. No sound from inside for a minute, the door opened suddenly and a pretty blonde in a white terry robe with *J.J.* monogrammed on one of the pockets in blue was standing there, my height, thirtyish, blondish, did I say that already? Holding a steaming mug, smiling brightly. 'Good afternoon,' she said. I asked her if John happened to be home, indicating the real estate folder. 'He wanted me to stop by and show him some properties he thought he might be interested in.' 'He isn't, as a matter of fact. He's in New York at the moment, but I'm expecting him back tonight. I'm Mandy.' I asked if she was Mrs. Illidge. Her smile widened, she transferred the coffee to her right hand, held out her left and let me behold the multi-carat diamond on her fourth finger. 'Not yet,' she said smiling down at the rock.

"I couldn't take my eyes off it. It had to be ten times the size of the ring he gave me. 'No worries,' I told her. 'I'll catch up with him in the next day or two, Mandy.' I handed her the insurance letter, turned and walked back to my car. 'Who should I say stopped by?' she called behind me. 'I'll let John know!'

"'The current Mrs. Illidge,'" I said over my shoulder, and left it at that."

# CHAPTER FOUR

# THE DEARS

SATURDAY OF THE THANKSGIVING weekend, John followed through on the invitation he had extended outside *Centro's* in August and "convened" a family gathering at his farm in the rolling hills south of Collingwood, Ontario, *Beinn Tighe* the Gaelic name ("house on the hill") given to it by the original owner, Murray Davis. Murray had bequeathed the country property to a lover he'd had many years ago, who was then living in Spain. As it turned out, the man had passed away some years ago; his partner, with no use for a 750-acre farm in Canada, asked Murray's executor, his sister Barbara Somers, if she could sell the property and send him the money—not that he needed it, but it was in fulfillment of Murray's wishes, so he wanted to follow through.

John handled Barbara's investments for her, had known Murray and been to the farm many times. Creating Beinn Tighe, which he had begun in 1960, disassembling a large circa-1830 log house he discovered near Guelph, Ontario, and reassembling the hand-hewn oak beams on a scenic piece of land he'd bought south of Collingwood had been Murray's life's work. Barbara wanted to honour that by keeping it in the family if at all possible. She appealed to John as the next best thing, a close family friend. He bought the place as is, kept Peter the farm manager (fifty head of Black Angus beef cattle to tend) and Holly the gardener (there were seven gardens around the property) as employees, everything inside the house left exactly the way it was the day a friend drove Murray to the palliative care hospital in Toronto, never to return.

Ellen and the girls arrived at Beinn Tighe a few minutes before Jill and I and our three children. Her girls went off together while she gave us the Cook's tour of the estate, which is what it really was—like something you might see in *Architectural Digest* or *Better Homes and Gardens*: the large, two-story log house with substantial wings on either side of the main building, fieldstone chimneys at each end, towering oaks overhead, a wide, well-treed lawn sweeping down to a pond, the barn just below, Angus cattle grazing in the adjacent field, the blue waters of Georgian Bay visible in the near distance.

Though my brother Peter and his wife Debi couldn't make it (they'd gone to Algonquin Park so Peter could photograph the autumn colors for an upcoming show), our sister, Judith, who lived fifteen minutes north in the town of Collingwood, showed up as the tour ended. She left her golden retriever Duncan outside to play with our kids, joking, when she came in the kitchen where Ellen, Jill and I were having drinks and putting lunch together, that it was so typically John: *'Come on up for lunch, and bring the lunch if you wouldn't mind.'* Judith wondered why, with the way John drove, he and my mother wouldn't have arrived yet. He'd gone to St. Catharines first thing in the morning to pick her up . . . in his Porsche. The four of us cracked up at the thought of a 78-year-old headstrong woman with bipolar disorder cooped up in a high-performance, two-seater sports car for three hours of John's no-speed-limit driving. The consensus was that she'd be breathing fire by the time she stepped out of *RSKY BZNS*.

And indeed she was. Twenty minutes or so after Judith arrived, Carson, twelve, opened the sliding door in the kitchen, poked his head in and wryly announced: "They're heeeeere . . ." The four of us drained our glasses, steeled ourselves for "showtime" (our term for the drama that Bev never failed to bring with her to family functions) then left through the sliding-glass door, following Carson around to the front of the house.

The passenger door of the black Porsche open behind her, my mother, massaging her legs with one hand, the other favouring her back, came around the front of the car holding forth to the six grandchildren dutifully assembled beside the car to welcome her. Wincing, one hand still favouring her lower back, the expression on her face was one of peeved indignation as she griped, "I'll tell you one thing, children, I'm never riding in a Porsche again! The worst drive of my life. The seats are so low I could barely see out the front window. The engine was so loud, I could hardly hear myself think. And your Uncle John's reckless driving—running up behind cars in front of us so the bumpers were practically touching. I don't know where he thought he was going. Grandma Illidge is lucky to be here in one piece!"

John's eldest daughter spoke sympathetically, "We're glad you are, Grandma." The others echoed the sentiment.

The kids dispersed, except Nicky, who hurried over to admire the Porsche. He was ten, loved cars and idolized his Uncle John.

John held the driver door open, let him sit behind the wheel, closed the door then said if he wanted, he could come with him in the Porsche when they reconvened at Judith's for dinner later on. A dream come true, Nicky hopped out of the car and ran off to tell his brother.

Ellen, pointing out various features of the property along the way, led my mother up the flagstone walk to the house, Judith and Jill following.

I remarked to John that he seemed remarkably stress-free after his three-hour ordeal. He lifted an overnight bag from behind the driver's seat, slung the strap over his shoulder, put a hand up to one ear and then the other, pulling out plugs. "What was that?" he mugged.

Jill let me know afterwards that my mother had rattled on irascibly, criticizing just about everything in the house throughout the Cook's tour. "Like she was jealous and resentful of the place, even suspicious that John would have had the money to buy such a magnificent property. The Porsche trip seemed to have put her in a foul mood, and she was pretty clearly furious with him." Jill wondered if that was it.

"It wasn't the ride," I said. "On the one hand, he wanted to impress her with the car and the farm, convey the message that if she kept her money with him (I'd explained the situation to her), the sky was the limit on how much she would make—her funds were in the best hands, hands that were clearly making fortunes for him and those lucky enough to be his clients. Make her think she won't find anyone else who was making the kind of money he was. But at the same time, it's his way of getting back at her. As I've told you, he enjoys nothing more than exploiting her guilt over the wrongs he feels she did him in childhood. Besides, switching to another investment broker is one thing, getting the money back from the fired one is another matter. Did you talk to him?"

"Not really. The *dears* were driving me crazy. It's gotten worse. Though not as bad as the *mothers* he uses with Ellen. Where does that even come from?"

"No idea. I never heard either word from any of the men in my mother's or father's family. I know Ellen's father Ed used to call Evelyn *mother*."

The problem was whenever our families got together, John would refer to any younger or older females present, other than his wife and daughters, as *dear*. His daughters he called by their names. To Jill it was always "nice to see you, *dear*," the same way he'd talk to our seven-year old daughter, Hannah. "Could you pass me the butter please, *dear*?" or "Watch your step going down the stairs, *dear*." To Ellen: "*Mother*, why don't you and Paul sit over here?" "I'd take another slice of roast beef, *mother*" or "*Mother*, you better let the dog out."

It had offended Jill since the first time she met John. He never spoke personally to her, never asked how she was doing, how things were going at Sick Children's, the hospital where she worked, or how her parents were. As far as Jill could see, he had no facility for normal small talk, no banter, no simple conversation, at least with women. He seemed to Jill cold, aloof, condescending, overbearing, in control, reserved—like he was playing it socially safe by limiting what he said to formalities, glib quips and trivialities. She felt insulted, intimidated, demeaned, so much so that she'd never quite been able to come to terms with it, never confronted him about it, never even kidded him—had never been able to because she felt such incredible hostility toward him.

As twelve of us prepared to sit down to lunch at the long pine table in the sky-lit, open-concept dining room with the eight-point, elk antler chandelier hanging above us from the cathedral ceiling, I told Jill I knew how demeaned she felt, but said, as we'd discussed before on numerous occasions, that The Dears wouldn't stop until she got the message through to John about how she felt. She understood that, but it was hurtful in the meantime: insulting, humiliating, just wrong. What made it worse, as far as she was concerned, was that John seemed oblivious to the belittling effect the term had on her or anyone else. How could he not know that—with three daughters?

We made a point of sitting at the opposite end of the table from him, well out of *dear* range.

My mother grew less agitated as we ate (she'd never really liked cooking; living alone now, she liked it even less), appreciating Jill's and Ellen's delicious Thanksgiving lunch, inquiring what the different grandchildren were up to, tossing in some history of Murray and the Davis family: the Davis Leather Company, started in Toronto in the 1830s—Davisville Avenue near Yonge and Eglinton was named after the family. They made all the boots, saddles and leather goods for the Canadian army in World War I. They were multi-millionaires; Barbara Davis married the composer Harry Somers; Murray and the youngest brother Donald founded the Crest Theatre in 1954. It ran until 1966. A *Who's Who* of Canadian, British and American actors, writers and directors starred there. The Davises put Toronto on the cultural map. *Everyone* went to the Crest—

"That reminds me," John said to me across the table. "Barbara wants to commission a book about the Crest. I'll call you next week and we can talk about it."

He then brought up the subject of his new wine fridge over by the wood stove. He wondered if we'd noticed it.

Yes, we had. Ellen pointed it out giving us the Cook's tour.

Jill asked how you could keep red wine in a refrigerator.

"It's a dual zone unit," John explained. "It has two separate spaces, each with its own temperature control. The reds are kept mildly cool as if they're in a wine cellar. The whites get chilled to perfection." The fridge, he informed us, was full to capacity: fifty-two bottles, two-thirds of them white, the rest red. John only drank white.

After lunch, he hitched his tractor up to a wagon and took the kids and anyone else who was interested on a hay ride. The kids urged my mother to come along. She was reluctant because her back was still sore from the ride in the Porsche. But everyone else was going. "You won't have any fun staying home by yourself, Grandma," one of the kids said in appeal. "It's Thanksgiving!"

She relented.

A sunny autumn afternoon, John drove for a few minutes on a sloping trail through spruce and pine woods behind his house. We came out in a grassy pasture, part way up the hillside, the house about a hundred yards below, grazing Black Angus, several of them with calves, quietly watching as John turned to head us higher still: the wagon bouncing wildly over furrows and gopher holes, the hay bales we were sitting on bouncing just as wildly, everyone laughing trying to hang on, the kids screaming with delight, John turning to me after a burst of gleeful whoops, winking, smiling, appreciating the moment, happy.

We left for Judith's house at four-thirty, Nicky, as promised, riding with John in *RSKY BZNS*. My mother went with Ellen and the girls.

Judith's house in Collingwood had a large backyard. She had set up her net for some badminton, a game that had always been popular in our family. Once drinks and snacks were organized on the back patio, John drew up and announced, only partly tongue-in-cheek, a roster of elimination matches he assured us was based on the same scientific ranking system that he had developed when scheduling games for the Madawaska County Badminton Championship of which he was the long-time reigning champion. (Madawaska was the lake where Ellen and John had owned their first cottage when their girls were young.) After a chorus of boos and catcalls from some of the younger competitors that John had rigged things in his own favour ("Who else's favour am I going to rig them in?"), the MCBC Championship got underway.

My mother, who had been a very good badminton player in her day, joined in the spirit of things, winning her first game against my daughter Hannah, losing the second to Ellen, but not by much. John as convener of the competition provided humorous play-by-play commentary during games, tossing in plugs for himself here and there as the *reigning and still undefeated champion.*

"You've been defeated!" his youngest daughter called out. "By me!" She almost beat John in one of the semi-finals. Jill beat me in the other. She would play John for the championship, best two out of three—two of the most competitive people I knew about to battle it out in front of the whole family. Both were good players with strong serves, smart clears, hard drives, sly drops, powerful kills. For both, winning wasn't everything; it was, as a famous coach once said, the *only* thing.

Jill started strong, was leading by four points—a solid lead in badminton—when John began working *dears* into his play-by-play commentary. Every few points at first, then between points. Heckling, teasing, razzing—"Bring it on, *dear!* It's no use, *dear!* I could play you blindfolded, *dear,*" pulling ahead fast as Jill's anger grew until at game point—

He jumped in the air, smashed the bird so hard it landed at her feet before she had time to clear, John taking the first game.

Jeers and taunts for John, clapping and whistles for Jill as they changed sides. "Don't give up mommy!" "Don't let him get to you, Auntie Jill! Make him hit backhands. It's his fatal flaw!"

And it was. Jill leapt out to an early lead in game two, moved faster, caught him off guard; she varied the placement of her shots so that he had no choice but to hit backhands, only half of them well. He seemed to clue in to the fact that her go-for-the-jugular play had something to do with the *dears*. So he stopped them. He grew more and more rattled by her intensity, began struggling to keep up with her moves . . . then when she took the game by a comfortable five points, he went psychological on her and announced that he had let her win to make things more interesting in the third game. "You ready, *dear?*" he asked Jill as she prepared to serve.

Not taking the bait, she said nothing, made her serve a sky shot, ran to the net and peppered her return at his head, the bird hitting his glasses with a *thwock*. "Sorry about that, *dear!*"

Cheers and applause from the spectators. "You rock, Auntie Jill!"

She kept on rocking, but John did too. Neither went ahead by more than a point in the third and deciding set. Eight times they were tied, both of them intently focused and concentrating on every shot, playing superb badminton, the game too close to call until John, who could play right or left, switched the racquet to his other hand, throwing Jill off. She tried but for some reason couldn't get him to hit backhands. He capitalized, made six points in a row, and won.

Boos, whistles, jibes, laughter, John doing a little dance on his way to the net, ducking under it, putting out his hand to shake. "Excellent game, Jill. Really excellent."

Though she'd lost, it seemed to me that the smile she gave him as they shook hands had a look of victory to it. No more *dears* . . .

It was mild enough to eat dinner outside, the kids at one picnic table, adults at the other, my mother sitting quietly between Ellen and me, ruminating about something that had come to mind, growing agitated about it, the petrified look coming into her face that always did when she felt she was losing control—then vanishing an instant later as though it had never been, and she'd rejoin the world. She helped clear the table, sat with the grandchildren for a bit after dessert, told them they'd have to come and see her at the seniors' residence where she would be living come December first.

"Will you be able to play badminton there, Grandma?" Hannah asked.

My mother laughed at the thought. "I'm not sure, dear. But if I am, and you come over to see me, we'll have a game."

We called it a night around nine-thirty since Ellen and the girls were driving back to Toronto. My mother staying with Judith, who would take her back to St. Catharines in the morning for church—John, Jill and I were heading to the farm for the night. Ellen reminded us that the Illidge Boxing Day dinner would be at Wilkett Road, the house at York Mills and Bayview they were renting while Ridley Boulevard was being restored after the fire in September.

Emma had been in her room one night talking on the phone, holding the end of her Bic over a candle she had burning, flicking the drops of hot plastic into her wastepaper basket. She decided to go downstairs for a snack, joined her sisters in the kitchen, the three of them realizing after a few minutes that it wasn't their toast that they smelled burning.

Fire damage on the second floor wasn't extensive, but water damage on the main floor was substantial. According to John, the insurance adjuster offered him $750,000 for repairs and restoration, which was unacceptable as far as he was concerned. He wanted $1.6 million, not a penny less, or he would take legal action since he knew for a fact that the actuarial tables showed claims paid out for house fires were the lowest in the industry. The insurance company duly coughed up the $1.6 million without blinking an eye, so John said, and was also paying the $12,000 a month rent on the Wilkett Road house. When all was said and done, he had Ridley Boulevard restored to the identical state it was in before the night of the fire, pocketing six hundred thousand himself *on the way through* with his threat to take the insurance company to court over its actuarial tables, tables that John led them to believe he knew all about, when the truth was—and where for him the beauty of the story lay—he knew absolutely zilch.

It had been a long day, everyone was pooped. Jill and I and the kids had to be up early and get home to put the Thanksgiving turkey in the oven. Jill's family were coming over for dinner. She and Hannah took the bedroom off the living-room wing, Carson and Nicky slept in one of the upstairs front bedrooms. I was to take the other.

The master bedroom was off the kitchen/dining room. John and I talked as he came and went getting ready for bed while I stood at the kitchen counter having a glass of Dujardin, a German brandy made from French grapes that had been Murray's favourite. John had been looking for an ironing board in the pantry closet one day about six months after Murray's passing. No luck finding an ironing board, but he hit the jackpot liquor-wise: five unopened cases of Dujardin, Murray's private stash.

Though officially the director of trading at Rampart as of December 30, because the markets were closed over New Year's, his first day in the office would be January 4, his forty-seventh birthday: over twenty years in the business, something he said he found hard to believe. He'd started at Greenshields Securities back in 1978 on his birthday. Brushing his teeth at the kitchen sink, he said he thought that augured well for Rampart. He felt the millennium would be good for them; he was bringing most of his trading team from St. James, a number of whom he'd worked with as far back as his Credifinance days in the early nineties. David Cathcart, Patricia McLean, Stafford Kelley, Dev Misir, Nick Tsanconakos were names I recognized.

Why the move to Rampart? It had experienced hard times off and on for the past thirty years, capital problems, management problems, a revolving door of directors, ownership changes, I.D.A. issues, nothing grievously serious, but still it left a taint. Now that John was CEO of the parent company, Rampart Mercantile Holdings, he could move into some of the new markets emerging with globalization. That's where the future lay. He also felt, from a personal perspective, that it was his mission to put the brokerage back on prosperous feet and restore it to its glory days of the 1960s, when our Uncle Bob, Robert C. Stone, my mother's cousin Mary's husband, started the original Rampart brokerage and became a Bay Street player. There was something about the name: **RAMPART**.

As things turned out, start he did on January 4, 2000, but to everyone's astonishment, he left the company three weeks later.

Someone had been taking money out the back door . . .

# CHAPTER FIVE

# ELECTRIC BOOTS AND
# A MOHAIR SUIT

I HAD JUST CALLED the kids for dinner when the phone rang in the family room off the kitchen. Carson, who had just got up from the couch to turn the TV off, reached back to the side table, picked up and said hello. A frown appeared on his face as he listened. He turned to me, holding the receiver against his chest. "A man wants to talk to *John Illidge's brother Paul*," he whispered. "He's crying. It took me a second to figure out what he was saying."

Pointing down the hall, I told him I'd take it in my office, and that he, Nicky and Hannah should start eating. There had been calls like this before. They could go on for a while.

I sat down at my desk, waited until Carson had hung up before introducing myself, continued waiting while the man regained his composure.

He did shortly, apologizing for the excessive display of emotion. It was just that he was a wreck. He'd been trying to reach me for months now, but what with my number being unlisted it hadn't been—

I cut him off. "Reach me? Why?" Not rude, not angry; from previous calls of this type, I'd learned that the forthright approach was the only approach you could take with *The Husbands* as I'd come to call them.

It caught him off guard. He hesitated. "Reach you about the affair your brother has been having with Patrici—with my wife," he quickly corrected himself. "It's been going on for nearly two years now."

"And you're just calling me now?"

"It's been on and off."

"Are you drunk?"

"No—"

"Stoned?"

"No!"

"Mentally ill?"

"Of course not."

"I'm going to hang up now."

"*Don't! Please don't!!* I'm sorry—it's got to me, that's all."

"What's got to you?"

I knew he needed to get it out, so I let him.

"The wining and dining, the high life your brother has my wife leading, romantic getaways, shopping sprees to the tune of thousands in New York, Miami, London. She says she's not in love with him, but she is. I know she is. How can she not be? Any woman would be. She's behaving like an infatuated teenager, not a forty-seven year old woman. She tells me she'll be away for a week on business. Her business doesn't involve travel. She tells me it's something new they've started. I had my suspicions, so I went to her office to check. She's not only not away, she works with your brother John. Their offices are next to one another. Everyone at St. James and now at Rampart knows about them. His wife Ellen even knows. She's known for several years."

"She told you that?"

"Not exactly."

"Never mind. Let's just take it that what you say is true, Mr. ...?"

"My name is immaterial."

"Not to me."

"I'd rather not give you my name."

"You could be making this whole thing up. Without a name, I can't take anything you say seriously."

"I'm not making it up if that's what you're thinking."

"I'm not thinking anything."

"Why would I go to all the trouble—"

"Back to the point. The purpose of your call."

"Very well." He paused, rattled I could tell. He cleared his throat nervously. "I want you to tell your brother to call off the affair. As you can imagine, it's pretty well destroyed my marriage. I'm trying to salvage what I can of it. I love her. I know in the end, she's going to get hurt—and hurt badly, at least from what I've heard through the grapevine about the way your brother's treated some of his ex-flings. I want you to tell him what I've told you then ask him for some respect, some understanding, some sympathy for what he's been doing to me and my family."

"You mean what your wife's been doing."

"If that's the way you want to see it, but—"

"I don't see it one way or another, sir. The only thing I see, and I'm sorry to say it, is that what my brother and your wife do is none of my business."

He raised his voice. "Tell him to leave her alone! You're his older brother!"

"Do you have an older brother? Are you an older brother yourself?"

"How is that relevant?"

"You overestimate the influence an older brother can have over a younger one. He's forty-seven years old, sir. I tell him some anonymous guy who refused to give his name calls me up and demands that, as his older brother, it's my responsibility to make him cease and desist with this anonymous man's wife immediately, and he'll laugh in my face. Which is what I'd do if the situation were reversed. How do I know you're not just a crank caller?"

"I don't want my wife to get hurt more than she has been already!"

"If she's getting hurt, why would she continue the affair? I'm sure she has more sense than that. You make it sound like he's got some power over her."

"He does! He's a con artist."

"And you know that how?"

"Everybody knows."

Silent for a moment, I gave him the response I'd given the others. "If you let me have your name and your wife's name, I'll mention to John that you called and relay your concerns."

"*You can't!* That would be the last straw."

"What would?"

"Using our names!"

"Well, there's nothing I can do then."

"She'll know I've been spying on her."

"You have been spying on her."

"It's not like that!" He pulled the phone away from his mouth. I could hear him breaking into sobs.

"Look, sir, I have to go. My kids are waiting to eat dinner. Can you leave it with me? I'll do what I can, but as I said, I can't promise anything."

"It's humiliating."

"I'm sure it is."

"How can I keep up with someone like your brother?"

"I've asked myself the same question, sir."

"Sorry for taking up your time. I'm desperate at this point. Can you understand?"

"Your wife's name is Patricia. She works in John's office."

Taken aback, he paused. "Yes, that's right," he said.

"I'll do my best. I promise you that."

"Tell him I didn't make any threats. I'm not the threatening type."

"I'll let him know . . ."

He stayed on the line. After a few seconds I hung up.

The kids were nearly finished with their lasagna. I brought my plate from the stove, sat down and started eating.

"Somebody looking for Uncle John?" Carson asked.

"Where is he these days anyway?" Nicky chimed in. "He's never been at the farm when we were there."

Carson, who had turned thirteen in February, had caught on through the phone calls and messages he sometimes took regarding John that there were people looking for him: wanting to talk to him, asking how they could find him—the sort of questions, Carson came to realize, that you ask of people on the shadier side. "Maybe he's gone to the mattresses, Dad."

Hannah screwed up her face. "The what?"

Carson, having watched *The Sopranos* for two seasons, explained. "What the Mafia do when a gang war breaks out and—"

"—they want to keep from being *whacked*," said Hannah, to our amusement. "Fat Tony's always talking about that." Fat Tony the smooth-talking, precisely enunciating but not too bright mobster on *The Simpsons*, Hannah's favourite show.

"Does somebody want to whack Uncle John?"

"Not that I know of," I said.

"Now," Nicky mugged, imitating Fat Tony's Bronx accent, "*Who's ready to sleep with duh fishes?*"

We cracked up . . .

Later on, Carson in his room doing homework, Nicky and Hannah watching *Seinfeld* in the family room, I went to my office to have a look at the documents my lawyer-friend Molly Conners had given me. Molly had worked for John at Credifinance Securities. Single, smart and pretty, she so intimidated John with her self-assurance and intelligence that not only did he never pursue her amorously, he came to look upon her and confide in her almost like a sister.

I met Molly completely by chance one Thursday night in my single days when she came into the lobby bar at the Mont Remy Hotel, an after-work spot popular with the downtown finance and investment crowd in the nearby business district. I happened to be sitting in that night for the house pianist Johnny Hutton, Jr., a friend of mine whose back was giving him problems.

Drink in hand, Molly *sashayed* (as she later described it) over to the piano as I was starting my second set. Elton John's "Benny and the Jets." She'd had a few and, drink in hand, was dancing her way over to the piano, motioning me to move over so she could sit down beside me, with a mischievous smile bringing her mouth up and saying into my ear while I continued to play: *"Electric boots and a mohair suit—what happened to Johnny Hutton, Jr.?"*

We got to talking on my break, laughed about the serendipity of it all, went back to her place, talked about it some more, then passed out about four. In a few weeks we became involved, after three months discovered it was hazardous to our friendship, so became un-involved and the friendship has stayed solidly intact to this day.

Molly had managed to obtain documents for me with the latest on the continuing Investment Dealers Association investigations, as well as transcripts of Securities Commission hearings on the bankruptcy of St. James Securities, and what looked to be the sudden demise and impending action against Rampart Securities on charges just out that the "conspiracies" John had masterminded at Credifinance and St. James were identical to the one he had now tried to put into effect at Rampart. Molly had highlighted key excerpts.

Since he'd been barred from buying and selling securities in Canada as a result of making fraudulent transactions on client accounts at St. James without having completed the required disciplinary measures imposed after his improper trading practices at Credifinance, he was now conducting similar trades at Rampart but through various "conspirator" surrogates— the "team" he had brought with him from Credifinance to St. James to Rampart.

The hearing transcript elaborated: "Illidge and his Co-conspirators colluded together and were active participants in a fraudulent scheme to 'pump and dump' penny stocks [notation by Molly: *Pumping and dumping* is buying million-share blocks of penny stocks, sometimes as low as a quarter of a cent, then pumping up interest in them through aggressive promotion. Buying pressure on stocks increases, pushing the share price up, unwitting investors believe the hype, buy the higher-priced shares, at which point the manipulators sell off their holdings, making a hefty profit, the price of the stock plummets, the manipulators cash out, while those left holding the stock incur heavy losses].

"The Co-conspirators participated in a similar practise with 'illiquid' securities [Molly: *low-priced stocks of little interest to anyone*], misrepresenting their value as substantially higher than what it actually was, falsely drumming up interest to justify obtaining loans from Rampart Securities client capital to purchase the higher value stock, with the intention and knowledge that their actions [Molly: *Keeping the proceeds of the sale of the falsely overpriced stocks themselves, maybe paying the loan back to Rampart, though probably not*] were stripping value from Rampart, causing the serious capital deficiencies that were driving the company toward insolvency."

"In other words," Molly joked in a further notation, "John had his Co-conspirators taking money out the back door for him!!"

The caller who wanted me, as his older brother, to stop John from running around with his wife had let slip the first part of her name and said she worked with John. Something twigged. I remembered a Patricia, the only female, being mentioned in the St. James conspiracy. Ellen had also mentioned a woman named Patricia, with whom he worked, as one of John's principal girlfriends for several years. By mistake, the husband had blurted the name. *Patricia.*

After some searching, Molly spotted the name in a court transcript: *Patricia McLean.* ". . . Evidence before the court clearly implicates Patricia McLean as an active participant in a number of peculiar and allegedly fraudulent transactions entered into as part of the alleged conspiracy of John Illidge and his assistant David Cathcart. She acknowledges that funds were improperly stripped, transferred and withdrawn from Rampart client accounts by the Co-conspirators to a loss approaching $18,000,000."

Further on in the transcript were details from a hearing in which Patricia McLean turned on her Co-conspirators, "voluntarily providing a large binder of exhibits to the hearing in which the Ontario Securities Commission was addressing concerns over the same type of conspiracy activity with stocks of Hucamp Inc., a junior gold mining company of which John Illidge was CEO, Patricia a director." The transcript recorded that McLean had ceased all contact with the conspirators, including John, except on a strained and adversarial basis." [Molly's notation: *They've broken up!*]

Maybe Mr. McLean would get his wife back, be proven right in his predictions that Patricia would end up being hurt and hurt badly. It seemed to me that this was the more operative question: would the long-suffering Mr. McLean be as eager to have her back, when he learned that John had left Patricia holding the bag as sole officer and director of now bankrupt St. James Securities, Ernst & Young the bankruptcy trustees suing her for damages in the amount of $25,000,000?

"Complicating matters further for Patricia McLean," so the affidavit went on, "Ellen Illidge, John's wife, has been in the process of pursuing matrimonial litigation to divorce John for two years now. The settlement figure arrived at by her lawyer was $9,900,000, though a separate action was underway against Patricia McLean. Ellen had reason to believe that as John's lover, she held substantial assets in trust for him through a company called Southampton Securities, a company McLean owned. She worked closely with John for many years, and carried on a long, clandestine romantic relationship with him.

"Ellen and her attorney contend that in the course of this dual personal/professional relationship, McLean helped John set up various corporate records to reduce debt and structure his affairs so as to substantially lower their value on paper, so he could give Ellen a lesser settlement in any divorce proceeding. McLean did this through a second incorporated company, of which Ellen says she owns 48%, with John saying he owns 86%. Whose position is correct? How will it be possible to determine? Why should a lovers' spat have any bearing on a fair matrimonial settlement for Mrs. Illidge?" Ellen's lawyer argued.

"People ask," Molly wrote in her final notation, "how John could have got away with doing what he did and not be facing any real consequences, other than losing his securities license for life and paying a fine. Here's a little diagram that will give you some idea of just how tangled a web he wove. As you'll see (and this is only the companies we know about), it's quite the labyrinth he's created for himself. Navigating it would test the chops of even the best forensic accountant. *Let's keep the money moving, baby!* Isn't that what he says to his troops at the beginning of the trading day? He did when I worked with him. The morning pep talk: Keep the money moving, kids, and remember, where she stops, nobody knows!

"Here's a selected list of companies John Illidge either owns or controls, or is directly connected with:

Charrington Business Consultants
Southampton Inc.
Conquest Capital
Beinn Tighe Holdings
Elkhorn Capital
Saints Trust
Provident Holdings
Rampart Mercantile

Atlas Securities Inc.
Rampart Securities
Platinum Equity Funding
J.J. Holdings
St. James Holdings
St. James Capital
Hucamp Mines, Ltd.
MYO Diagnostics
Medallion Capital Corporation
Northern Securities
Financial Matrix
Beinn Tighe Properties
Sloop Securities

"On his instructions the 'team' keeps the money moving between these companies. And, like he says, where the money ends up, only John knows . . ."

I called Molly the next day to thank her for the material and let her know about the phone call I'd had from Patricia McLean's disconsolate husband.

She picked up before the second ring.

"I was just about to call you."

"No kidding?"

"Guess who I got a call from?"

"I was going to ask you the same thing."

"Really? What's up?"

"Patricia McLean's jilted husband tracked me down."

"Wanting what?"

"His wife back."

"Looks like he'll get his wish, now that things have run their course with Don John. Let's hope Mr. McLean can help her with the $25 million lawsuit John left her saddled with."

"*Have a nice life—if there's anything left of it.* What's your news?"

"Your brother phoned me about an hour ago."

"Has he gone to the mattresses?"

"If so, they're expensive ones."

"Where was he calling from?"

"New York, or so he said. 18 East 68th Street at Fifth Avenue to be exact. The Thomas Crown house."

"The what?"

"The brownstone townhouse where Pierce Brosnan lived in the film *The Thomas Crown Affair*. John says he got the place for a steal."

"A brownstone on the Upper East Side would have to be worth a few million."

"It would."

"I remember the original Steve McQueen film—wasn't Thomas Crown an art thief?"

"He was. But he wasn't motivated by money. He stole for the sheer thrill of the crime."

"That's not John."

"I wouldn't say so. He loves his cash. I've seen him kissing the stuff. There seems to be something more to it than that."

"What else did he have to say?"

"Not much. Reminiscences of *the good old days* at Credifinance."

"The good old days before people discovered what he was up to."

"He claims he's perfectly innocent of course."

"Naturally."

"Do you think he's really in New York?"

"Molly. Come on. Check last night's TV listings and I bet you'll see *The Thomas Crown Affair* was on. He finds the address of the brownstone. Some photos. And tells you he just bought it. He does this all the time. It's make-believe, but who ever bothers to check and call him on it? Who would even know how to? They just take his word and stand in awe of him. It's his pathology. Always has been. I'll ask him about the movie when I see him tomorrow."

"Where are you meeting him?"

"Rampart."

"What's the occasion?"

"He's giving me fifty-eight thousand dollars."

# CHAPTER SIX

# THE WOLF OF BAY STREET

I HAD NO IDEA WHY John wanted to meet me at the Rampart office when I'd been told he was no longer working there, but Molly reminded me of the Securities Commission report: it was John's company; he could do whatever he wanted except buy and sell securities, which he was still doing, of course, just through his protégé David Cathcart and some of the other conspirators, as the I.D.A. and Securities Commission referred to his "team." Molly said I'd probably get to meet them; they were bound to be hanging around the boiler room.

*"Boiler room?"*

"The room where brokers work the phones to generate sales, using, let's just say, questionable tactics. Pump-and-dump chiefly, as the investigations termed the practice: hard selling penny stocks, private placements, deals that regulators, if they dig further, will deem wholesale fraud—of the kind *frère* John seems to have been involved in committing."

On my way downtown, I stopped in at Elliot's Used Books on Yonge Street and picked up an item he had put aside for me on fraud, a subject in which I had become increasingly interested the more I learned about John's activities. The book was a memoir called *Catch Me If You Can* by Frank Abagnale, Jr., an American serving several sentences in federal prison for a string of notorious frauds during the 1970s. With no education, he assumed the identity of, and was accepted as a bona fide surgeon, a lawyer and a commercial airline pilot among other things, forging and kiting checks in the names of the fictitious identities he assumed—all before he was twenty-two. *His secret?* According to the book-jacket, Abagnale had *a winning smile, charm, confidence, high intelligence, plus an energetic and captivating personal style.* So good was he at what he did that it took the FBI years to

58

apprehend him, and even then he managed to escape from custody twice.

A friend of mine, who worked in publishing and who also knew John, had read Abagnale's book when it originally came out and told me that except for the fact that he wasn't as good-looking, Abagnale reminded him a whole lot of John. I wanted to see for myself.

Back on the subway, I read the first line: *A man's alter-ego is his favourite image of himself,* and was immediately hooked. That was so John, always projecting his favourite image of himself, an image that to him was more real than the one he would have seen in a mirror if he ever looked into one, which he hadn't for years. John hated mirrors, as did I. The result of a traumatic experience when we were boys.

I raced through thirty-five pages before I reached King Street Station—nearly missed the stop trying to finish a chapter. The book was compelling, the similarities between Frank and John being positively uncanny. Listening to Frank talk in his writing was like listening to John. Right from the start, Abagnale was open—as John always was—about his three main obsessions: class, finesse and style. Money was merely the means to obtaining them and, as Frank described it, "They're so universally admired by most people that almost any fault, sin or crime will be judged more leniently if there's a touch of class involved."

I recognized in Frank what I was coming to understand more clearly about my brother John. Both presented all the aspects of narcissism: the inflated sense of their own importance, intelligence and invulnerability; the deep-seated need for attention, respect and admiration; the history of troubled relationships; the lack of empathy for others; and hiding behind masks of extreme confidence a fragile self-esteem. That was John to a T.

Stepping out of the subway car, my shoe caught in the door-opening. In my panic, I dropped *Catch Me If You Can* on the platform, yanking the shoe free a second before the doors closed.

A folded piece of paper that had slipped out of the dust jacket started to blow away along the platform in the rush of wind from the departing train. I scooped up the book, dashed toward the edge of the platform, stepped on the paper, stooped and grabbed it. I unfolded it as I headed for the exit: a creased, slightly soiled photocopy of the top section of what looked like a nineteenth century newspaper page: *The Philadelphia Saturday Courier, June 1843,* printed in the ornate scroll that ran along the top of the page:

### Diddling as One of the Exact Sciences

n. Diddler: a cheat, an embezzler, a confidence trickster.
—*Oxford English Dictionary*

Not only have there been diddlers since the world began, the principle of diddling is peculiar to man. A crow thieves, a fox cheats, a weasel outwits, a man diddles. To diddle is his destiny. A diddler is a man who was made to diddle. He is a composite of nine ingredients.

*Minuteness*: — Your diddler is small-scale in that he's never tempted to magnificent speculation. His business is retail, for cash.

*Interest*: — Your diddler is guided by self-interest. He always has an object in view. He regards always the main chance. He looks to Number One. You are Number Two.

*Perseverance*: —Your diddler perseveres. He is not readily discouraged. He steadily pursues his end, and never lets go of his game.

*Ingenuity*: —Your diddler is ingenious. He is creative, and understands plot. He invents and circumvents. Were he not what he is, he would be a maker of patent rat-traps.

*Audacity*: — Your diddler is audacious, the boldest of men. He proceeds straight on, conquering all by fearless assault and no small measure of blarney.

*Nonchalance*: — Your diddler is nonchalant. He is not at all nervous. He is never put out, remains always cool, cool as a cucumber, calm, easy-going.

*Originality*: — Your diddler is original—conscientiously so. His thoughts are his own. He would scorn to employ those of another. A stale trick is his aversion. He would return a purse upon discovering that he had obtained it by an unoriginal diddle.

*Impertinence*: — Your diddler is impertinent. He swaggers. He sneers in your face. He eats your dinner, he drinks your wine, he borrows your money, he pulls your nose, he kicks your poodle, and he kisses your wife.

*Grin*: — Your true diddler winds up with a grin when his daily work is done, a grin nobody sees but himself. He goes home. He locks his door. He divests himself of his clothes, puts out his candle, gets into bed and, placing his head upon the pillow, grins as he drifts off to sleep.

—Edgar Allen Poe

Edgar Allen Poe? *Masque of the Red Death? Murders in the Rue Morgue?* Creator of the murder mystery but here dissecting the fraudster psyche— in 1843? It seemed to me Edgar Allen had down pat, even if he did make frauds sound more like conniving rascals than calculating criminals.

The thought remained with me as I headed into the Warburg Building at Bay and York Street. I wondered, as I rode the elevator up to the twenty-seventh floor, in which of the two categories I would have placed my brother if I'd been asked. Probably both. The rascal covered for the criminal. And *grinned as he drifted off to sleep* every night as John often boasted.

The receptionist let him know I was there. In a few minutes, he appeared at a door to my left, waved me in, held the door open for me, then we walked down a corridor with offices on both sides. We entered a larger room where maybe a dozen people were working, some standing while they talked on the phone, some roaming, others sitting at desks, light laughter, people chatting, cups of coffee in hand, an easygoing atmosphere in what I guessed was the Rampart boiler room.

Several people glanced over offering friendly smiles as we came through. John stopped in front of a set of double doors with polished brass handles. The boardroom. He opened the doors, led me into a spacious, blue-carpeted, wood-paneled room with high ceilings, oil paintings on the walls, a crystal chandelier that came on automatically, sparkling above the long mahogany table, chairs for sixteen around it, a view of Lake Ontario out the south-facing windows where a ferry was crossing to Center Island.

A half-dozen men sauntered in and joined us beside the boardroom table, whether of their own accord or at a signal from John, I couldn't say. A friendly bunch, in shirts and ties, no jackets, several with their sleeves rolled up, they put out their hands in turn, introduced themselves and we shook, names I recognized from the Investment Dealers and Securities Commission reports as those of the *co-conspirators*, though I tried not to let the recognition show.

"So this is where it all goes down," I said, trying not to sound glib.

"Well, *where it all goes up* is the way we think of it," said Nick Tsaconakos.

"Do you play the market?" David Cathcart asked with a look to my brother. "Does the trading gene run in the family?"

"It depends who you ask," I said. "I only bought stock once. My broker recommended one called Quebec Sturgeon, a gold mine in northern Quebec. Guaranteed to go up, he told me. I'd make a killing. The latest core samples were looking excellent. I asked him about a stock called

Cherokee, an oil company. I said I liked the name and thought that was the one I should buy. The broker said you can't invest in a stock because you like the name. So I ended up with shares of Quebec Sturgeon, which we referred to as The Fish. Unfortunately, The Fish couldn't swim very well. It went up a bit the first few days, then dropped, and continued dropping. During the descent, I kept my eye on Cherokee, rising as fast as The Fish was sinking. I cashed out before I lost my shirt. Well, my thousand dollars."

"Who was your broker?"

I paused. "My brother . . ."

A good laugh all round, including from John. He sat down. The conspirators drifted back to the boiler room, all except a Chinese fellow named Eddy Ing, in his late fifties at the time, the oldest of the group, wondering if he could have a quick word.

John smiled up at Eddy, looked to me. "Eddy and I have made some money together, haven't we Eddy?"

"You could say that," Eddy grinned modestly, he and John chuckling at an in-joke of some kind.

In that moment, I recognized the same look on his face that I'd seen in the faces of the other guys from the moment they walked into the boardroom. They not only had a high degree of respect and admiration for John, they seemed to revere him. His capabilities, his cool confidence, his charisma, trusting him blindly, from the looks of it, as if worries he would ever lead them astray were the furthest thing from their minds.

Leaving them to talk, I walked over to the south-facing windows, Bay Street twenty-seven stories below. Streetcars, buses, taxis—early-afternoon stop-and-go traffic snarled in all directions, no relief in sight.

I gazed out over the lake, watching a tugboat chugging toward the eastern gap—recalled the cover of a business magazine with a similar photo of New York Harbour on it as seen by someone we're meant to think is Jordan Belfort standing at the window of his south Manhattan office overlooking the harbour and Statue of Liberty. The photo was for a feature on the notorious stock market manipulator who defrauded thousands of investors to the tune of $200 million during the 1980s with aggressive pump-and-dump schemes. Belfort had been indicted for securities fraud and money laundering and was about to begin a stint in federal prison.

As an accountant and an investment lawyer, Molly had followed the case closely. Besides the recommendation that I read the Frank Abagnale, Jr., book to better acquaint myself with financial fraud and fraudsters, she had given me a stack of business magazines and newspaper articles covering the Jordan Belfort story. Molly had a theory that John's own pumping and dumping had been inspired by Belfort, whose nickname was "The Wolf of Wall Street."

According to Molly, John knew all about Belfort. May even have met him and talked to him at some point. The two of them had come up in the investment industry at around the same time. When Molly worked for John, he apparently mentioned Belfort frequently and paid close attention to his fraud and money laundering case as it unfolded during the early 1990s. Molly's theory was that John saw himself as "The Wolf of Bay Street" (Toronto's equivalent of Wall Street), only a lot smarter than Jordan Belfort about business because he didn't do drugs, and he wasn't a party boy, the two things that had brought Belfort crashing down—

"*Okay!*" the Wolf called over. He had his pen and checkbook out. "Do you want the fifty-eight thousand as a lump sum, or separate amounts?" he asked as I sat down.

"Separate amounts, thanks. Twelve thousand for my lawyer, Tom, so he can send my files to the new lawyer, Charlotte, who I had to retain since according to Tom, you have to use a female lawyer in family law cases now. Twenty-one thousand for the two credit card balances Jill ran up on her lawyer's instructions to "frustrate" me in settlement negotiations. Ditto with the fifteen she juiced up on our line of credit."

"You knew nothing about any of these?"

"She hid the bills and overdue notices."

"What did she spend the money on?"

"Clothes and booze."

"Right. Bingeing. I remember you telling me."

"This latest one has gone on for six months. She used to be able to cover them up, but she's lost the knack and can't pull it off anymore. When she's not drinking, it's almost as bad. *Dry drunk* they call it at Al-Anon. She needs treatment, but her family won't admit there's a problem. They're certainly not going to cough up for a private facility, which a case like hers needs."

"Ninety-five percent of patients in those places are back doing what they were doing within two years of treatment, Paul. The success rate is miniscule. Money down the drain."

"May be. I talked about it with the Al-Anon support group—told them I wanted to go to her family and ask for help. Explain that something had to be done for everyone's sake. My wife was becoming unmanageable, dangerous to herself and others. I needed help. The group supported the move, but they warned me to be prepared: *Hell hath no fury like an alcoholic outed.* I went to the family. They brought on the fury."

John chuckled. The checks written, he opened a file folder that had been sitting on the table. Took out two copies of a promissory note for the fifty-eight thousand dollars, payable to him. Slid one copy over to me, left his pen where I was to sign.

"I thought this was coming out of mom's money."

"It is. For business reasons, I need a promissory note from you to prove that I didn't take the money out of the company for personal purposes."

"But it's mom's money."

"Exactly. As far as her portfolio is concerned, I have to account for it."

"Mom didn't mention anything about a promissory note for fifty-eight grand."

"It's just a formality. It won't be enforced."

Knowing what I did now about his business practises, I was uneasy, sure there was a catch, a snag, a hitch that would come back to haunt me down the road. I knew John was no longer power of attorney for my mother. She'd revoked it and given it to Judith, who had no idea that John had mingled my mother's money with other clients' and was treating it all as his own, let alone how to go about retrieving it from within the corporate labyrinth John had constructed to hide his tracks and prevent anyone from ever getting their money back.

I relented; it was none of my business. I needed the money to take care of the accrued debts. I signed.

He walked me back to reception. He asked if I was going to Beinn Tighe with the kiddies on the weekend.

"I was hoping to."

"I want to get up there, but it's been crazy here. Maybe I'll shoot up on Saturday. My girlfriend will be in town. We'll have a big dinner."

"Is that Patricia?"

"Patricia?" he said vaguely, frowning as if trying to recall someone by that name.

"Patricia McLean."

He frowned for a second then recovered with an uneasy laugh. "Where did you hear that?"

"Ellen told Jill something about it."

John shook his head, apparently amused.

"Which reminds me. I got a letter from a Patricia McLean the other day asking me to return three laptops she said you'd given me and *assorted family members.*" A wary look came into his face. "Apparently, she's doing asset recovery for St. James Securities and says I and other family members are in possession of company assets and are required to return them. —Didn't she come with you here to Rampart? I think that's what you told me, you were bringing your team over?"

"I did," he said evasively, "but Pat's the CEO at St. James now. I'll be talking to her. I'll take care of it."

"I'll alert the assorted family members just in case."

"Her name's Tammy," he said.

Off my confused look he added: "My new girlfriend. You'll like her."

"I'm sure I will."

"Don't worry about the promissory note!" he called after me as I walked to the elevators.

He didn't make it up to the farm that weekend. Or any other weekend. Except for the Illidge Boxing Day dinner, I didn't see or talk to John for the next sixteen months—until a hot afternoon in late August. The door bell rang. I opened up.

There he was.

# CHAPTER SEVEN

# DEEP THROAT

"How would it be if I moved in with you and the kids for a while?" He stepped quickly inside: tan slacks, burgundy loafers, floral-patterned Tommy Bahama silk shirt. Moving into the living-room, he got right to the point. "Thing is, I need somewhere to stay when I'm in Toronto." He ran his eyes around the room, appraising the carpets, the furniture, the walls and the art I had on them.

"You in a pinch or something?"

"No, not at all. Trying to decide if I should move to Ottawa or not."

"Kind of a long commute, isn't it?"

He took me literally. "It's not that. I've just bought this moving company in Oakville, and I need to be around. Didn't I tell you about it?"

"Not in the last sixteen months you didn't."

Sarcasm noted. "Has it been that long?" he said, studying the carpet.

"Except for the Illidge Boxing Day dinner, and you were still stock-brokering then. But back to the moving company. You own it and somebody else operates it?"

"I do both," he said, only half-listening.

Into the dining-room, again assessing the walls, the carpet.

"Full time?"

"Nine to five, Monday to Friday."

"That's a little out of left field, isn't it? For you, I mean. What about the investment business?"

"Finito. This was too good to be true. No stress, cash business, more customers than you can shake a stick at, what with the growth of Oakville north of the 401. It's a gold mine."

We walked through the kitchen.

"Cash business? Moving's pretty expensive. You have a mob clientele?"

"No, you jack the prices up, offer a great discount if they pay cash. It's a trip to the bank. They go for it every time."

He stepped into the family-room, picked up the TV controller and turned it on. Changed a few channels.

"You on satellite or cable here?" He shut the TV off.

"Cable."

"You've got what, five bedrooms?"

Upstairs we went. He checked out the master bedroom, Hannah's and Nicky's rooms, Carson's, the bathroom beside it then the spare bedroom, a bright ten-by-ten room with hunter green broadloom, two windows overlooking the front lawn, no furniture in it except a bare glass-topped desk and an office chair. John slid the mirrored closet door open, had a peek inside then threw me a distressed look. "What's all this?"

The shelves were brimming with Bankers boxes, stacks of paper, crammed file folders, manuscripts, books, magazines, photo albums and miscellaneous odds and ends.

"Don't panic," I said, sensing his discomfort. "I'll clear it out *before your arrival.*" His relief was palpable.

Downstairs we went, arrangements were made. I felt somewhat guilty about the whole thing. The criminal overtones. Knowing there was a lot John was conveniently not telling me, knowing the trouble he was in with investment regulators, maybe even the police by that point—which very likely had something to do with him not having been seen or heard from for sixteen months. Yet there I was, the big-hearted older brother, letting him *hole up,* as I saw it, with me and my children, making them accomplices, aiders-and-abettors too—

"Tammy will be here, too, some weekends if that's all right," John said opening the front door.

"Tammy's more than welcome."

"She likes her job, hates Ottawa, but her father's there, her mother and stepfather. A move to Toronto could be in the works. In which case we'd get our own place of course."

"Stay as long as you need to." I knew I was safe being so magnanimous: John never stayed anywhere for very long. "Only rules are no smoking, no pets, and lights out at eleven o'clock."

The quip caught him off guard. "What?"

"When should we expect to see you?"

"Maybe a week or so. I'll call beforehand and let you know."

Then he was gone, down the drive to the black Jaguar XJ he was driving that day, a sizeable dent in the front quarter-panel on the driver's side.

"Fender bender?" I called to him.

He shook his head. "Emma hit a pillar in a parking garage. I'm making her save the money to have it fixed."

I wondered, as I closed the door, why he wouldn't let insurance handle it. Have Emma pay him back for the repair to teach her a lesson, if that's what he was trying to do. I wondered, too, if it was really Emma who hit the parking garage pillar. Since their sixteenth birthdays, John's daughters had always driven their own vehicles. In fact, they teased him for being Mr. Scrooge when it came to letting them even test drive one of his *deluxe darlings*—which prompted further wondering: if he did, in fact, own six cars, why on earth would he be driving around in the one with an ugly dent in its front quarter-panel, when that was something a person with a fetish for class and style like John's would never do?

It came as no surprise when I didn't hear from him after a week, or a second week. The kids and I began to wonder if he'd actually show—if maybe this was another one of those times when John talked something up, committed himself to doing it and made all the right motions toward following through, but in the end, for reasons he never made clear, failed to do so. Whatever was supposed to happen didn't and was never spoken of again. . .

The morning of August 29, two days before the Labour Day weekend, I had stepped out of my office to go to the kitchen for a second cup of coffee, when the *beep-beep-beep* of a truck backing up in my driveway stopped me in my tracks.

The doorbell rang. Rang again before I could open up. When I did, John was standing there in a white button-down shirt, no tie, navy suit pants and black loafers. A body-built black man in his mid-thirties stood behind him. Byron. We shook hands. Over his shoulder, I could see a white box truck backed up in the driveway and onto the interlocking brick front walk almost to my front porch:

OAKVILLE MOVERS
*The best move you will ever make!*

He explained quickly that he had just bought the company to make some easy cash while he decided what his next move in the investment business would be.

Not a minute to lose, according to John, Byron and his helper Jimmy, a not quite so body-built white guy with a goatee in his later twenties, had the ramp in place from the truck to the porch and my front door—the moving blankets, furniture pads and floor runners laid down and the unloading well underway in less than ten minutes.

John directed the whirlwind operation from the front hall: a large couch, wing-chairs, side tables, lamps, carpets, a queen-size bed and frame, dresser, clothing bags, large and medium-size oil paintings, a steamer trunk, dozens of cartons, boxes, suitcases, and assorted household items.

As for things of mine that he was replacing, Byron and Jimmy toted them down to various rooms in the basement. The job completed in just over an hour, Byron and Jimmy drove off in the Oakville Movers truck following behind John in his dented black Jaguar: *The best move you will ever make!*

Time would tell . . .

The kids and I left for Beinn Tighe Friday morning. After lunch, we visited Judith in Collingwood. While the kids swam in the YMCA pool (Judith was director of the Collingwood Y), she let me know she'd decided to try and recover my mother's money. She'd hired a new accountant who had had some forensic experience. The previous one had quit in frustration at not being able to make sense of what little paperwork John had given my mother over the years, most of the documents—including numerous government ones— turning out, as far as the accountant could tell, to be fake, forged and counterfeit. The man claimed he just couldn't afford the time on the phone and in correspondence required to obtain any kind of legitimate information on my mother's investments, which she needed for income tax purposes.

Apparently, the new accountant, after looking matters over, felt confident he could make headway. As he saw it, there was a fair chance of developing a fraud case to take to the police, though he said it would be a slow process because of the difficulties of communicating with John: he had already complained to Judith that there was never an answer on any of the phones whose numbers he had been given to call; he couldn't leave messages because his voicemail was always full, and there was no current mailing address. (The one on his driver's license was Ellen's.)

Now that he would be living with me, Judith wondered if she could give the accountant my address. I told her that was fine; I would keep my eye out for his letters. However, I made sure to add there was no guarantee they wouldn't go in the garbage like just about everything else John received. Mail had begun accumulating the week before he finally arrived at my place, two grocery bags full. He'd gone through them before he and the movers left—kept several clothing catalogues, two car magazines and a few advertising brochures, but gave me the rest to throw out. I reminded Judith of what Ellen had said about him years ago: *mail is something John just doesn't do.*

He and Tammy had arrived in the dented black Jaguar by the time the kids and I returned to Beinn Tighe from Judith's. Hannah was the only one to notice. "Do you think he hit an animal, Dad?"

"Hope not," I said.

Nicky had heard her. "That's rust," he said, surveying the damage. "From a collision."

The two of them ran inside to see John.

After introductions in the kitchen, the kids leaving after a few minutes to go outside, the three of us talked over a glass of wine, a Stony Hill Chardonnay from John's wine fridge. He pulled a replacement bottle out of a Stony Hill carton and placed it in the empty slot.

Tammy (not short for anything she let me know) was pretty, an ash blond, John's height, easy to talk to and not a bit self-conscious at being thirteen years younger than him. She even teased him about it, got him laughing and tossing back digs of his own, which I thought was a good sign for their relationship. Dinner would be a combination of food they'd brought and things that I'd picked up in town. Tammy said she'd assemble it. She knew John wanted to show the kids and me his *latest toys.*

We went out front, walked around the side of the house into the woods a little way, Nicky running ahead, ecstatic when he saw—

"ATVs!!"

Sure enough, there were two brand-new Yamaha all-terrain vehicles, one blue, one red, each chained and locked to the trunk of a spruce tree.

Nicky hopped up on one, gripping the handlebars, ready to ride. Carson jumping on the other, I lifted Hannah onto the seat behind him.

"How 'bout we go ATVing tomorrow?" John asked the kids. "Any takers?"

A resounding *Yes!*, though Nicky in his enthusiasm politely wondered why we couldn't go for a quick spin after dinner.

"Because Uncle John's too pooped." He ruffled Nicky's hair, heading us back through the woods.

"Impulse buy?" I asked him.

"Couldn't say no to the deal. The pair for fifteen thousand. I could resell them tomorrow for thirty."

"Is Tammy an ATVer? She doesn't really strike me as the type."

He chuckled. "We'll find out tomorrow. Seven-hundred and fifty ccs of pulsing power between her legs, I'm betting she'll like it."

The first time in my life I'd ever heard him make a sexual joke; I laughed at that more than I did the joke.

We came out of the woods onto the lane leading to the north pasture. Turning back toward the house, John led us down the lane to an open-sided wood shelter where he chopped and stored his firewood. He kicked away the logs that were holding down the four corners of a blue polyethylene tarp covering something next to one of the woodpiles. Grabbing the tarp by the top, he whipped it off like a magician to reveal a new Yamaha 450 cc. dirt bike, white with slashes of purple, green and black on the frame and fenders.

Nicky ran over, eyes popping out of his head.

John asked him if he wanted to go for a quick spin.

He turned to me for permission.

"What about helmets?"

John wheeled the bike out. "We'll just go as far as the road and back. I'll stick to the speed limit."

He started it up, I helped Nicky on, making sure he had both hands on the passenger strap since, as I knew he would, John revved off down the sloping lane at a good clip, disappeared down the lane around the cedar grove, the whine of the engine quieting when he reached the road, turned around then hit the gas hard for the engine-roaring climb back up the hill.

Tammy had come out to tell us dinner was ready. She watched the motorcycle pull up, the engine crackling and sputtering as it idled, the dazzled look on Nicky's face as he hopped off, adulation in his eyes when he high-fived John, thanking him profusely for his *first ever motorcycle ride!*

"He's Junior John!" Tammy called to me above the sound of the engine, a warm smile, eyes back on Nicky; Hannah, Carson and I watching too as John accelerated up the lane, leaned back into a wheelie and, to cheers and applause, sustained it until just before the woodshed, when he lowered the front of the bike, turned right and scooted inside.

We went ATVing the next morning, Carson and Nicky getting solo turns (with helmets) down the lane to the road and back several times, across the lawns and around the pond. I took Hannah for a short ride that she really didn't enjoy. She found the engine way too loud, as did I. I'd never driven an ATV before, and I haven't since.

After lunch, John and Tammy drove to Judith's. *Shrek* was playing at the Collingwood movie theatre. She was taking the kids to the matinee then bringing them back to the farm for dinner—which left me on my own to do research on the Crest Theatre. John had told Barbara Somers

I was interested in talking to her about a book on the history of the theatre. We had spoken briefly on the phone, Barbara inviting me over to her house a week from Tuesday so we could decide on terms, discuss her ideas for the book, how we could get it published, and so forth.

I cleaned up after lunch, went into John's bedroom, found the laptop computer John told me I could use—*Property of St. James Securities* (one of the laptops Patricia McLean had been looking for), then set myself up at the kitchen table facing the south windows with their panoramic view of the surrounding countryside, the same view that I know Murray would have enjoyed countless times over the years, life here at his country retreat an important part of the theatre's history that I would have a first-hand opportunity to capture.

The only email was from Molly, "Deep Throat" in the subject line. *"Are you free to take a call? I've got the goods."*

*"Call away,"* I replied.

I had phoned her the morning John stopped by the house to talk about lying low with the kids and me, which I was sure he was doing. I felt I needed to know more about what was going on. Could she get the lowdown for me? She thought she could.

"Sorry to disturb your weekend in the country," she said, when I picked up the phone.

"Everyone's out and I'm doing research on one of the stolen St. James computers I found stashed away."

"Ahh . . . are you going to let Patricia McLean know you've hunted it down?"

"I don't know if that would be wise. I'm trying to protect my cover."

She laughed. "And why is that again?"

"Tolstoy said happy families are all alike, but that every unhappy family is unhappy in its own way. What did he believe made the difference between happiness and unhappiness?"

"Money."

"You know your Tolstoy."

"You're afraid you're aiding and abetting his activities by having him in your house."

"He owes people serious money, Molly. People who want to know where he's at so they, or someone working for them, can get it back. He leaves trails of anger, fear and unhappiness behind him wherever he goes. I don't want him bringing any to me and my family."

"Of course not."

"But at the same time, he's my brother. I know why he's doing what he's doing. I feel sort of responsible, guilty in a way. That was always my job as the eldest: keep John from behaving badly and upsetting my mother. *Making her sick again*, as we were always warned—"

"Stop!" she said, cutting me off. "You have to let that go, Paul. You're enabling him. Rationalizing not having said *No*."

I knew she was right. "Let's hear the goods."

"Are you sitting down?"

"That sounds ominous."

"Seems the day Johnno was casing your house as a prospective bolt-hole, Rampart Securities declared bankruptcy, Rampart Mercantile a week later, then John filed for personal bankruptcy the week after that. And it looks like St. James Capital, one of his prime holding companies, will be in the same boat by Christmas. The meeting for creditors on the personal insolvency arrived at ninety-six million owing: the largest sum to a one-time partner named Robert Salna for twelve million; ten million to Ellen; two point five million to a lottery winner and his wife who gave John their winnings to invest, but never saw the money again; plus hundreds of thousands to dozens of clients whose funds it appears he mingled with his own. There are no company books, or at least accurate ones. No records, a handful of files, virtually nothing you could call a paper trail.

"A total for the Rampart bankruptcies has yet to be established. Ernst & Young, the bankruptcy trustees, went to court and obtained a Mareva injunction against the 'Co-conspirators,' as they're now referring to them, which means a judge ordered an injunction freezing assets of both Rampart Securities and Rampart Mercantile to protect them for creditors. In other words, based on evidence from the I.D.A. investigations, the court felt there was a high likelihood that without the injunction, the bankruptcy trustees would find the Co-conspirators had made off with the assets.

"The court transcript (I'll mail you a copy) shows how the bankruptcy came about and who was culpable. The Mareva injunction was granted on the basis that the '*Co-conspirators were active participants in a planned fraudulent scheme to misrepresent the value of illiquid securities in order to obtain margin loans from Rampart, with the intention and knowledge that their actions would strip value and/or capital out of Rampart, causing injury to the company and thus contributing in large part to its bankruptcy.*'"

"Money out the back door . . ."

"History repeats itself," said Molly, then continued: "Evidence for Ernst & Young's fears of what would happen without an injunction came in counsel's documents showing that transactions by the Co-conspirators from the early '90s to the early 2000s alone increased Rampart's capital deficiency from $253,000 to $14,219,000, the overall loss of value to clients and shareholders as of August 12th when client accounts were frozen, somewhere in the neighbourhood of $20,000,000."

"So I *am* harbouring a criminal."

"A criminal who, despite his sea of troubles, as they say, manages to keep himself comfortably afloat. I heard about the Oakville Moving Company purchase. He's not at the moving company nine to five. And not every day. When he's not there, he's set himself up with a new surrogate to do his trading for him, a man named Stafford Kelley."

"I met Stafford Kelley when I was at the Rampart office."

"John's been paying Kelley eight thousand a week to use him and his company, Medallion Securities, to manipulate the share price of Hucamp Gold Mines, which John still owns. He and Kelley are using high closings, wash trades and jitney trades to pump the stock's price, the two of them moving money back and forth between their respective companies to cover their footsteps, or at least John's footsteps. Stafford Kelley does trading for John through a company called Elkhorn Capital. At one point, Kelley needed to meet the Elkhorn principals to talk through a deal. John introduced him ostensibly to the CEO and CFO of Elkhorn, with Kelley unaware that they were friends of John's he'd primed to play parts—unaware, as well, that the actual owner of Elkhorn Capital was John Illidge, the person with whom he was trading shares of Hucamp Mining stock to take a final haul *out the back door.*"

"How convenient. I remember Kelley. He was an older guy."

"Seventy-five."

"So John's using him for cover."

"Excellent cover. The kind you get for eight thousand a week. How much business must he be doing to be paying that out? As to Oakville Moving, the details are out of *National Enquirer.*"

"I'm all ears."

"On a tip from Jack Kelsey at Long, Sternberg & Williams, I did some due diligence on Oakville Moving. The owner was a man named Earl Lindegard, fifty-eight, divorced, nice guy, good businessman, bit of a drinker. Apparently, he met and started a relationship with a thirty-year-old stripper named Honey Sue from Fort Lauderdale, Florida—"

"Are you telling me this with a straight face?"

"Trying to."

"Is Honey Sue her stripper name or her real name?"

"Jack didn't know. But Earl is head-over-heels smitten with Honey Sue and can't live without her. He hears about John's interest in a cash business and they meet. Earl accepts John's offer of fifty thousand cash that will allow him to follow Honey Sue to Florida and keep her in a style to which she's become accustomed since meeting Earl. John agrees that he will sell Earl back the company in six months, the amount of time he gives Earl to blow the fifty grand, get dumped by Honey Sue and come back to Canada with his tail between his legs. John will give him back the company for one dollar so the guy can get back on his feet. In the meantime, the weekly profit at Oakville Moving is his to keep, $15,000 on a bad week, $25,000 on a good one, cash. Earl showed him the books."

"Who's going to do the books for John?"

"Nick Tascanakos."

"One of the co-conspirators."

"He's acting as chief financial officer and treasurer."

"What happened to Earl's treasurer?"

"He drove to Florida too. Seems Honey Sue has a sister she wanted him to meet."

"Speaking of romance, how's the future Mrs. Illidge?"

"Fine. Very pleasant. I think she gets him."

"His criminal ways?"

"I don't think she knows much about that yet. But as far as I can see, she's got his number. In a good way."

"That's quite the surprise."

"I thought so."

"Is 'Tammy' short for something?"

"No, it's Tammy. She was right up front and firm about that. Tammy."

"Well, I'd better go."

"Let's have dinner next Wednesday night."

"What's the occasion?"

"Does it have to be an occasion?"

"Just asking."

"It's a surprise."

"Give me the details on Tuesday."

"One thing I meant to ask. Have you got the creditors' list there?"

"I do."

"Can you see if there's a woman on it with the initials B. S.?"

I heard her shuffling papers. "There is. Barbara Somers. Isn't she the woman you might be writing a book for? About her theatre?"

"That's the one. What's John into her for?"

Molly paused. "Three million."

# CHAPTER EIGHT

# KING OF CANDYLAND

A VOICEMAIL MESSAGE from my mother was waiting for me, when the kids and I returned from Beinn Tighe around noon on Monday. In a voice that fluctuated in a listless monotone—the effects of anti-agitation medication I knew her doctor had prescribed—she murmured more than muttered *Happy Birthday* . . . cleared her throat quietly then reminded me of the fireworks . . . Labour Day Monday, 1951 . . . *Do you remember I went into labour early Labour Day morning?* (How could I forget? she'd been reminding me for years.) That from the window of her hospital room that night she had watched the Labour Day fireworks a block south of the hospital at Toronto City Hall? *I'll always remember those fireworks* . . . her voice drifting off as if she'd pulled the receiver away from her mouth—resuming suddenly with *Have you talked to John lately?* which was, of course, the real purpose of her call. I wondered if she knew he'd moved in with me. Would Ellen have told her? The only person I'd talked to about it was Molly, who pointed out that in spite of his assorted houses, his farm, his cottage, his place in Palm Beach and any number of other places, real or imagined, where he might have hung his hat at the end of the day, no one for the last ten years or so had ever really known where John actually resided. He'd become a kind of nomad; either that or, as Molly said, homeless.

I erased the message before listening to the end, made the kids some lunch, drove them down to the Beach for a stroll beside Lake Ontario on the boardwalk, something I liked to do on Labour Day if at all possible, say goodbye to summer with school starting the next day. Having grown up in the Beach, I usually bumped into someone I knew who was either living in the Beach or making their Labour Day pilgrimage to the boardwalk for old times' sake as I was.

A sweltering late-summer afternoon, the kids and I walked as far as the lifeguard station at Kew Beach but decided that with the oppressive heat, the crowds and dogs packing the boardwalk, we'd turn around, walk back to Beech Avenue then head up to The Goof on Queen Street for a cold drink. (The Garden Gate was the restaurant's actual name, but in the early 1960s it had been dubbed "The Goof," when the green neon letters -D in GOOD and -OOD in FOOD on the overhead electric sign over the front door burnt out but were left unrepaired for so long that the nickname became a part of Beach lore.)

I had opened the restaurant's glass door and was holding it open for a man and woman who were leaving. The woman threw me a beaming smile as she stepped outside: *"Paul Illidge!"*

*"Linda Gordon!"*

*"Sledge!"* her husband Doug said, walking out behind her, using my nickname from high school. Putting out his hand, we shook.

"Long time no see. How are the kids?" I introduced them. Doug and I had a quick chat.

We were the same age, had been good friends in high school. Linda, two years younger, had been behind us, in the same class as John and Ellen. A bridesmaid at their wedding, she had been one of Ellen's best friends. Doug apologized that they really had to get going, wished me luck at school in the coming year (he was a teacher too), before I could tell him that I'd quit in June—Linda calling back as they started across Queen Street: *"That was terrible about John!"* Doug waved, put his arm through Linda's and rushed to beat the red light.

Carson asked, when we were seated in our booth, what was terrible about John?

"I'm not sure what she meant," I told him.

"Is he in trouble?" Nicky asked.

"If he is, I'm sure he can find a way out of it," I said. "You know Uncle John."

"Beauty guy!" exclaimed Kenny the smiling Chinese waiter arriving at our table. He'd worked at The Goof for over forty years. He knew me and most of my friends. His smile fell. "What your rascal brother up to these days anyway?" Not waiting for an answer, the smile returning, he held up his pad, clicked his pen and took our order.

Early to bed for everyone except me that night. Tuesday was the first day of school for the kids, Carson starting ninth grade, Nicky going into seventh, Hannah in grade four. Before heading to Oakville Movers, John was going downtown for a meeting. Tammy had to be in Ottawa by noon.

As the only one who didn't have to be somewhere, I treated myself to some Dujardin, plunked myself down on the living-room couch with which John had replaced mine. Feet up on the matching ottoman, it occurred to me in a kind of revelation that this was the first September I wouldn't be returning to an educational institution of some kind in forty-six years. I'd started kindergarten at four, went through elementary school, high school and university in successive years then taught English for the next twenty-six years. It was sobering to realize that I'd spent ninety-five percent of my life up to that point—nearly half a  century—in schools of one sort or another, either sitting at a desk in a classroom as a student or standing behind one as a teacher. The same routine every year: rising for the national anthem every morning, hormone-rich adolescents, textbooks, tests, essays, exams, sports, theatre, staff politics; with time measured out by the clock and the ringing of bells at precise forty, then in later years, seventy-five minute intervals for seven hours per day, every day.

When people found out I was quitting teaching to write for my living, a dream I'd secretly harboured since high school, they told me, with a few exceptions, that I must have been out of my mind. Single parent to three children? A sizeable mortgage? Monthly bills? Taxes? What was I thinking? Couldn't I see that I was committing *financial suicide?* They thought I loved teaching.

I did. Sure I did. Or rather I had. But with the rise of the *Administrative Complex* and *Systems Education* in the 1990s, I'd come to the realization that the teaching of adolescents had, in fact, become counter-educational. The school where I was teaching, the largest in the school board, became a template for all that was wrong with modern education—making administrative power and compliance with its bureaucratic directives, rather than academic excellence, the goals of education.

The previous year had been the worst of my twenty-six year career, to the point that returning this September would have been hazardous to my health so contaminated had relations become between "The Admin Team" at Laurel Downs Secondary—the principal, her three vice principals and all new to their positions—and the hundred and sixty staff.

By the end of the first week of September, the school had descended into grim, black comedy chaos from which the administration (Leora the principal and her first assignment, vice principals Gary and Mike, rookies as well, and Fred, an old friend of Leora's, who had been bounced from another school board for illegally strip-searching a male student) seemed incapable of extricating itself: starting at the end of the first week of school, fire alarms went off two and three times a day for a month and a half, followed by two weeks of bomb threats at the end of October. It was sheer madness evacuating the school's nearly 2,700 students and staff to the football field behind the school each time the fire alarms sounded (some days it felt like we spent more time on the football field than in class), the increasingly perturbed fire department rushing to the scene, conducting their twenty-minute investigation (it was a huge building), the all-clear given after thirty or forty minutes with not a whiff of smoke detected.

The perpetrators (though a rumour was rife that "Pyro Man" and "Bomber Boy" were the same person) were never even witnessed, let alone caught, despite *state-of-the-art surveillance technology* the Admin Team warned in a PA announcement at the beginning of the second month that the police had installed in one of the vice principal's offices. Though the information was withheld from students, we staff were informed that certain fire alarms had been rigged with paint-spraying devices that would cover the front of the perpetrator's clothes. It was only a matter of time before he or she was caught and brought to justice. Idle threats no one outside of Leora and her Three Stooges took seriously, as the disruptions continued unabated.

People's nerves frayed. Teachers and senior students in particular were reaching their breaking point, falling so far behind in their curriculum that credits for the semester were in jeopardy. Half the graduating class wouldn't apply, or wouldn't be allowed to apply, to college or university.

You'd have been hard-pressed to find a teacher, a student or parent who wasn't angry and fed up with Leora and her Admin Team for losing control of the school. How were teaching and student learning supposed to go on in an atmosphere where one never knew when an alarm might shatter studious silence? That was the other thing: the fire alarm at Laurel Downs was an eardrum-shattering electric buzzer blast every other second so loud and grating you thought it was the call to battle stations on an aircraft carrier. People joked, only half kidding, that the blaring sonic buzz was seriously affecting their hearing. *Huh? What???*

As staff coordinator (liaison between teachers and the Administrative Team—an elected position), people came to me with ideas, suggestions and complaints they wanted discussed at the next staff meeting. I would prioritize the items, present them to the principal, Leora, who then drew up the staff meeting agenda: many of the items I'd presented were conspicuous by their absence on the agenda she gave me to hand out, composed as it was of Leora's secondary, tertiary and incidental items that avoided any mention of the problems, crises and turmoil enveloping the school.

I went to Leora's office in mid-October and submitted the staff's preferred agenda points. She gave them a quick glance but set the paper aside, folded her hands on the desk and levelled her eyes at me, the paranoid aggressive look that I'd come to recognize as a sign that I was in trouble.

*Dissension among the staff*, she announced, was getting out of hand; a group of troublemakers were plotting a *rebellion* against her, a rebellion of which she had good reason to believe I was the ringleader.

"*Illich*, isn't that a Russian name?" she asked me two days later, after—as I knew it would be—a disastrous staff meeting that devolved into teachers throwing paper airplanes at Leora as she delivered some pointedly heated remarks, castigating them for their increasingly disrespectful and generally unprofessional behaviour toward her as principal—

Two paper airplanes suddenly sailed at her from either side of the room, one sticking in her hair. Outraged, she shrieked: *You people are acting like children! I won't put up with it any longer! Grow up!!* at which point she turned from the podium, stormed toward the door of the lecture theatre where the meeting was being held, ordering me to follow her to her office. Someone shouted just before she hit the crash bar to open the door: *Do not pass go, Leora! Do not collect two hundred dollars!* the heckle drawing derisive, humiliating laughter throughout the room.

In her office, ignoring her ridiculous question about Illidge being a Russian name (Vladimir *Illich* Ulyanov, aka Lenin, led the Russian Revolution), Leora berated me for not controlling the staff better in meetings, accused me of enabling the deterioration of staff/principal relations to the point that things were now completely out of hand as a result of my operating behind her back to turn the faculty against her, something she said she knew I had been doing since the beginning of—

I interrupted her to say that I wasn't the one who had insulted the staff by calling them children and telling them to grow up. How did she expect adult professionals to react to a demeaning comment like that? Being blamed for what were her and her Admin Team's failures—

That did it. Leora shot to her feet, informing me that she was putting another reprimand in my file; one more, so she informed me, and I'd be placed on *administrative review*, unofficially known as the *termination track*, i.e., on track to be fired, in my case for *insubordination*. The reprimands were always for insubordination. I had no doubt another would be coming my way sooner rather than later.

They were always for the most absurd things, so absurd that there was no point arguing with Leora about the reasoning behind them, because there was none. The best illustration was the reprimand she'd doled out shortly after Pyro Man's false alarms ceased, when there really was a fire, and by chance I was the one who happened to have put it out.

A student had started it in the recycling bin of an empty classroom next to the one where I was covering for an absent French teacher. A student I knew named Jesse walked past the room, spotted the smoke pouring out the open door, ran back to my class and shouted at me to come right way, there was a fire next door. This was a month after Pyro Man, the phantom fire alarm puller's reign of terror. I told Jesse to cut it out. It wasn't a joking matter. He should know better. Jesse pleaded with me, *swore* he was telling the truth. A good kid, and from the urgency with which he said it, I knew he was. We ran next door.

Flames were leaping out of the blue recycling bin and licking the lower shelf of the wall unit, stacked with hundreds of pages of photocopy handouts, the bottom ones already starting to burn.

I grabbed the fire extinguisher out of its bracket by the door, told Jesse to go into the hall and pull the fire alarm.

"No way, sir! Are you kidding me? They'll think I'm Pyro Man!"

*"No, they won't!* I'll vouch for you. Get cracking!"

He waited to see what happened with the extinguisher. I pulled the pin, held it up, pointed it down at the bin and squeezed the trigger and kept squeezing it until the jet of white chemical powder snuffed out the flames. *"Good work, sir!"* said Jesse as we ran out.

Back in class about forty minutes later, word had circulated that Pyro Man was back and had struck again. The PA blipped on as I was explaining to my tenth grade class what had actually happened. Leora's secretary, Ginny, summoned me to her office. *"They're going to congratulate you, sir!"* one of the kids called to me as I went out.

"Maybe there's a reward, sir!"

As it turned out, I didn't get as far as Leora's office. She and the captain, in full firefighting gear, hat on, were standing with the three vice principals outside their offices, the fire captain livid, as I could see by the reddening of his face as I approached.

He did the talking.

"You were the one who put the fire out?"

"I was."

He glared at me. "It's not your job to put out fires. That's our job."

"I put the fire out, Captain, because a recycling bin filled with paper had been set on fire. Above it there were three shelves stacked with course handouts, hundreds of sheets of paper. They were already starting to catch and burning fast—"

"You're not listening," he cut in.

"There was a fire. I put it out. Isn't that what's important here?"

His aggravation rose. "I'll decide what's important."

"What's the point of fire extinguishers if they're not to put out fires?"

"It's *not your job!*"

"Respectfully, Captain, if I hadn't put that fire out, we wouldn't be standing here having this conversation."

Leora erupted. "With *that,* you've just bought yourself a reprimand, mister!"

"For putting a fire out?"

"For insubordination."

"To whom? I put out a fire, Leora."

"I'll speak with you in my office later."

I considered myself dismissed, left and went back to class. But I didn't show up in her office later. The war brewing between us had finally broken out into the open. I needed to plan my strategy carefully.

Or did I? On the drive home, I contemplated Leora's staff meeting tantrum of a few weeks earlier, the threats she levelled at me in her office afterwards confirming her obsession with having me fired for what in her book was the crime of crimes: *insubordination.* She held all the cards. The union could delay the process, but they couldn't protect me. She could harass me with impunity—had already tried to rattle my cage when she had me summoned to a vice principal's office out of the blue one morning, two regional police detectives interrogating me as to the source of letters to the director of the board of education from a group calling itself the *Dead Poets Society*: complaint letters with examples of negligence, incompetence, unsafe practices and fraud on Leora's part; they had to be from someone with *inside information.* The letters were libellous! I could do jail time! My teaching career would be kaput! All that could be avoided, however, if I told them I was the person who had been sending the poison-pen letters, the ringleader of the *Dead Poets Society.*

I foiled their attempt to get my fingerprints by handling the clear plastic "dusted" sleeve containing a copy of the letter I'd supposedly written, by holding it between my knuckles. The bad cop seethed when he noticed what I was doing, exploding in my face when I gave him back the un-fingerprinted sleeve. *This wasn't the end of things by a long-shot!* He slammed the door behind me so violently when I walked out that the walls in the outer office shook so hard, several pictures popped off their hooks and crashed to the floor.

On the way back to class I did my own shaking, not the frightened kind, mind you, but the angry kind, an anger like I'd never felt before, mixed with a despairing feeling in the pit of my stomach; a sense of helplessness because, under the circumstances, there was absolutely nothing I could do to mitigate the adversarial situation with Leora.

Things grew considerably more tense when it leaked out that Leora had been altering the provincial school records of some graduating students who had been in one of my senior English classes. Whether she was changing the transcripts for money or not couldn't be ascertained, according to my friend Andy, the Head of Guidance, who arranged a clandestine early-morning meeting with me in the woods two blocks from the school, where he turned over photocopies of the provincial record transcripts Leora had told him she'd had to "correct," along with copies of my original records with the final failing marks. She had bumped up some students' English marks by as much as forty-percent; in the case of one boy whom I had failed for serial plagiarizing, by fifty-three percent—from a mark of 43 to a new mark of 96—an astonishing thing to have done on an official government record, when her falsifying act brought the suddenly brilliant student the school's coveted senior English prize.

Thanks to my friend Andy, I had the evidence I needed to expose Leora and take her down if I wanted to. But the question was, did I want to? Would it be worth the aggravation and stress that would descend on me if I were to go to the media and reveal the truth?

Driving home with the incriminating documents, I made my decision: teaching wasn't for me anymore. It was pretty simple, really. My twenty-six year career at four different high schools had been an extremely good one. I loved my subject, I loved the kids; some days I couldn't believe I was actually getting paid for what I was doing when I enjoyed it so much. But in the previous two years, it had gradually stopped being enjoyable and become really hard work coping with the culture of complaint that Leora had introduced to the school. She bullied and harassed good teachers and ignored the bad ones who were fully protected from termination by the union. I resolved not to let Leora have the satisfaction of terminating me. I'd take matters into my own hands and resign, slipping photocopies of the false records and my originals (attested to by my friend Andy in Guidance of course) in with my resignation letter just to let her know that the tables had turned: her fate was in my hands now. It would remain there as long as I wanted it to and, best of all, there was nothing she could do about it.

I'd had enough of Leora. And I'd had enough of an education system that placed someone as unqualified, personality-disordered and morally bankrupt as her in charge of a high school in the first place—a system that had come to have everything to do with catering to the whims and stroking the egos of career "educrats" (education bureaucrats) and little or nothing to do with fostering a safe, secure, stimulating and exciting learning environment in which teachers could do their jobs effectively, and where kids could enjoy learning, having fun in the process and preparing for their future.

In September, I'd be turning fifty. A colleague had tipped me off that the Teachers Pension Plan was offering a retirement window for people who were turning fifty before the end of the calendar year. The window would allow qualified teachers to retire early but still receive full pension.

I put in for mine, valued at $412,000 according to the person on the phone, $48,000 in yearly income, $24,000 less than the $72,500 I'd make if I kept teaching.

There was income tax to pay, of course, and the medical-dental family benefit deduction was $575 a month: *$7,000.* My forty-eight thousand shrinking fast, I thought about it for a day then contacted the Teachers Pension people again and told them I was opting out. I wanted my money out of the plan. I was through with teaching; I wanted to be through with their pension as well.

There wasn't a single doubt in my mind that I was doing the right thing. Still, it seemed worth talking to an actuary, just in case.

I went to see a man named Ben Dibben, the actuary who had evaluated my pension for divorce financials the year before. After outlining my five-year plan for a full-time writing business, explaining to Ben that writing for my living was something I'd dreamed of doing since I was fourteen, he said he applauded my decision. Said I couldn't go wrong if I was an able money manager, especially in the first few years until I got the writing business up and running: in general, a business of any kind takes about five years to succeed if it's going to. "The key, in your case," he said, "is believing in yourself, in your talent and ability, and above all, in your *resourcefulness*," an interesting word for him to have used, I thought, since if there's anything I'd been all my life it was resourceful.

"Besides," he added matter-of-factly as he walked me out of his office when we were done, "teachers, on average, if they retire at sixty-five, which most of them do, only ever use about seven years of their pension." It took me a second to understand. I looked at him. He nodded.

"Why didn't you tell me that when I made the appointment, Ben? I could have saved myself a hundred dollars!" He smiled benignly. "Forget the hundred dollars. You're a starving artist now. Just put me in one of your books."

All seemed good until the last week of May, only a month to go before *Liberation Day*, June 30th. The Teachers Pension Plan notified me in a registered letter that they had revised my pension estimate and I would now be receiving only $312,000 from the fund, no explanation as to where the other hundred thousand dollars had gone and why.

In a panic, I called the Pension Plan to inquire about the missing funds, asking the woman with whom I was speaking on what basis a hundred thousand dollars would have disappeared. Surely there had been a mistake.

"No," she came back. "This happens from time to time. There really isn't anything we can do about it. Whoever was handling your file must have discovered an error in the original valuation."

I asked if I could talk to that person to find out more about the error.

Unfortunately that wasn't possible. She had no way of knowing exactly who was handling my file.

Dazed, confused, searing mad—how could a hundred grand simply vanish?—I called the father of a friend who had at one time been the CEO of the Teachers Pension Plan and explained. Ted asked me what retirement date I'd put down on my original application to withdraw the pension funds. June 30th, I told him, adding that the Pension Plan person I had talked with initially said that "retirement date" referred to the last day of the school year. Ted chuckled. "Change it to July 3rd," he said. "It has to do with the price of thirty-year bonds."

"Why wouldn't someone have clarified that for me?"

A wry chuckle. "The Plan doesn't like people taking their money out. They have their ways of hanging on to you."

I made the change and, sure enough, a week later my hundred thousand was back.

At the end of August, I paid a low six-figure sum in income tax, had $200,000 invested according to government regulations in what was called a LIRF (Locked-In Retirement Fund) with a friend from university's wealth management firm ($2.7 billion under management), telling Sandra, the adviser my friend had set me up with, that my puny investment must have been one of the lowest in company history. She assured me it wasn't. Noting my last name, she frowned slightly, looking away from me as if she had put two and two together and was silently wondering whether—

—"John Illidge is my brother?"

"Sorry," said Sandra with an embarrassed shrug.

"Don't be," I kidded her. "Every family can use a little infamy in its life," a flippant remark that would come back to haunt me . . .

Tuesday morning, the day after Labour Day, once everyone had left the house, I poured myself a second and then a third cup of coffee, revelling in the sense of freedom I was experiencing for the first time in nearly fifty years, an ease of mind, a calmness, a contentment that seemed to have come over me in the previous twenty-four hours that I found . . . *clarifying* was the word that came to mind. I could see clearly where I wanted to go, how I would get there, and what I was going to do when I did.

After breakfast, I phoned my bank to let them know I'd be coming into the branch at 10:30 the following morning to withdraw $50,000, half of the $100,000 payment the Pension Plan had stipulated I take in cash. The money had been deposited into my account the night before. I was told to ask for Sharita, the assistant manager, when I came in. The person with whom I was talking asked about denominations. I said I thought hundreds would be best.

The branch was in the Beach, not far from the house where I grew up. I must have attached a subconscious meaning to this return to my roots at a time when I was about to plunge into the most uncertain of futures.

I found myself parking on my old street, a few doors down from "*327,*" the house where I lived until I was eighteen and moved downtown to live at the university while my parents, brothers and sister moved to St. Catharines, Ontario, on the Niagara Peninsula, when my father took a new job there. I hadn't been on the street in over thirty years. It surprised me that the house looked much the same as I remembered it the day in 1970 when we moved out.

Nearly 10:30, I walked quickly down the street, went a block east, my Royal Bank branch the fourth building along on the north side: a narrow storefront between the Bethel Gospel Temple and a store named *Arleigh's* that sold fur coats, both buildings that had been there when I was a boy.

I found no one about when I stepped inside, went past the closed door of the *Manager's Office* into an open area to my right that was really just a small grey room with four teller stations, all deserted, no one at the reception desk, security cameras trained on the entrance and the teller stations.

Things stayed this way for several uncomfortable minutes. Something didn't seem right. There were no customers, and the bank had just opened at ten o'clock. I got a strange vibe looking up at the security cameras. The silence was unnerving. Was the staff hiding in a room somewhere watching me? Were they thinking I had come to rob the place?

A door noisily flew open down the hall to my left surprising me, several women hurrying out laughing. Two of them went to teller stations and opened up, the third continued toward me smiling.

"Sharita?"

No, she wasn't Sharita. "Are you Paul?"

I told her I was. She led me down the hall, opened the door to a room across the way from the one she and the two other women had just come from. We went inside. Sharita would be along shortly, the woman said, then left.

It was a small, bare room, a bare desk with an office chair behind it, two chairs in front, no phone, no computer, nothing on the grey walls. I took a seat, growing nervous again about the set-up, which had an increasingly Alfred Hitchcock feel to it. I waited for what felt like ten but was probably closer to five minutes for a woman without a name tag but who I presumed was Sharita, the assistant manager, to show up, five banded bundles of bills in her one hand, five bundles in the other: five hundred $100 bills in all, $50,000.

No introductions, no request for identification—which struck me as a little strange—Sharita spread the bundles in a neat row across the desk in front of her, about six inches between each bundle. She raised her eyes from the money and looked at me.

"Ready?"

"Let the counting begin," I joked.

No smile, she slipped the band off the first bundle, licked her thumb and began counting the crisp new bills.

It took all of five quiet minutes, after which she put the bills back in two stacks of five, pressed the bundles together and slid the cash across the table.

An awkward moment, I realized when I looked at the bundles that I had nothing to carry them in. Walking the street in broad daylight with $50,000 stuffed in my pockets probably wasn't the wisest thing to do.

I asked Sharita if she had an envelope of some kind. She searched the desk drawers, came up cold, no envelopes, had an idea, leaned down and checked the bottom drawer again.

"What about this?" She held up a purple felt Crown Royal whisky bottle bag with the gold tasselled drawstring.

"Perfect!"

When I pulled in the driveway at home a little after 11:30, John was just opening his car door. He must have come home for something. He waited till I got out of the car, caught a look at the Crown Royal bag and chuckled.

"Drinking during the day now are we?"

"It's for a friend."

We laughed.

"I'll be home around five—can't miss *Blind Date!*" He hopped in the Jaguar, backed out and booted it up the street, Oakville-bound to check on things at the moving company.

I went straight to my basement office, to the closet where I stored my manuscripts, financial records and personal papers in nine-by-twelve by five inch white boxes my printer supplied me with. At the time, there were thirty-six boxes of material on the shelves, numbered and titled on both ends in black magic marker.

With John in the house now, I was taking no chances. It wasn't said about him for nothing that he had a nose for money. I knew he did; he'd always had one. My hunch was that he'd catch the scent of my $50,000 in no time flat wandering around the house whenever I wasn't home. Like my mother, John liked to snoop.

In the opposite corner, beside my desk, I had a filing cabinet stuffed to the brim with fifteen years' worth of old bank statements, cancelled checks, warranties, utility and phone bills that Jill had insisted on storing for some reason. Burying my treasure within a drawer crammed with old household bills seemed the ideal thing to do.

The filing cabinet wasn't the locking kind, however. I reconsidered. Theory would tell you that no one would think anything valuable could have been kept in a drawer that didn't have a lock and was full of paper which should have been shredded years ago. However, John, with his talent for concealing things, would recognize the hide-in-plain-sight ruse. He'd go straight for the filing cabinet—the top drawer of which was open an inch or so and I hadn't left it that way. Had he already been in for a snoop?

New plan. I went over to the door-less closet, white printer's boxes, thirty-six of them stacked, titled and numbered on the three shelves I'd built on the back wall. I took manuscript box 19 down from its place in the center of the stack on the middle shelf—copies of a screenplay that I'd written five years earlier called *King of Candyland*. An action drama about Owen and Oliver Henry—the O. Henry brothers—confronting a dark secret from childhood that has haunted them ever since.

Inside there were five bound copies of the 118-page script. I lifted them out, laid the ten bundles of hundred dollar bills on the bottom of the box, spaced evenly apart, then put four copies of *King of Candyland* on top. I slipped the fifth copy, which I'd removed to make room for the bill bundles, into the script box below. The *Candyland* lid back on, five manuscript boxes back on top of it, I took the Crown Royal bag upstairs and slipped it in a kitchen drawer, mission accomplished.

Further security measures would be necessary, but I breathed a sigh of relief for now. I wouldn't have minded a shot or two of Crown Royal. My nerves were frayed by the surprise encounter with John. With what I was coming to know about his embezzling ways, was it just a matter of time before he'd root out my stash? And if he did, how would I manage to get the money back from him when it was now clear to me that no one else ever had?

# CHAPTER NINE

# SOMETHING WICKED
# THIS WAY COMES

JOHN SETTLED EASILY into family life, something that surprised me considering he had only lived sporadically with his own family in the last five years. I figured there might be a period of adjustment, that he'd find the everyday routines of domestic life with three children hard to get used to. Yet, there he was living with us and, as far as we could see, enjoying himself: sharing bathrooms, eating breakfast and supper with us, watching TV; joking, laughing, always ready with entertaining anecdotes, stories, tales of his past exploits that even my kids knew, from long experience, were too tall to be true, yet his dramatic talents were so compelling they would hang on every word.

Monday to Friday the kids were off to school by 8:30, I was in my office working by 9:30, the time John, a late-riser, either headed downtown for "meetings" at Medallion Securities with Stafford Kelley, the stockbroker whom he'd been paying $8,000 a month to do his trading for him, or to Oakville Movers, his ride now a new Mercedes S500, black of course, the *RSKY BZNS* licence plates resurrected *now that he'd sold the Porsche.*

What of the dented Jaguar? With the new Mercedes in the garage, it sat, no license plates, rusty dent and all, in the driveway beside my Honda Accord.

At the end of the third week he was living with us, a Thursday night, everyone else asleep (John never went to bed later than ten o'clock), I was lying in bed reading a not very interesting book, losing the battle to keep my eyes from closing—when the doorbell rang and they shot open: 10:55 by the alarm clock on my bedside table. I hopped out of bed, threw on my

90

robe, hurrying downstairs to answer before the bell rang again.

I flicked on the porch light and opened up to a black man in a black turtleneck under a black leather coat, maybe in his early forties, well over six feet, a fine-featured face, soft-spoken, pleasant.

"Is John here by any chance?"

"John who?"

"John Illidge."

"Bit late for a house call, isn't it?"

He looked at his watch then back at me. "Not eleven yet."

"How can I help you?"

"I'm picking up his Jaguar. I wondered if there was anything in it that John might want. Can you wake him?"

"That might take a while," I said. "He's a sound sleeper. I'll check for him." I stepped over to the hall table to get—

"Don't need the keys," said the repo man. "Just informing him."

He turned, headed down the walk. I slipped on my shoes and followed him.

The Jaguar's four doors were open, the cab lights on inside. A blue clunker of a sedan had parked at the foot of the drive, a bald, burly white guy in jeans, cowboy boots, a white T-shirt under a Cincinatti Reds windbreaker leaning back against it watching me, arms crossed over his chest, a cigarette in his mouth.

The black guy walked down to him, taking out and lighting a cigarette, the two of them smoking as I went through the car collecting John's contents, a second wave of belongings that he hadn't yet brought into the house because there was nowhere to put them; his bedroom was already packed to the gills.

A partial inventory of the salvage went as follows: two Montblanc suitcases (full by their weight), four expensive-looking leather brief bags, two brown, two black (all packed tight with documents), three leather attaché cases, two of them open on the back seat, their contents scattered around: file folders out of which legal papers, bills and correspondence had spilled, several dozen check books on different accounts from major banks, twenty or more boxes of business cards, some with their tops off, cards strewn around, fourteen pairs of shoes, dress, casual, athletic, some new and in boxes, some with shoe trees in them.

In the trunk, a golf bag with a full set of clubs, a pair of spikes, an umbrella, two badminton rackets, a can of feather birds, a neon green Frisbee, a squash racket, one ski pole, a motorcycle helmet, two empty 40-ounce bottles of *Absolut* vodka, a fully taped Titan Pro hockey stick, a yellow plastic grocery bag with the *RSKY BZNS* license plates in it.

Working fast, I had the Jag empty except for some fast food bags, coffee cups, pop cans and assorted garbage in about ten minutes, the two repo men at the foot of the drive smoking and talking quietly while I worked, in no hurry to be on their way knowing the repossession had been successful and they would be paid. I picked the Jaguar keys up off the hall table and took them outside.

Closing the trunk, then the doors except for the driver's, where the black repo man came to stand. He gave his partner a thumbs up before turning to me.

"We'll be off then."

I held up the keys. "You want these?"

"Nope. Souvenir."

"How did you know he was here?"

"Your sister-in-law. We went there first."

"Thanks for letting me get his stuff."

"Anytime." He snickered at something private, hopped in the Jaguar and closed the door. He waited until his partner had backed out, backed out himself, the two cars moving off slowly down the street, one of the Jaguar's tail lights still burnt-out I noticed.

Before I turned off the light in my office—just curious, a reward for my efforts as I saw it—I tried the locks on all the bags and suitcases. Most of them were open. But I'm a respecter of privacy, snooping something I've always been against, so I didn't look inside; I didn't peak at any of the legal correspondence either.

The only thing I did that you could construe as nosy was done out of necessity: when I was picking up business cards off the back seat, I had to note the company names in order to return them to the proper boxes. It was no surprise each name exuded Trust, Security, Integrity, Steadfastness—many sounding like they came from the same sturdy template as Rampart.

John was Chief Executive Officer on all the cards, *International Finance, Investment Banking, Leveraged Buyouts* and what the various companies did, their offices in global business and financial hubs like New York, London, Paris, Zurich, Hong Kong and Tokyo, with Montreal, Miami or Toronto substituted occasionally—credentials to impress even the most reluctant of investors.

But noticing the many similarities in the way all the company cards were designed, and that John was listed as either CEO, president, or occasionally both at every firm, it was easy to see that the cards were fake;

they were printed up as part of a repertoire of deceptive targeting techniques John used to attract investors to one of the high-return securities firms he was promoting—where they were guaranteed to receive higher returns than anywhere else—all along unaware that the companies they were handing thousands, hundreds of thousands and in some cases millions to, consisted of nothing more than staunch-sounding names he had dreamed up and put on business cards, and the only one making money on the transactions was John . . .

Tammy would come to Toronto one weekend, John would drive to Ottawa the next, the kids and I heading to Beinn Tighe on those weekends at John's request to keep an eye on the place. A local roofing company was replacing the slate shingles on the kitchen and living-room wings of the house, both rooms with several skylights in them through which the roofers would be able to see inside. According to John, they were already hosing him on the price, charging him *rich-guy-from-the-city* rates, something all the local contractors did. Plus, John had noticed a couple of them eyeing his two new ATVs and Yamaha dirt bike chained to a tree in the woods, which could only be seen from the roof of the house. He said he felt better knowing someone was around when, so the police had told him, break-and-enters by contractors and people connected to them were on the rise.

After school on Fridays, the kids and I would drive to the farm, stopping to buy groceries for dinner on the way. Saturday morning, I'd take them to my sister Judith's in Collingwood, where they'd hang out with her until after lunch on Sunday, leaving me plenty of time to work on the book about the Crest Theatre that Barbara Somers had commissioned me to write. To be here at the home of the person about whom I was writing was a rare and fascinating privilege: I found little notes in the books of Murray's extensive library, in personal letters, diaries, notebooks going back fifty or more years to the time when he and his brother and sister were hatching the idea of a first-ever Canadian professional theatre company.

My initial meeting with Barbara, one of *the first ladies* of Canadian theatre during the 1950s and 60s, according to the Canadian Theatre Encyclopedia, seventy-nine at the time and still a formidable *grande dame* with "all her faculties intact" as she liked to joke, resulted in one of those *where I was when it happened* moments that you never forget.

Traffic on the 401 lighter with the end of rush hour, I drove down the Don Valley Parkway, got off at the Bayview extension and wound my way through Rosedale till I found Barbara's house. I parked in front, was ringing her doorbell at 9:15, staring at the red, gold, blue and green stained-glass mandala in the upper half of the door—when it flew open: Barbara was standing there in a white cable knit sweater, her hair done, lipstick matching the color of her large frame red glasses.

A distressed look on her face, she motioned urgently. "Come in! Come in! You have to see this."

The small television on the kitchen counter was showing the World Trade Centre in New York. Dark smoke was pouring out of the windows in the middle stories of the two buildings.

"Jets have just crashed into them," said Barbara. "Terrorists they think." She took two mugs out of the cupboard, set them on the counter and poured the coffee. My cup filled, she glanced across at the TV while filling hers. "My God," she said.

I turned my eyes to the TV. Neither of us spoke. I put cream and sugar in my coffee.

"Maybe we should put this off to another time, Barbara."

"What, and let the terrorists win? Not a chance. Shall we?" she said, pointing me to the living-room.

We talked for two hours, a captivating conversation about all kinds of things: the fact that today was her deceased husband Harry's birthday, about whom she'd had a haunting dream the night before in which Harry had weirdly warned her with an eerie line from the witches in *Macbeth* that *Something wicked this way comes*; the benefits of a new touching technique for pain relief that her friend Lila was coming over shortly to demonstrate; an extensive list of names, addresses and phone numbers from several well-worn address books of people that had been affiliated with the Crest Theatre in some capacity during its thirteen-year history, and who would be more than happy to talk with me about their experience, her one hope for the book that it could be ready for publishing in October 2004, the fiftieth anniversary of the theatre's founding. She wondered if that presented any problems. Three years to write a book? I assured her that gave us plenty of time.

She wanted me to know that there were absolutely no strings attached, I was free to write the story in whatever way I saw fit, warts and all, *publish and be damned*, as her brothers Donald and Murray, who managed the theatre, used to say to critics threatening them with bad reviews. She said she trusted me completely to see the theatre's numerous achievements for what they were, and write about them accordingly. For years she'd wanted a book done about the Crest while *people were still around*, so to speak. She was relieved and grateful that John had brought us together.

As to money, she asked if $15,000 was enough to get me started, what with research, traveling to do interviews, original production photos from Robert Ragsdale, the theatre's long time photographer . . . I would need funds for all that. When I needed more, as she said she knew I would with a publishing world that was nothing like what it used to be, I merely had to ask. She would alert John to let me have the money right away. "He handles my investments for me, which I suppose you know." She paused. "Speaking of which, what is he up to these days? I know he's left Rampart. I haven't heard from him in a while. Do you know if he's still living in Toronto?"

"His girlfriend's in Ottawa," I managed awkwardly, strictly speaking not a lie but avoiding her question.

"Girlfriend? What happened to Ellen?" She seemed confused.

"Well," I said, trying to cover for my slip. "It's sort of confidential right now. They're talking about a divorce, but quietly, because of the girls."

"Of course."

We went back to the kitchen for more coffee. We needed it. Her hand shook, she had to steady herself while spooning the coffee into the filter.

"Should we turn on the TV?" I asked, I don't know why, except that I hadn't really grasped the enormity of events in New York.

"It's ghastly," said Barbara, "I can't see there's any reason to."

I lied and said I had no interest, yet as the coffee maker steamed and sputtered, neither of us could keep our eyes off the dark screen.

Lunch was a spicy curry made from a recipe Barbara's friend Laura Davies had given her years ago. Born in Britain, Laura moved to India soon after the war, opened a women's clothing store in the Taj Mahal that had enjoyed many years of success. She was coming for a visit mid-October. Barbara wanted me to meet her. She would let me know the date and the three of us would have lunch. *Though not curry!* she said. *I can cook other things.*

I didn't know then but later found out that one of the reasons for Laura's visit that autumn, rather than in the spring, when she usually came to Toronto, was to talk to her lawyer about John's bankruptcy: she'd met John through Barbara ten years ago, decided to invest $75,000 with him, $75,000 that her lawyer had told her was among the smaller claims against John, which meant she stood little chance of recouping her money.

A slow drive home up the expressway toward the 401, there were dozens of jets stacked up in holding patterns to the west toward Pearson International Airport, probably grounded because of the New York attack. I left the radio off, put in a Cuban music CD instead, wondering, as I would more frequently in the next few years, what people like Laura

Davies might think of me, how she would judge me when Barbara introduced me as John's brother. *You rub shoulders with infamy,* as the French writer Albert Cossery once said, *and some is bound to rub off on you.* I'd always worried about that—guilt by association, people stigmatizing me because of my relation to John and, as always happens with stigmas, holding their suspicions against me.

John wanted to treat us to dinner that night, *a break for Daddio,* as he'd come to call these dinners on him that he was nice enough to recognize the need for, at least one night a week. That night, he said, it would also help take our minds off the disaster in New York.

As we drove to *Mr. Greek,* which, along with *Swiss Chalet, The Keg* and *Kelsey's,* was one of his favourite eateries. John forgot about the purpose of going out to keep our minds off New York and made a point of letting us know that he'd been in the World Trade Centre plenty of times in the last twenty years. He knew people that had probably been killed that day. Hundreds of billions of dollars, maybe more, had been lost. The weirdest thing: he was scheduled to have a meeting at the "WTC" in two weeks. I was tempted to ask with whom, but knew that he probably had a name ready. John liked to keep one step ahead of you.

Nicky, twelve at the time, the FBI's *Ten Most Wanted* list for some reason one of his current fascinations, remarked at dinner that Number 8 on the list, Osama bin Laden, was probably high on the FBI's suspect list.

It baffled John that Nicky would know something like that. He jumped on it, asking Nicky if he wanted to bet.

"On what? I'm just saying he could have had something to do with it. He's a known terrorist."

"But do you want to *bet* on it, Nicky Bo-bicky?" John teased. "Put your knowledge to the test? Make some money?"

Nicky looked across the table at him and grinned. "How do I know you'll pay up when you lose?"

John cracked up. "When I lose . . ."

Home from work most days between 4:30 and 5:00, John generally came into the kitchen when I'd finished my writing day and was cleaning up the kitchen before starting dinner preparations. We'd chat while he removed his tie, set his suit jacket over the back of one of the kitchen chairs before grabbing a highball glass and fixing himself a vodka on the rocks. (I didn't drink vodka, he bought his own, *Absolut,* the same brand as the empties I'd found cleaning out the Jaguar . . .)

He'd take the drink with him into the family room, locate the remote, bring it back to the armchair he always sat in and, after a sip of his drink, turn the TV on to his "shows," those being *Blind Date* at five o'clock, and *The Fifth Wheel* at five-thirty, reality dating shows where, in the *Fifth Wheel's* announcer's words, *"Strangers become lovers, and lovers become bitter suicidal exes all in the same show."*

Though they were some of the tackiest, if not the trashiest shows on television at the time (even by reality TV standards), John was addicted to them. He'd sit back in the chair, drink in his right hand resting on the arm as he ruthlessly hollered at and heckled the characters on screen, all the time keeping up a biting, sarcastic commentary, first on the *Blind Daters,* then the double-dating couples on the "more sophisticated" (according to John) *Fifth Wheel,* which featured date-swapping and secret liaisons with a provocative male or female *fifth wheel* who joined the two couples, and the fights began—cameras following every move while commentary in the form of subtitles, animations and sarcastic thought bubbles which popped up, mocking the bad behaviour of the four daters.

John would polish off three or four vodka on the rocks while absorbed in what he called "his shows," freshening his drink during the commercials.

Hannah and Nicky, having smelled dinner cooking, would drift downstairs a little before six at the tail end of *Fifth Wheel.* They'd sit down on the couch laughing, not so much at the on-screen high jinks as at John's eviscerating and, by that time, drunken play-by-play: "I don't know how you can even watch this stuff, Uncle John," Hannah said to him at one point. "It's an acquired taste, honey," he came right back, not a hint of irony, eyes glued to the TV.

There was always an air of excitement on the Fridays when Tammy came to town. She would arrive at the house about 4:30, John already home, Nicky and Hannah in the family room with one eye watching television, the other on Tammy and John when they sat down at the kitchen table for The Count, Tammy taking a few moments to sip the tea that I'd made for her, John nursing a vodka.

When ready to start, Tammy would set her tea down, off to one side, then remove her diamond engagement ring and slide it to the other side so there was plenty of room. This Nicky's and Hannah's cue that The Count was about to begin, Tammy would wait for them to come into the kitchen and sit down, John finishing off the routine joking: "Let the games begin!"

Picking up the first of the four or five Manila envelopes that John had placed in front of her, she'd take out a handful of bills (some loose, some bundled with paper straps or elastic bands), lick her thumb and forefinger and begin counting John's cut of the weekly *take* at Oakville Movers.

The kids and I kept our eyes glued on Tammy flipping through substantial wads of cash expertly, not too fast, counting to herself with each snap of her thumbs, twenties, fifties, hundred-dollar bills, the process, depending on that week's take, usually done in fifteen or twenty minutes, after which the money was wrapped in elastic by denomination, returned to the envelopes, at which point Tammy would look to John, the size of her smile corresponding to the size of the take—ten-thousand dollars on a slow week, fifteen on an average one, twenty thousand plus whenever business had been especially good. Tucking the money in her purse, Tammy would take it back to Ottawa on Monday morning, depositing it, so John explained, in their Ottawa bank account.

Immediately after The Count, or at five o'clock, whichever came first, John would freshen his drink, Tammy would top up her tea and they'd move into the family room where they'd sit together on the couch (Hannah and Nicky having gone downstairs to watch TV in the rec room) and tune in *The Shows*.

Dinner Friday night followed when *The Shows* were over, courtesy of John for the first six weeks, or rather courtesy of Ellen in that the prime rib roasts, beef tenderloins, free-range chickens and crown pork roasts John brought home on Friday night were purchased from *Bruno's*, the gourmet grocery store in North Toronto where Ellen continued to shop, unaware that Bruno had neglected to remove John's name from the account, therefore he could still sign for things. And sign he did. When I told John one night after boasting about his ruse that I thought it was a jerk thing to do, he pounced on me like I'd hurt him. "Every dollar counts these days. Why shouldn't I take advantage, when I've been the one footing the bills all these years? Besides, she can afford it."

I wasn't going to argue. I called Ellen the next day and that was it for *Bruno's* . . .

Sometimes Tammy would stay until Tuesday, or arrive Thursday so she could type up John's latest stock deals on my computer. Penny stock companies that he agreed to *pump* in exchange for two or three million shares in the company, shares which he would *dump* once his repertoire of trading manipulations sent the price high enough for him to make three- or four-hundred thousand dollars when he cashed out his shares, leaving the owners of the company holding deal contracts worth nothing by the time the share price plummeted lower than it had been when John originally became involved. Later, I would hear this referred to as a "predatory practice designed for the sole purpose of committing fraud." And there was his service fee of fifty thousand dollars, of course, which the companies paid up front, in cash.

I told him to get Tammy a laptop; I refused to have my computer used for criminal purposes. He insisted there was nothing criminal about anything he was doing. "People just think that because the business is doing so well. They're just jealous," was his defence.

Tammy continued using my computer, of course (John not having talked to her about our conversation), but he made a point of telling me the files were all accessible to me anytime I wanted to look at them—something John insisted I do so I could see everything was *on the up-and-up* and *above board* (which I knew very definitely it wasn't), long before he began asking me to type up deal documents whenever Tammy couldn't make it to town.

I went along and admit knowingly that I aided and abetted what he was doing. Why? Because I wanted to find out what was really going on in these deals—to learn and understand exactly what my brother was doing and confirm what Molly said made it criminal, loosely with the idea of creating a paper trail showing his intent to commit fraud, with which I could go to the authorities at some point. That was where the risk lay, of course. Proving intent.

As Molly pointed out, with John living and operating out of my house—counting the Oakville Movers money at my kitchen table, for starters, now typing up his stock deals—it would look pretty clearly like we were in cahoots, partners in crime: that I was complicit, very much part of his pump-and-dump scam.

What could I say in my defence except my fraternal relationship with John had ceased years ago? I had no subjective personal feelings for or against him. We'd managed to objectify things between us when we were teenagers. Any communication we had was conducted entirely in dispassionate superficialities: jokes, teasing, gossip and short exchanges about perfunctory matters. It had to be, because of the tacit understanding we shared about a traumatic incident involving our mother when we were young which had been hushed up, as such things were with families in those days, but which we had long ago come to understand there was no relevance in discussing.

Colluding with him was the last thing I was doing, or so I told myself. I was a journalist writing the profile of a criminal psychopath whom I happened to have known since he was a boy, nothing more. I saw myself as an honest observer gathering inside information that no one else had access to, evidence that could be used against him if ever an opportunity arose. In the meantime, I was only the typist.

John assumed that I knew nothing about the securities business, trading stocks or how the market worked, and I kept it that way. I let him explain how completely legitimate and innocuous the documents I typed up were. I asked nothing but simple questions to which I already knew the answer, from legal material Molly had me read. I took everything in, learning as I went, conferring with Molly regularly to understand John's modus operandi.

He knew nothing about computers. I saved the templates Tammy had created for his various companies' deal documents, copied each one into a file she would never think to open. I wondered at the time if she had any idea what John was actually doing. I had my doubts. According to John, all Tammy cared about was money. That's why he *picked* her. . .

She was working in the same building as John. He spotted her one day and made a point of riding the elevator with her every morning, exchanged the odd interested glance with her, an occasional smile.

One day, he noticed she'd had her hair done a new way. He said to her as he got off the elevator with what she apparently took as sarcasm: "Nice do." As the doors closed, she yelled, *"Fuck you!"* John said that's when he knew he had her.

After a few dates, the grooming began. Tammy, as John predicted, had a spending problem. Her office administrator salary allowed her barely enough to cover the minimum monthly payment on her credit cards. She was applying for other cards to pay off the original ones. John got her to admit that she needed a financial adviser. Rather than go to a stranger, whom she'd have to pay for the advice, why not let him come up with some strategies to help rebuild her credit?

In six months, with help from John, the credit card balances not only came down, they came right down to the point that not only was Tammy's credit restored to A-1 status, she was entitled to companion cards. For John, of course.

That had been the plan all along . . .

Faxes would come in on my office fax (I'd never given John the number that I could remember, but apparently he'd found it) consisting of bank correspondence, stock deal documents, *Without Prejudice* lawyers' letters that I would dutifully take up to his room and leave in a pile on his meticulously made bed.

Some days there were phone calls to my home number from people identifying themselves as so-and-so from *Company X, Bank Y, Investment Group Z,* wondering if the lower six-figure sum of money they were expecting (it varied between $200,000 and $400,000) had been deposited into their account yet. I would politely defer, telling them John would be happy to call them back, hanging up before they could leave their number.

Several times men phoned asking breathlessly: *"Is this Linda, or Suzanne, or Carol?"*

"Do I sound like Linda, Suzanne or Carol?" I'd reply sarcastically, wait through a few seconds of embarrassed silence, then end the call.

One day a woman called from the bank in Miami holding the mortgage on his Palm Beach, Florida, house (the one across the street from golfer Fred Couples's ex-wife) inquiring, with obvious concern, when a payment would be made on the mortgage account, since it was currently eight months in arrears. In fact, the bank was looking to foreclose unless immediate arrangements were made by Mr. Illidge to bring the account into good standing.

I thanked the woman for drawing Mr. Illidge's attention to the matter, gave her all three of what I believed were his latest cell phone numbers, and told her to have a nice day.

One morning at breakfast, two months after my meeting with Barbara, I asked him as he was getting up from the table if she had spoken to him about letting me have fifteen thousand from her account to get started on the Crest Theatre book. Could he give me an idea of when I would receive the money?

This was the conversation that I'd been so dreading; I had put it off for much longer than I should have. Barbara was asking if I'd been paid. I told her I had, no idea why. I knew that John would have an airtight *it's-not my fault, things are slow right now* alibi ready, the kind he never failed to come up with when he was due to give you money.

Because of the bankruptcy, *all his funds were frozen.* It was impossible to get access to them. And the trustees for Rampart had slapped a Mareva injunction on him, meaning he couldn't access any of Rampart's accounts.

I asked him how that applied to Barbara's money.

"It applies to all my clients' money."

"So what are you doing for cash in the meantime?"

"I've squirreled some away here and there to keep me afloat."

*"Here and there?"*

"Everything's legit. Like I said, it's just a little difficult getting to it right now."

"Nothing shady?"

"Nothing shady."

"Squirreled away where?" This caught him off guard. "The Cayman Islands?"

He became even more off guard. "Someone in my position can't just zip down and make a withdrawal without attracting attention."

"How so?"

"The bankruptcy trustees would be on me like pit bulls on a poodle."

"Wanting to know about these other accounts . . ."

"Exactly."

"Offshore, in other words."

He didn't appear uncomfortable talking about it, so I continued.

"Isn't there someone who could go to the offshore bank and retrieve some of it for you—those millions in net worth you're always talking about?"

He gave me a look, not defensive, more like he was trying to figure out what I was driving at. He considered. "Why would someone be willing to accept five hundred thousand dollars for all the risk involved in bringing me back five million? Why would someone do that, Paul?"

"You could find somebody reliable, don't you think?" I gave him the names of three people we both knew in the investment business whose reputations were impeccable.

"Dealing with offshore banks isn't the kind of thing impeccable people do."

"So there *is* something shady."

"I just have to be careful, that's all."

"Why not let me go down?"

"To the Caymans?"

He laughed, amused at the thought, or so it seemed, until he sat down at the table again, a serious look on his face that said he was interested in hearing more . . .

# CHAPTER TEN

# THE PLAN

**M**ONDAY NIGHT, just before ten, my phone rang. I picked up after the third ring. A man in a casual almost friendly tone, who pronounced G's at the end of words as K's, introduced himself as Gerhard Gurdler, trustee in bankruptcy, *jokink* clumsily that I was a hard person to reach, however, now that he'd succeeded, it was his duty to inform me that I owed him fifty-eight thousand dollars, two promissory notes to John James Illidge in that amount *havink* been signed in a *meetink* with John at Rampart Securities—*somethink* which he, Gerhard (people called him Gerry), didn't particularly like the thought of *doink*, but no matter, as personal bankruptcy trustee for John, he was professionally obligated to collect the fifty-eight thousand at his earliest opportunity, or (he paused for effect) he'd pursue litigation where, unfortunately, I would lose to his Bay Street lawyers, so why didn't I just get the money together for him, thereby *savink* myself the trouble and expense of *goink* to court—

I cut him off. "I think you have the wrong number. Good night."

Five-minutes later the phone rang again. Gurdler. I answered it.

"Wrong number," I said, turning my phone off this time.

I managed to catch John mid-morning on Tuesday at the Medallion number that he'd given me. No answer. I hit redial. He picked up after the first ring. "Gerhard Gurdler called at ten o'clock last night threatening that I make good on the promissory notes for fifty-eight thousand, or else."

John laughed. "Or else what?"

"The money was supposed to have been from mom's account, John."

"It was."

"But the checks were from Rampart."

"Business personal checks."

"I've never heard of such a thing."

"My CEO account at Rampart. I drew the fifty-eight thousand from it, so I had to replace it with money from mom's account."

"And did you?"

"Of course."

"Well if the money was returned to Rampart, what's Gerry still doing with the promissory notes?"

"You'd have to ask him. I guess he found them going through my files. I thought I threw all that stuff out."

"Call him off. Tell him the truth, that it was mom's money, to tear up the notes."

"I wish I could, but that's obstructing justice. I'll go to jail."

"Have him call her up then, so she can verify the money came from her, not you."

"She won't remember."

"You know that's not true."

"Fine, I'll mention it to her."

He didn't, of course. Three weeks after he gave me the $58,000, my mother had removed his power of attorney and transferred it to my sister.

"Tell Judith to check Mom's Rampart statements. The fifty-eight thousand would have shown up there. I have no access to any of that now."

Obviously uncomfortable with the conversation, to lighten things up John told me not to worry about Gurdler. "He's harmless. Just rattling your cage."

"He's an asshole."

"First class, I agree."

"Why did they saddle you with a prick like him?"

"They didn't. You pick your own bankruptcy trustee. I picked Gerry because I knew right off the bat he wasn't as smart as he thought he was, and he had serious self-esteem issues. You can get your way with people like him pretty easily if you stroke their egos and let them believe they're smarter than you. Besides, he owes me."

"Money?"

"A favour."

"Why's that?"

"I met him a year ago, when I knew I was going to declare bankruptcy and had to line up a trustee. He was fifty-two, had bags of money, had never been married, let alone had a girlfriend, but he was obsessed with finding and marrying a blue-eyed Swedish blond, an Aryan fetish or something, which is weird since Gerry's Jewish. Trouble is, he's only five-six with his shoes on. At the time, he was obese for a man of his size, had thinning hair, a face just this side of ugly, and he wore thick-lens glasses. He confessed the deep, dark Swedish blond fetish to me after three martinis, when we went to lunch to discuss him becoming my trustee. I saw an opportunity, told Gerry I thought I could help him if he really wanted to change his life around—maybe even introduce him to a Swedish blond—but only if he dropped eighty pounds, got contact lenses, grew a moustache and goatee (it would be blond, but it drew attention away from his near baldness), started working out regularly, burned all his old clothes and bought a completely new wardrobe that made him look like someone a Swedish blond might consider looking at if she saw him in the VIP lounge of the right downtown clubs. He shed the pounds through Jenny Craig, grew the goatee, bought the clothes, got the contact lenses, joined a fitness centre, and came along with me to the right clubs, where I gave him tips on how to walk, talk, stand, sit, and flash a three-grand wad of hundreds and fifties whenever he could.

"When it came to the point I thought he was ready, the occasional woman giving him second glances—looking his way, maybe a little curious—I introduced him to a Swedish woman I knew named Sidse, a knock-out blond: eighteen years younger than Gerry, extremely pretty, in good shape, a flight attendant for KLM on layover in Toronto and happy to party the night away with us.

"I left about eleven. According to Gerry, Sidse went back to his place, skipped her flight the next morning, and a week later they were in love, Sidse even talking about moving in with him. Euphoric, Gerry gushed that she was the woman of his dreams, just like I'd predicted. He said he didn't know how to begin thanking me. I told him to take his time. One day he'd find a way."

"You pimped a wife for him?"

"It wasn't easy, believe me."

"He wants to marry her?"

"He's hoping to."

"Will it happen?"

"Sidse's not exactly the marrying kind . . ."

"Of course she isn't."

"But everybody's happy in the meantime."

"And Gerry, to show his gratitude, finds a way to bend the bankruptcy rules for you now and again on any money you make, a chunk of which he's supposed to be sending to your creditors every month, isn't he?" I'd been reading up on bankruptcy fraud to learn how the process worked.

"I wouldn't call it bending, exactly, massaging maybe . . ."

"A matter of semantics."

"Of what?"

That night, a little after ten o'clock, Gerry called again.

I waited till he'd said hello then hung up on him. I turned off my phone.

Thinking he'd catch me off guard, I guess, he beamed in Wednesday morning at seven-fifteen just as I was waking up and turning on my phone. I held the receiver aloft, let him spout for thirty seconds before shutting off my phone.

During the day, he left a battery of voicemail messages, some of them so lengthy he had to continue in follow-up calls. With no interest in what he might have been going on about—the man was a lunatic as far as I could see, impossible to take seriously—I erased the messages unheard after the first few, on the basis of which Gerry later accused me of having aided and abetted John's frauds, warning me that as an accomplice, which he felt sure I was, the police would be interested in talking to me. Fifty-eight thousand dollars in promissory notes to John, maybe they'd find more! Maybe I was laundering the proceeds of crime for him right now, something Gerry thought he could make a strong case for, based on my aggressive, antagonistic and evasive responses to his requests for the money I owed. It was obvious to him that I was hiding something.

By eight o'clock Wednesday night, the phone call barrage continuing, it became clear that creepy Gerry's behaviour wasn't just harassment, he was stalking me—relentlessly, ruthlessly, obsessively, in his efforts to have me repay money that, as far as I was concerned, had already been repaid.

I kept my phone off until nine, turned it on a few minutes after and waited for the expected call: it came at nine-twenty. I picked up.

"My mother instructed John," I said before he could speak, "as her power of attorney, to give me fifty-eight thousand dollars out of her account at Rampart that I needed for a personal matter. I didn't want to sign the promissory notes. John made it a condition of getting the money. The check he gave me was drawn on his Rampart CEO account. Rampart went bankrupt, the fifty-eight thousand disappeared, my mother's fifty-eight thousand ended up in one of his holding companies. The fifty-eight thousand is still there. He set me up. Get it from him."

"That's not my problem," Gerry came back. "I'm sitting here with two promissories in your name. I want the money. And I'm determined to get it."

I toyed with hanging up; I'd said my piece. "Are you, Gerry?"

"What's that supposed to mean?"

"You're being stupid. You should be nicer to me."

"Why's that?"

"Even though it's a drop in the hundred-million-dollar bucket, my fifty-eight grand is an easy get for you. A year on the job, little to show for it, according to John, after your monthly fee and expenses are paid, you need something to prove to his creditors that you're working hard to get them results, when the truth is you have no idea where John's money is, no idea even where to begin looking for it, and John isn't offering you anything in the way of clues. If you'd stop being such an asshole and ask me nicely, maybe I could give you some."

And I hung up.

As predicted, he called back instantly. I let it go to voicemail. Then go there again a minute later. The third time I answered.

*"Okay, okay!"* Gerry said in a panic. *"I get it!"*

Apparently, I'd hit a nerve.

"Meet me this Friday, *Fran's*, at College and Yonge. You know it?"

"I do."

"Noon hour. Sharp. Bring me something I can use. And don't be fucking with me. I'm not someone you want to do that with."

I was going to say, *that's not what I've heard,* but settled on an obsequious *I'm sure you're not, Gerry,* stroking what John had warned me had developed into a *tumescent ego,* now that he was getting spanked regularly by the woman of his dreams . . .

*The Plan.* I worked on it all day Thursday, didn't mention to John any of the other calls I'd had from Gerhard, or about our upcoming meeting. I was clearly on my own in this. There really was nothing John could do at this point anyway. Even if he wanted to pay the fifty-eight thousand to Gerry himself, he couldn't: bankruptcy law prohibited you from writing promissory notes to yourself. Getting Gerhard Gurdler out of my life was something I'd have to do alone.

Though the meeting wasn't until noon, I came up from the College Street subway station at 11:05, crossed with the lights at Yonge and hurried the half block to *Fran's,* a diner that I knew well. I went up the alley that runs beside the restaurant, in at the kitchen entrance, a clock on the wall as I walked through showing 11:10.

In the restaurant, I caught the attention of the waitress serving the six tables in the large front window looking out on College Street, taking a seat at one of them that was unoccupied. When the waitress came over, I asked if she could do me a favour: I told her I was meeting my ninety-year-old grandmother for lunch at eleven forty-five, wondering if I could reserve this table so she wouldn't have to stand in line when she arrives, she uses a walker these days. I said I was happy to pay her to hold the table for us if—

Absolutely not. She said she was happy to save the table.

I asked if it was possible to leave a birthday card on the table to be there when she arrived.

She said to go right ahead.

I stood up, took the oversize pale-pink envelope marked "Gerry" that I'd brought with me—it did contain a birthday card—and set it on the table. I mentioned to the waitress that my cousin would be joining my grandmother and me. If she saw a short man in his early fifties with a blond moustache and goatee looking for someone, perhaps she could bring him over to the table.

In case Gerry had shown up early himself, I made it fast along the alley that runs behind *Fran's*, went down the lane beside police headquarters to College Street. I crossed to the south side at the Atrium on Bay and headed back toward Yonge, ducking into a nook beside the Art Deco revolving doors of the west entrance to College Park Mall: directly across from *Fran's*.

I stationed myself so that I had a perfect view of the table through the front window.

At 11:55, hazard lights flashing, a white Lincoln Town Car swung out of traffic and pulled into the No Parking zone in front of *Fran's*. The driver's door staying closed, the passenger door and rear doors opened, two heavy-set men in topcoats that looked to be a size too small stepping out, followed by a short man with a neatly-trimmed blond moustache and goatee in a double-breasted belted beige trench coat having what appeared to be a heated conversation with someone on his phone. Gerry Gurdler, I had no doubt.

He finished the call, took the phone away from his mouth, slipped it in his coat pocket, glanced up and down the street before looking at his watch, had a quick word with one of the men with him then the other, checked his watch again, broke away from the two men and headed inside. Twelve o'clock. Sharp.

In a minute, he appeared in the window, the waitress walking him toward the table. She stopped, smiled, pointed it out to him and left.

Gerry spotted the card right away, picked it up, looked around, tore open the envelope, opened the card, catching and unfolding a photocopy that had fallen out, a fax I'd asked my mother's lawyer to write for her and send me regarding the missing $58,000:

> The $58,000 which bankruptcy trustee Gerhard Gurdler is currently asking my son Paul to pay in honouring two promissory notes to his brother John, was money to have been given to him from my own trading account at Rampart, not from Rampart Securities itself. Nothing about the transaction involved Rampart. John was merely acting as my power of attorney, power which I revoked three weeks after he'd taken the $58,000, along with all the other money that disappeared into his companies over the years.
>
> Sincerely,
> Beverley Illidge
>
> cc. Alea Gould, LL.B; Brad Wallace, C.A.; Det. Les Vuyk, Niagara Regional Police

Gerry was irate, whether because I'd been a no-show, or because of the contents of the letter, I couldn't have said. I saw him corral the waitress as she was passing with the fresh coffee carafe. He questioned her fiercely. She shook her head, shrugged. A waste of time, Gerry fuming, he held on to the letter but flung the birthday card and envelope at her. A corner of the envelope caught her in one eye. Her hand went to her eye. She dropped the coffee carafe. Gerry rushed off.

I stepped out of the nook, walked to the revolving doors and went into College Park, rode the escalator down to the subway, pleased with the way The Plan to have Gerry back off had worked out . . .

The phone rang at ten-thirty that night. My nerves rattled until I checked: it was my mother. It had been a harrowing week. I didn't want to talk to her, so I let the call go to voicemail: *"I almost died today. Can you and your brothers and sister come and see me tomorrow? I don't know how long I'll last."*

## CHAPTER ELEVEN

# PROMOTED TO GLORY

"WE'LL FLY," John said when I relayed what sounded like my mother's last request.

Billy Bishop Airport on Toronto Island was home base for the two Cessna T182Ts that his company Aviation Holdings owned; however, he'd recently moved them to the Collingwood Airport (where, presumably, they'd be less visible to Gerry and others looking for assets to liquidate).

"We'll drive to Beinn Tighe in the morning, leave around two, the flight only takes about fifty minutes. I'll have taxis waiting when we land for the drive from Niagara Regional to the Loyalist Lodge, maybe twenty minutes, then they'll return us to the airport after dinner. We'll be home by ten o'clock at the latest."

My brother Peter drove from the farm with the kids and me, Judith met us at the airport and we waited while John went to pick up his pilot, Graham, at the motel outside Collingwood where he was staying for the weekend, flying two clients home to Toronto Sunday morning, happy to kill time with a flight to St. Catharines and back.

I'd never met Graham before, but I knew his history and how John came to hire him in the mid-1990s. He'd been a celebrated, revered music teacher and band conductor for twenty-five years at Oakwood Collegiate Institute, a public high school in Toronto. In April 1991, he was arrested and charged with twenty-seven sexual abuse and abuse-related offences. The following week, more kids came forward. The number shot up to forty. Charges went back as far as 1979, and they involved male students. He flew boys who played in the school band to his cottage on Georgian Bay for special "rehearsals," served them alcohol, then molested them once they were drunk.

He was convicted on all counts and sentenced to three years in prison.

A registered sex offender, the only job he could find upon release was as a charter pilot and flight instructor at Toronto Island Airport, John one of Graham's first flight students.

After getting his pilot's licence in 1995, John decided to buy two Cessnas and start a premier charter company with Graham as his chief pilot. John knew his story. It had been in all the media. But as far as he was concerned, the man had done the crime, served his time and was trying to put his life back together. He deserved a chance. Besides, he was a superb pilot, the kind you need working for you when you're flying rich, heavily insured clients and celebrities around.

John and Graham arrived. After introductions and some talk about seating arrangements for load purposes, Judith, Nicky and Hannah boarded Graham's plane, Peter, Carson and I, John's. We took off into a cloudless blue sky, levelled out at six-thousand feet heading south-east, a golden autumn sun warming the cabin, the engine droning bearably loud, not a hint of turbulence. Carson and I gazed out our windows at the landscape passing below, while Peter, the technical wizard, peppered John in his usual way with mechanical questions about the plane, wondering about specs and details which John knew nothing about. "I don't build them, Pete! I just fly them," he said to end the interrogation. Peter laughed, unpacked his camera, made some adjustments to the lens then started taking pictures for an autumn-themed photography show he was preparing.

We flew over the town of Creemore, New Tecumseth, Mansfield Hills, the Hockley Valley, over Etobicoke in south-west Toronto where we started across Lake Ontario. I felt a sudden anxiety at being high over water in a small, single-engine prop plane, and I guess it showed. John picked up on it, telling me with a straight face that we had nothing to worry about: there were lifejackets in the back of the plane "if the crash doesn't kill us." Strangely enough, I found the droll humour reassuring, relaxed and enjoyed the ride.

Two taxis were parked on the tarmac when we landed. John gave one driver my mother's address, Judith and the kids heading off. Peter and I waited with the other driver while John and Graham discussed something: Graham's plane had developed a mechanical issue during the flight. He thought he knew what it was, but needed a mechanic with whom to discuss repairs. Whether the issue would be resolved by the time we were done visiting my mother was hard to say. Fingers crossed.

We arrived at my mother's building, Loyalist Lodge on King Street in downtown St. Catharines, just after four. My mother picked Loyalist not because it was the newest of the senior residences in town, but because it had been built on the site of the Bell Telephone Company building where my father had worked for twenty-three years.

As the first dinner sitting wasn't until five, my mother gave us a tour of the residence: for the benefit of the kids, she said, who had seen the place before, of course, but showed polite interest in what Grandma Illidge was saying as she proceeded a few steps in front of us—the beginnings of a stoop, downcast eyes, wringing her hands, chewing her lips, along with dry voice and throat-clearing—side effects of the medication she was on. She was certainly pent-up about something, enough to have convened this rare family conclave: all four of her children together with her at the same time, something that, as I thought about it, hadn't happened since my father's funeral. Yet there we were on what would have been his seventy-eighth birthday, one big happy family . . .

Dinner was roast beef, Yorkshire pudding, peas, carrots and Parisienne potatoes, with lemon meringue pie or strawberry shortcake for dessert. Conversation consisted mostly of my mother's reminiscences about John, Peter, Judith and I when we were growing up, stories the kids had heard before in one form or another, delivered now in a voice that was little more than a murmur, so faint at times we couldn't figure out if she was talking to herself or to us, not that it would have made much difference.

Then, just like that, she segued into questions for the kids about how they were doing, what school was like, what they and their friends were up to. Their answers given, there seemed to be nothing else to say. Even when we turned the conversation to Canadian politics, she gave one- and two-word responses to questions that not so long ago she would happily have taken fifteen fierce minutes to answer.

I recognized the agitated look storming her face. It came my way, reminding me of what I was expected to do before broaching the source of the panic that had drawn us all here: she didn't want to talk about it in front of the kids.

On the one hand, I was determined not to capitulate *just like that*, telling the kids to snap to it and get down to the recreation lounge for some ping-pong so the adults could talk. I'd discussed mental illness with my children enough that they understood Grandma Illidge suffered from one. As they saw it, that's why her behaviour was sometimes so eccentric. It was really no big deal to them. They didn't mind having a slightly off-kilter grandmother. They had told me it made family events more interesting and sometimes dramatic and helped them better understand that family relationships can be more complicated than we think. There might not be many more opportunities to see their "interesting" grandma. They were part of the rescue team; it seemed to me they deserved to hear what all the fuss was about.

At the same time, I couldn't expect her to understand that discussing something like mental illness with your children had become a healthy thing to do nowadays; that people were trying to stop treating it as something dangerous, to be feared and kept secret as she and my father had always done with my brothers and sister and I, never acknowledging, even in adulthood, the impact my mother's illness had taken on our mental health, and was continuing to take: proof of which surely lay in the fact that we had again reacted to one of my mother's distress phone calls in the usual Pavlovian fashion by immediately dropping everything and rushing straight over to St. Catharines, only to listen to her recount yet another fraught tale of near-death experience, this one, ludicrously enough, at the hands of a hotdog.

Nevertheless, I made her wait before giving in, five minutes of silence that was uncomfortable for us all. Her brooding becoming more fretful by the minute, I caught John's eye and told the kids they could go play ping-pong if they wanted to. Off they went.

"So Mom," John said on cue, "What's up? Why have we convened?"

She came to life instantly. Bright with sudden energy, she sat up in her chair, leaned forward, hands folded in front of her, no longer wringing them and, after clearing her throat a few times, explained about the hot-dog.

"Yesterday was hotdogs for lunch. Sometimes, I have trouble swallowing hotdogs. A bite became lodged in my throat and I started choking. The aides couldn't dislodge it. I was turning blue, I couldn't feel myself breathing. I continued choking, things went dark and I lost consciousness. That's all I remember until I woke up in bed in my apartment. They'd revived me despite the *Do Not Resuscitate* order on my medical record. I didn't want to be revived. I wanted to go. They ignored the DNR. What's the point of having one if they're not going to respect it? When I asked the director why, she said choking was a medical emergency, and by law they had no choice but to resuscitate in medical emergencies. My point was that if you're dying, and it doesn't matter how, that's a medical emergency, isn't it? What ways of dying are there that aren't medical emergencies? There's really no situation where you can use your DNR, because it's always a medical emergency, and they'll always revive you. What's the point of even having a DNR order? Do Not Resuscitate means *Do Not Save*. At this point in my life," she said growing evangelical, "I don't *want* to be saved!

I'm not *worth* saving!"

"Don't say that, Mom," said Judith.

"Have you told Reverend McKinley that?"

She made a face. "Reverend McKinley." The minister at her Anglican church, with whom she often tangled in dogma disputes brought on by my mother's belief that Michael McKinley was actually a Roman Catholic trying to convert his Anglican congregation to go over to the Dark Side. *"I want to go,"* she said firmly, like it was a proclamation. "I want to be *promoted to glory* like the Salvation Army says."

"Death as a promotion," said Peter. "It's kind of a nice concept . . ."

As morbid as conversation like this at the family dinner table would seem to most people, it needs to be understood that my brothers and sister and I were used to such talk from my mother on the subject of Death, her own, of others, the general principle. She'd been obsessed with the topic on and off for much of her life, and it was something about which she talked with no compunction, as if views on death, on heaven and hell, and the afterlife were things that all families discussed as a matter of course. I don't know if she ever expressed it to my siblings, but my mother had told me on numerous occasions throughout my life that she didn't fear death. She had faith. She believed in God, the resurrection, the life everlasting—that she looked forward to the day when she'd be *At Rest*, the words she wanted inscribed on her gravestone, the same ones she had put on my father's. *"At rest,"* she would say when musing about it, *"is something I've always wanted to be."*

"—Maybe you could avoid choking by taking smaller bites, Mom," said Peter.

"Chew them more," John suggested.

"Drink a glass of water while you're eating."

"Just stop having hotdogs, Mom," said Judith. "They'll bring you something else."

"I like hotdogs."

"Why don't we forget about the hotdogs," I said. "What is it you want us to do, Mom, now that we've rushed over to see you, thinking there was a crisis."

"What I want you to do is check and see if the *Do Not Resuscitate* order is still in my records. If it's not, tell them I want it to be; if it is, tell them to follow through on it next time, even if it's a medical emergency."

"To let you die . . ."

"What about the aides whose arms you die in? How are they going to feel? It's not fair to them. Have you thought of that?"

"It's human instinct to want to help someone in distress."

"Why did you want a DNR in the first place?"

"I get lonely."

"Who doesn't?"

"Nobody comes to see me . . ."

This was the lead-in to the Guilting Story: the rant that she'd let loose at some point on these to-the-rescue missions: why we didn't visit more often, why we never called, how we'd abandoned her to live cooped up in an *old folks' home* without a car—

John's phone rang. He took the call.

He turned to my mother when it was done. "We have to be on our way, Mom."

"Is everything all right?"

"Everything's fine. We want to get in the air while it's still light."

Residents were lining up for the second dinner sitting. After we finished our coffee, I went to the recreation lounge and rounded up the kids. We walked my mother back to her apartment, chatted for a minute outside her door, reminding her it was only five weeks until Christmas when we'd see her again. She watched us go down the hall to the elevator, waved when it came, the kids calling *Bye Grandma!* as they hopped on.

Things weren't fine at the airport as it turned out. Graham was still waiting for the mechanic he'd called to show up. The repair could take a few hours, maybe longer.

John made a phone call. Fifteen minutes later, a black stretch limousine appeared. A uniformed chauffeur stepped out. John explained to the kids that Graham's plane had to be fixed, nothing serious, but the mechanic would be a few hours working on it. They could drive back to the farm in the limo with Judith. Peter and I would go with him in the other plane, and we'd reconvene at Beinn Tighe in a few hours. He peeled two hundred-dollar bills off his wad, handing them to Judith for pizza and snacks on the way. *"Ándale, Ándale!"* he joked, hustling everybody into the limo.

A late-night Saturday, the kids stopped for snacks twice, when the limo driver left the highway, he got lost on the dark country roads. It was close to one by the time they finally pulled up at Beinn Tighe.

We slept late, had brunch and drove home early Sunday afternoon. The mechanical issue dealt with, John stayed at the farm so he could talk to Graham when he returned from St. Catharines about what had gone wrong with the plane.

He didn't come home to my house that night, or if he did, it was after I'd gone to bed. I missed him Monday morning, was working in my office transcribing an interview that I'd done for the Crest Theatre book when Judith called to say there'd been a break-in at the farm during the night. The police were investigating, trying to get in touch with John.

Apparently, a neighbour driving by early in the morning reported a Yamaha dirt bike lying on its side in the middle of the road about thirty yards from the foot of the Beinn Tighe driveway, no damage to the bike, a helmet nearby, a key in the ignition switched to *ON*, half a tank of gas, no sign of a driver having been thrown into the brush by the side of the road. The police were stumped.

They traced the registration, found John's name and the Beinn Tighe address about twenty yards back along the road. They walked up the lane to the farm, found the front door wide open, assumed there'd been a break-in during the night. They found Judith's name and Collingwood phone number on a Post-it note beside the wall phone in the kitchen labelled "Emergency Contact." The police asked what her connection to John James Illidge was. She told them, and they asked if she had a telephone number where they could reach him. Judith gave them the five she had in her book, having no idea which ones were still in use or not. Some were, but the police said the voicemail message boxes were all full.

Judith drove down and met them at the farm. The first thing they pointed out to her was a set of men's boot prints in the light snow under one of the living-room windows, the sash closed but, as one of the officers pointed out, unlocked. He lifted the sash then lowered it. This was how the thieves must have gained entry.

The place hadn't been vandalized by the housebreakers in any serious way. Far from it. A few lamps had been knocked over, a couple of side tables and some chairs had been overturned, books pulled from cases and scattered on the floor, broken dishes in the kitchen, some paintings hanging cockeyed on the walls, two appeared to be missing, several ivory table sculptures were knocked over—more mischief than anything else, so the police said. A $69.95 Walmart ghetto blaster that John kept on the night table beside his bed and a naval telescope that Murray's grandfather had used in 1916 at the Battle of Jutland seemed to be the only things of any value missing. According to Judith, it didn't seem like that big a deal overall, except for the wine fridge.

The glass door closed, the key was in the lock, but there was no need for it: the red wines were still there, only the shelves of the other compartment—where John kept his prized whites—were empty. Judith pointed this out to the officers, who joked that they were dealing with a very selective group. As to how they had found the key, the police surmised that while working on the roof, they had been able to see the wine fridge down below. But the key to the fridge? How could they have known where that was kept? The police suggested that at some point, they must have seen him retrieving the key from its hiding place in the kitchen. Judith pointed out that they couldn't have: John kept the key on a hook in his bedroom closet. This left the police baffled.

She led them around the side of the house into the woods: the chains that locked the ATVs to the trees had been broken with a bolt-cutter: both were gone. Cut as well was the chain lock for the motorcycle. The officers couldn't figure that one out. The thieves knew where in the house to find the key and a helmet, drove the cycle down to the road, leaving it, as well as the helmet, off to the side of the road about thirty yards from the foot of John's drive. They wondered why thieves would have done something like that. Judith wondered why they were only puzzled rather than suspicious when to her the whole situation had the look of a staged break-in.

She and one of the police officers walked down to the road. The officer took pictures of the motorcycle, as did Judith, who noted that the gas tank was half full. They lifted it up; Judith hopped on, turned the key and the bike started with no problem. Holding the helmet, the officer climbed on behind. They drove up the hill to the house.

The other officer said he'd reached John and told him what had happened. He was in Toronto, but leaving for the farm immediately.

Over the next two weeks, the police carried out an investigation, the roofers, who had finished six-weeks earlier, emerging as the prime suspects.

The insurance adjuster told John such things happen with local contractors sometimes if they haven't been paid. John assured him these guys had been paid in full.

A friend of Judith's whose cousin worked for the roofers said they were livid at being considered suspects. They'd only just finished the job. How stupid would they have to be to rob the place knowing they'd be the first ones questioned? They were an old family company, they all had alibis; there was no way they could have robbed Beinn Tighe. Besides, the owner of the roofing company told the cops, they hated white wine.

The claims adjuster was baffled by that one. Why would only the whites have been stolen? What could the thieves have had against red wine, especially when the adjuster, who said he had sommelier qualifications, explained that among John's reds, he had noticed some very impressive labels.

In the end, the police report advised the insurance company that the investigation of their only suspects, the roofers, proved inconclusive. There would be no charges. The case was to be considered closed.

The adjuster proposed a settlement of $128,000 for the stolen ATVs, the white wine collection, three missing paintings, some property damage. John countered with $155,000. They split the difference and settled on $142,000, more than five times what the roofers had soaked him for on the shingle repair.

John crowed with delight when he received the insurance check. Everything had worked out just fine. Three days later, he finally gave me the fifteen thousand dollars from Barbara Somers that I'd been waiting for since September, in cash.

# CHAPTER TWELVE

# AFTER THE GOLD RUSH

W ITH THE LEASE ON my Honda Accord set to expire in January, trips to Montreal and Stratford for Crest Theatre book interviews, plus a full slate in Toronto before leaving for Los Angeles in early February, I called Glenn Morrison, the leasing manager at Toronto Honda, and explained the difficulty. "Not a problem," Glenn said. "Come in any time, renew the lease and pick yourself out a new vehicle. You can pick it up in a couple of days. I'll even waive the December payment and throw in a full tank of gas. How's that sound?" It sounded pretty good to me.

As I turned to leave my office after hanging up, John was standing in the door. How long he'd been there I couldn't say. My back was to the door when I was on the phone.

He stepped aside when I came out to the hall, followed me into the kitchen. He'd overheard me talking to Glenn and, as it happened, he was in the process of hunting down a car for his daughter Emma. Why didn't he come along to the dealership with me when I went in to renew? Emma had mentioned a Honda, the CR-V Crossover appealed to her. He could look around while I met with Glenn.

That was John. On you before you had time to think about saying no. How could I say I preferred to go by myself rather than help him out? It was a harmless enough thing for him to ask, though it did seem to me it was something he should have done with Emma since she'd be the one driving the car. Besides, visiting auto dealerships and test-driving vehicles as though he was an interested customer had always been an obsession of his, a compulsion he'd had from the moment he got his driver's licence. Why on earth would he want to tag along with me?

But that's just what he did, even insisted that we take my car rather than the Mercedes, which caught me off guard and, frankly, made me nervous. John never rode in other people's cars. He couldn't stand being a passenger. If John was in a car, he had to be doing the driving, that's just the way it was with him: what I'd come to learn, over the years, was another control feature of his personality. Yet there he was, sitting beside me in the passenger seat of a four-door Honda sedan for perhaps the first time in his life. I wondered why.

Renewing the lease took all of fifteen minutes. I went with an Accord again, Hunter green this time instead of dark blue. The same monthly payment, same four-year term, I could pick it up on Monday if I wanted.

"Piece of cake," Glenn said shaking my hand at the door of his office. "See you Monday!"

I went off to look for John.

He was nowhere in the showroom, not outside on the lot. I thought he might be negotiating a deal in one of the sales offices, so I wandered over, giving the CR-V Crossover a look as I passed by, $36,900, light metallic blue—

"*Sold!*" John called out behind me. Glenn and one of his salesmen were escorting him into the showroom, each with a contract in hand. "Emma will love it!" he called again as he walked up. "Ron here has worked out a deal with Glenn to add it to your lease. I'll give you the monthly payments."

"One thousand, one hundred and fifteen a month for the two cars," said Ron, turning to me. "The CR-V alone is a forty-thousand dollar vehicle, all-in. Like your brother says, it's a great deal."

The next thing I knew, I'd signed Glenn's contract adding the CR-V to my Accord lease, and put my banking information on Ron's as the person responsible for the monthly payments, the one on the CR-V a hundred and seventy-five dollars more than mine.

"Even better," said Glenn, "we'll skip the December payment on both cars. Don't pay a cent till January 1st. How's that sound?"

John talked most of the way home, about what, I don't remember. I wasn't listening. I was busy beating myself up for not telling Glenn to tear up the CR-V lease—that I wouldn't be on the hook for the monthly payments. I couldn't be. My mortgage payment alone was only $35 more. Beating myself up, too, because I knew even as I was signing the double-lease that the arrangement would never work. That John had no intention of giving me his half of the monthly payment. That the car wasn't for Emma and never had been. Tammy was the one who talked all the time about wanting a Honda CR-V Crossover, and now I'd just bought her one.

We picked the new vehicles up on Tuesday, John presenting Tammy with the CR-V when she arrived on Friday. *"And it's the light metallic blue that I wanted!"* she cooed when she saw it.

December being our free month, I started pestering John for the $695 January 1st payment on Boxing Day at the family dinner, reminding him about it twice the day after, my hopes of getting a check from him dwindling with each fruitless request, to the point that I stopped thinking it was going to happen and wondered what my recourse would be, or if I had one—until as he was leaving to drive downtown the morning of the twenty-eighth, he handed me a personal check for $695.

I went straight to my Royal Bank branch, met with Maria the manager, to whom I'd previously explained the situation with the double-lease. She was happy to oblige. Since it was a Royal Bank check, she called up the account. No surprise, the check was rubber. The account had been shut down four years ago for unspecified "irregularities."

I rushed downstairs to the *Candyland* closet the moment I got home, opened the box where I'd hidden the checkbooks from the back seat of the Jaguar on Repo Night and rummaged through them: I'd kept one checkbook from each box, along with a sampling of business cards thinking they might come in handy at some point.

There it was: a book of Royal Bank checks for *John James Illidge*, address 162 Golfdale Road, the house he'd lived in with Mandy, the would-be Mrs. Illidge that Ellen met. The branch address was King Street West, two blocks from Rampart's offices.

That night, I told him the check had come back, that the account had been closed four years ago. I didn't ask about the irregularities.

A frown, a chuckle as he looked over the check, he said he must have forgotten. If I wanted, he could write me another one on a different account . . . or he could give me the cash tomorrow night. Whatever works best.

Knowing another check would be just as bogus as the first one, I saved myself the aggravation and opted for the cash—not altogether surprised when he didn't come home the following night.

I laughed at myself as I made coffee the following morning. *What had I been thinking?* There would be no cash. There was no point in trying to reach him. This was John letting me know that he expected me to cover the payment for him and I could get it back from him later, which of course I'd still be trying to do when the time for February's payment came around. That was the whole point.

Except sitting there having my coffee—out of nowhere, or so it seemed at the time—I made a decision.

It was New Year's Eve day. Call it an early resolution, but six hundred and ninety-five dollars wouldn't be coming from me. If the payment was made, so be it. If it wasn't, so be it as well. My enabling had to stop. I had to let go of what wasn't my problem but which, as usual, John had managed to make mine; I resolved, too, that from now on when it came to dealing with him there would be no more acquiescing, no more accommodating, no more acceding to his duplicitous requests. Two could play at this game, and I was a lot better at it than John knew. As Adriano at *Centro* said: *You got the brains, Paolo!*

I called Maria at the Royal Bank at four to tell her it didn't look like the money would be coming through; that I'd changed my mind and didn't want her to let my overdraft cover John's $695 payment. Maria said she understood the emotion behind wanting to do that, however, she couldn't see there was any way—

The front door opened, slammed shut.

I told Maria to hang on.

Obviously in a hurry, John said, *"Hey!"* stepped out of his boots and, keeping his coat on, ran straight up to his room, came downstairs a few minutes later with his suitcase, bound for Ottawa *to stay at Tammy's until after New Year's*. I moved to stand in front of the door, blocking his way. He gave me a wry smile, slipped his hand into the inside pocket of his suit jacket, plucked out six one-hundred dollar bills, four twenties, a ten and a five and with a grin handed them to me.

"Keep the change," he quipped.

I thanked him, but said there was something else: that I had enough to worry about at the end of every month for him to be playing games like this. I told him he'd put me over a barrel I didn't want to be put over. We needed to make other arrangements. "Tammy's driving the car," I said, "why doesn't she handle the payments?" I knew why: he'd made out, of course, the car was a gift from him. How could he ask her to pay for it?

"No worries," he said. "I'll take her to the dealership next Friday. Have Glenn put her on the lease so she takes over the payments as of February 1st. *Happy New Year!*" he said cheerily, and was out the door.

I made arrangements for the kids to stay with their mother for the two weeks that I'd be in Los Angeles doing interviews for my Crest Theatre book. On February 12, four days into the Salt Lake City Winter Olympics, I flew into LAX, the airport relatively quiet except for Olympics latecomers connecting to the ninety-minute flight north to Salt Lake. Only four months since 9/11, rumours I'd heard about tight security and armed military presence at major American airports turned out not to be true in L.A. Aside from a pair of soldiers with submachine guns slung over their shoulders patrolling the terminal looking bored, you would hardly have guessed America's "War on Terror" had begun.

Not all business, this was my first solo holiday in years. Free to do whatever I wanted according to my own schedule—if I even wanted a schedule—I packed as much into the next two weeks as I possibly could. My first interview was to have been with James Doohan, who went from acting at the Crest to playing Scotty on *STAR TREK*, but when I called to confirm the interview his agent told me Jimmy had been taken to hospital two days earlier and so would be unavailable while I was in town.

I had a telephone interview with Broadway *Camelot* star Robert Goulet in Las Vegas, who had begun his acting career at the Crest Theatre a few years before ("Paul, babe! How are you?"), and one with British actor Patrick Macnee in Palm Springs. Patrick had been in the Crest's very first production in October 1954. He went on to play a distinguished upper-class gentleman spy in the popular 1960s TV drama *The Avengers*. ("Charming to hear from you, my dear boy.") On the show with him was Honor Blackman, the Bond girl Pussy Galore in *Goldfinger*. She, too, had been in the Crest's first production, about which I was hoping to talk to her.

Brent, the screenwriter friend with whom I was staying, loaned me his car so I could drive up to a palm-tree lined street off Laurel Canyon Boulevard in Studio City and spend the afternoon with the Canadian-born playwright and screenwriter Bernard Slade and his wife, Jill Foster, who had met while working at the Crest Theatre in the early 1960s.

The Crest had made Bernie think that he had some talent as an actor and writer, and gave him the confidence to pursue it professionally. He wrote his first play between acts in the dressing room of the Crest, received a positive enough response from an agent in Hollywood so he moved to Los Angeles, wrote successfully for television and became the creator of well-known 60s and 70s television shows like *The Partridge Family*, *The Courtship of Eddie's Father*, and *The Flying Nun* among others. He wrote plays in the second half of his career, two of them Broadway hits. "My retirement fund," he joked, holding up three envelopes that had come in the mail while we were talking: checks from German productions of his Broadway hit, *Same Time, Next Year*. Bernie had grown up in St. Catharines, Ontario, where my parents had lived. Not only had Jill grown up in the same Beach area of Toronto as I had, she had gone to the same high school—in the same class as my Aunt Mary.

A friend from Toronto emailed to say that a producer at Madonna's

Maverick Studios would be happy to talk to me about a script I'd recently sent him. I called the producer and arranged a time, drove over to the studio in Brent's car the next day. He had warned me there'd be no parking within a three-mile radius at that time of day in that part of L.A., but not to panic: with his handicapped sticker—Brent had a bum left leg from the knee down—I could park at a meter right in front of the studio.

The meeting with the producer went well. They were looking at potential projects for Jessica Simpson, who was transitioning from singing to films. He liked my writing. He liked the story of a strong, smart young woman who's too much of a rebel for her own good, but, how could he put this? The producer felt they'd have trouble selling blond, buxom Jessica Simpson as a woman as smart as my lead character was, if I knew what he meant. I did. He liked the title *After the Gold Rush*; in fact, he'd always liked the Neil Young song, especially the version done by Linda Ronstadt, Dolly Parton and Emmylou Harris, which he hadn't heard in a long time.

Come on, he said, and headed me down a hall to the audio department, to a recording studio where he had the engineer cue up the song. We sat down. The engineer plugged in and handed us headphones. We closed our eyes. Linda, Dolly and Emmylou's high voices in three-part *a cappella* harmony: *I was lying in a burned out basement, with the full moon in my eyes. I was hoping for replacement, when the sun burst through the sky . . .*

Thinking I'd get a kick out of it, Brent, who was the same age as me, took me to lunch one day at a local diner with his friend Barry Livingston, who had played Ernie, Chip's younger brother on the popular 1960s TV comedy starring Fred MacMurray, *My Three Sons*. There I was sitting in a 60s diner that could have been the set for a *My Three Sons* episode, talking and laughing not with Barry Livingston but Ernie Douglas, whom my two brothers and I had watched faithfully every week when we were boys.

The night after the Olympics closed, my friend Trina and her partner Greg picked me up at Brent's. (As fans of the *Tremors* comedy-horror films which Brent had written and helped produce, they were thrilled to meet him.) We drove to a restaurant in Venice called *Hughie's*, which a chef-friend of Trina's had recommended. According to the friend, it not only had some of the best food around, but hadn't been discovered by the paparazzi yet, so prices hadn't been bumped into the stratosphere.

Her father a 1950s and 60s movie icon, Trina had grown up in Hollywood and was extremely cynical about the place and the shallow, celebrity-obsessed culture it had engendered. Five years ago, she had moved two hours north to Santa Ynez in Santa Barbara County, vineyards, wineries and horse farms in the foothills of the San Rafael Mountains. She had time to work on what she ironically called her magnum opus now—maybe not an opus, but at well over six hundred pages already, it was definitely going to be magnum—a book about the unknown, yet illustrious, history of horses on the silver screen. She had time for riding as well when she wasn't teaching, trails through the foothills and the Los Padres National Forest, Greg accompanying her when he wasn't painting—oil painting as well as house painting: in fact, he and Trina met when she hired him to paint her house three years earlier, a friendship developed, became more than that, Trina inviting him to move in with her when he finished—the two of them now leading the simple, quiet life they didn't know they wanted until they found it.

During dinner, we talked about what some of our mutual friends were up to, some of the movies I'd seen at the American Film Mart while I was in town, the Crest Theatre book, what we saw the digital twenty-first century holding for us at the age of fifty, and of course about John's burgeoning fraud career.

The description left them dazzled by his conniving audacity, the ease with which he was able to get away with what he did, and with impunity through the charisma of his sociopathic personality, targeting people as victims to make up for his own deficiencies and inadequacies at never having measured up to someone else's—usually a parent's—expectations. Trina felt that, from the sounds of it, John's dysfunctional relationship with my mother, where he was always trying to measure up only to find that she'd raised the bar again, was where his fraudulent tendencies probably stemmed from.

"There was nothing he could do to win your mother's approval, so he had to take it out on someone. Were most of his fraud victims female?" She said she bet they were. She knew the type. Hollywood was teeming with them. Teeming.

Trina spoke candidly about growing up in a similarly dysfunctional family. She could relate to the can't-measure-up kind of abuse, for that's what it was. Nobody had measured up in her family either, and her father took it out on her mother and two brothers.

On her, as the only girl, it was a different kind of measuring up, she said of the memory.

The day after Trina's father died, she explained, Bill Clinton had phoned her mother's house in Santa Barbara, north of Los Angeles, where she and Trina had gone for some privacy. Trina wasn't going to answer. The number was unlisted so it could only have been a family member or friend. But her mother was exhausted and having a nap, and Trina didn't want the ringing to wake her. So she picked up. It was President Clinton calling. Thinking Trina was her mother, he launched into an impassioned eulogy to her father, his stature as an actor, the quintessential Hollywood giant, an *icon* in his time, a fine man that Clinton said he had looked up to—

Trina couldn't listen to another word. She threw the phone down, went to her bedroom, packed a suitcase, left her mother a note, drove back to Los Angeles and caught the first flight to Hawaii.

There was the President of the United States worshipping, venerating her *icon* father—how she hated that fucking word—a man who had been anything but an *icon* for her, her mother and brothers when they were growing up.

She stayed in Hawaii for three weeks. Came home, Trina said, when she was sure the *icon* was really gone.

"Sorry for getting heavy," she said.

"No need," I said. "You're the first person who's ever talked to me about abuse in their family. I always thought ours was the only one." I told her how validated I felt, something I'd given up hoping for a long time ago. It just wasn't something people wanted to hear about. We toasted to validation. Our waiter appeared. We ordered dessert. I excused myself and went to the bathroom.

Apparently, actor Matt Damon, in the entertainment news a great deal just then for the upcoming release of *The Bourne Identity*, had the same idea. I entered to find a drunken fan cornering Matt at the sink as he was washing his hands. The drunk had a scrap of paper but no pen. He'd lost his pen. But he wanted an autograph. *Somebody* must have a pen, he bellowed. Who's got a pen? he whined drunkenly, positioning himself in front of Matt so he was trapped.

I met Matt's irritated look in the mirror.

"I've got a pen," I said, coming around between Matt and the drunk. I took the scrap of paper, put it on the counter and handed Matt the pen. He leaned down and signed, I handed the paper back to the fan, waited till Matt had gone before guiding the drunk over to the door. I went back, used the facilities and went out after washing my hands.

Standing off to one side, there was Matt Damon. Holding up my pen.

Trina teased me when I returned to the table. "You and Matt best friends now?"

"For*evah* . . ."

Our waiter leaving the bill after refreshing our coffee, I took out the American Express card that I'd brought with me. Spotting it, Trina insisted she and Greg were paying for dinner. I told them we could talk about that, but I wanted to conduct a little test first. I explained that my brother John, in a gesture of magnanimity had loaned me the American Express card in case anything came up in L. A. *in the way of emergencies.* I explained that it was a companion card he got through his girlfriend Tammy's account. He had five other companion cards. A bankrupt and he has six credit cards!

I put the card on the tray with the bill and waved the waiter over.

A good five minutes passed until he returned and, with a politely embarrassed look on his face, handed me back the American Express card, but Trina, Greg and I were laughing as, before the waiter could speak, we shouted out together: *"Declined!"*

# CHAPTER THIRTEEN

# ON THE RUN

I T WAS LATE AFTERNOON by the time the airport limousine dropped me off at home. I came in the door to find the kids had sorted the mail and left it on the console table in the front hall as I'd asked them to: a plastic grocery bag for mine, maybe one-third full, if that, while the bag with John's was stuffed, more lying loose on top.

After a quick peek in my office—the computer on, legal letters and crumpled stock contracts in and beside the wastebasket, a ribbon of paper curling from the fax machine down to the floor—I went across the hall and ran downstairs to the *Candyland* closet to check the rudimentary security system that I'd devised to see if The Snooper had been in while I was gone.

I lifted the thick, bristled rug that I'd strategically placed on the floor in front of the manuscript shelves so that anyone wanting to check the contents of the boxes would have had to stand on the rug, crushing the nuggets of Captain Crunch cereal that I'd positioned strategically underneath. The rug was thick enough that the crunching couldn't be heard.

I crouched down, lifted a corner of the rug and had a look.

The Captain had been crushed in quite a few places.

Out came the *Candyland* box, off came the lid. I ripped open the Crown Royal whiskey bag, slipped the paper strap off a bundle of bills, licked my thumb and started counting . . . to my relief all fifty thousand dollars present and accounted for.

Talking to Molly about it, once she stopped laughing, she said she found my Captain Crunch security method hilarious; that I could probably start a thriving business saving people thousands on alarm systems for just the cost of a box of breakfast cereal.

128

She felt it made sense that he scoped my office out. *The beast had to be fed*, and the various investigations underway were cramping his style. Why not take advantage of the situation? Go hunting for the money he'd overheard me mention on the phone the night before I left for L.A., when I was reassuring a friend concerned about how I was managing financially, that I had a chunk of money in the bank and another chunk stashed away. There were only so many places you could stash money—

"He's done far shittier things than that."

"According to the kids, he wasn't around very much."

"You think he has his lucre tucked away somewhere and just can't get to it?"

"That's the impression he gave me when we talked about it."

"What did he say?"

"He wanted me to check it out."

"Check what out?"

"Going to the bank for him."

"As in offshore?"

"Cayman Islands."

"Check it out how?"

"He mentioned impersonating him."

"Are you serious?"

"Perfectly. He said he could get me a forged passport and I.D. in his name. Our features were close enough. I'd darken my hair, and with a pair of glasses on, he didn't think I'd have any problem passing for him. He'd give me the passwords, brief me on the account, as well as the bank manager who I'd be dealing with. And put me in touch with a small-plane pilot who could fly me back to Miami immediately afterwards."

"Wouldn't the bank check fingerprints for something like that?"

"Only in James Bond movies apparently."

It felt like a James Bond movie just talking to her about it.

"You would be the mule. I believe that's what they call it?"

"He thought three million would do to start with. Maybe five the next time. He'd give me a million on this first run."

"Next time? This would become a regular thing?"

"It sounded that way."

"Do you think he'd actually have you go through with it?"

"Molly . . ."

"I know, I know. I fall for it every time."

"Who doesn't? He's so good at believing the delusions he creates for himself that he gets us believing them too, as though reality doesn't figure in. I checked on securities law in the Cayman Islands just to see what I might have been in for if I'd played along with the impersonation scheme. Just asking whether a person has accounts at a Cayman bank brings the same gunpoint police action as someone trying to rob it. You're thrown in jail until the authorities decide whether or not you're worth prosecuting, their decision made according to the amount of money you're capable of raising for *defence costs*."

"How did you learn that?"

"I made a phone call to the Cayman attorney general's office. The man I talked to was pleasant and forthcoming, but very firm about it *not being a good idea*."

Molly laughed. "Yet, John led you to think the whole thing was doable."

"He smokes people out."

"'Smokes them out'?"

"Leads them to believe one thing when the opposite is the case. It's a control thing. No one ever knowing exactly where he is, what he's doing and with whom."

She thought for a moment. "So the talk about you bringing three million back, five million, whatever, the smoke out is that there's probably no million."

"While Gerry Gurdler, Ellen's divorce lawyer, and all his creditors think he has millions *squirreled away* as John terms it."

"The hidden fortune is a lie, then."

"Bold-faced."

"But not to John."

"Everything he believes has to be true, otherwise, he wouldn't believe it. The rest of us start believing him because he's so convincingly positive it can't be a lie. And no one knows the difference between the truth and a lie better than John.

We held the thought.

"So what's he doing for cash then?" Molly wondered. "He's obviously strapped if he's snooping around your place looking for buried treasure. The beast obviously needs to be fed, yet, the pressure's on and being ramped up on all sides. I can tell you that Ernst & Young, the bankruptcy trustees for the Rampart companies, are on the asset-recovery warpath but getting nowhere, nor is Gerry Gurdler. I went to the hearing where they put John on the stand to explain how he was generating income, which they know he has been.

"His lawyer, Colin James, who manages to extricate John from these sorts of situations with a combination of bully aggression and wronged-victim sympathy, objected, saying John didn't have to answer that question, even if there hadn't been an inference that he was being deliberately deceptive. 'John Illidge is a private businessman. He's being as forthcoming as he can at what is a difficult and stressful time for him.' The judge bought it. Back to square one on asset recovery."

I wondered myself what he was doing for cash. No more Stafford Kelley at Medallion trading stocks for him. No one else willing to be his surrogate, what with the IDA and the OSC investigating him and, from what I could see on my computer, no more pump-and-dump stock agreements—worst of all, no weekly *vig* from Oakville Movers. He'd had to step away from the company in early February when the chief financial officer that he'd installed, Nick Tsaconakos, came under investigation by the IDA and the OSC for regulatory infractions he'd committed while working with John as a registered trader at Rampart, and before that at St. James. Nick was apparently under heavy pressure to *sing* on his former boss in return for a lesser fine and a reduced suspension from securities trading. Nick had a wife and three young children. He'd been ruthlessly loyal to John in the years they'd worked together.

Talking to me about developments one night after he'd had one vodka rocks too many, John said he was confident he could count on Nick to be *discreet* and not to *crack*, but in the meantime, he needed to move on to happier hunting grounds. *The beast had to be fed.* He couldn't sit around waiting for Nick.

He began spending more time in Ottawa, sometimes three or four days a week talking to people who *wanted to buy his expertise.* He claimed to be thinking of moving there. Was marriage in the cards? I asked him. He and Tammy had talked about it.

"Of course he'll marry her," Molly said. "Wives can't testify against their husbands . . ."

Times when he was back in Toronto, he drank more heavily, not just while watching his Shows. Always vodka on the rocks, always a bottle of wine with dinner, only he'd switched to red for reasons which, when I asked him, he was unwilling to explain.

No more jokes, wisecracks, snappy patter or comic banter now. He was under duress, being pursued in both professional and personal quarters. Like someone had pulled the plug on his easy-going good humour, he became volatile, mercurial, swinging frantically from one mood to another, denouncing his detractors as crooks pursuing him for money he denied vehemently that he'd ever had. He was paranoid that people around him were conspiring against him, determined on ruining him when he'd gone out of his way to do plenty for them when they were in a similar position.

Anger, hostility, and self-pity flared after three or four vodkas so that they enveloped you before you could get out of the way. Stolid, brooding, uncommunicative one minute, as boozers do, he'd fly into a vehement rage the next and become what my friends and I used to call a "snarly" drunk, whom it was unpleasant and often disturbing to be around. His sociopathic tendencies had taken over. He could no longer distinguish fantasy from reality. People were looking for him. He was on the run.

One day, I mentioned that I'd heard Barbara Somers' cousin Carol was going after him for the money (in the neighbourhood of five hundred thousand I'd been told) that had gone missing from Barbara's accounts over the years. "Someone I was talking to asked me about the case in connection with the Crest Theatre book, and the fact that you're my brother—"

"Okay!" John erupted like he was on the stand, and a cross-examining lawyer had just drawn a confession out of him. *"So I did a little mingling! The money's still there!"*

*Still where?* I might have asked if I hadn't been so shocked: it was the closest thing to an admission of guilt that I'd ever heard from John.

The next moment, he put his drink down. Got up from the couch, walked out of the family room and down the hall where I heard him pick up his car keys and go out. He'd left the TV on. *The Fifth Wheel* was back from a commercial. *Where strangers become lovers and lovers become bitter suicidal exes all in the same show . . .*

Toward the end of March, I received a call from a detective with the fraud division of the Niagara Regional Police Service named Les Vuyk, asking if he could meet with me to discuss a *will-say* for the court case the Crown prosecutor in St. Catharines was thinking of bringing against John for the theft of my mother's money. Something in central Toronto would be his preference since he was driving in from St. Catharines. We agreed to meet at the Toronto Reference Library at Yonge and Bloor, where I was doing Crest Theatre research in the Canadiana Collection on the fifth floor.

In his late thirties, I guessed, personable and easy-going, casually dressed, Detective Vuyk ("like Buick with a V") told me to call him Les, as I brought him to the table where I was working. He was impressed with the panoramic view of the library we had from five floors up. And you couldn't find a quieter place for an interview—which it really wasn't, Les hastened to add. As he'd said on the phone, before she could proceed, the prosecutor needed *will-says*, written witness testimony she could use in court if the case goes forward. There was no real rush for mine. He just wanted to get the ball rolling. At the moment, they were in a holding pattern. The prosecutor had some concerns about the prospects of conviction . . . more from a mental health point of view than an evidentiary one.

He asked if he could be frank. I told him he could.

"Your mother's history of mental illness, added to the fact she's seventy-nine, her memory not the strongest, her tendency to be easily confused, the prosecutor's afraid of her falling apart on the stand under what John's lawyer would make sure was a brutal cross-examination. He'd have her trembling and in tears, make her look like a senile basket-case whose testimony to anything related to her financial affairs with John couldn't be relied upon. Cruel, yes, but that's the way it would work.

"Your mother was duped by your brother," he continued, "into joining a Ponzi scheme that, from what I can tell, he's been running since 1991, when she first invested with him. Those *taking-money-out-the-back-door* scenarios at the various companies where he worked that you told me about on the phone were nothing more than Ponzi schemes as well. Are you familiar with Ponzi schemes?"

"I'm learning more about them all the time."

"Your brother's a master at the game. He takes people's money under the pretext that he's investing it in very profitable enterprises that will bring them a hefty return, and fast, because of his expertise . . . unless, of course, they want to let it stay in the fund and continue to grow—which everyone does—sending them the occasional five- or ten-thousand dollars as a way of keeping them happy, leading his unsuspecting investors to believe in the mounting value of non-existent assets that they continue to believe they own.

"The money he's making, the proceeds of crime as we call them, are going into his own accounts to underwrite his *Big Player* compulsion with the upscale lifestyle to prove it. The con is based on people thinking he's rolling in money, and they'll be rolling in it too if they invest with him. There's no paper trail, or not much of one. And that's okay with his investors; they let it slide, it will be worth it. John charms them; they like being associated with him, the enthusiastic self-confidence he exudes, the boundless energy of his personality. With the big money he constantly alludes to, why would they ever consider cashing out?

"What we find is that people don't exercise due diligence. When you're expecting to make money, and maybe a lot of it, with someone promising the world the way John does—but then after a while you wonder why—"

"—there're no statements, no transaction records."

"That's right. Nothing to verify you even invested with John in the first place. Your money has disappeared—"

"—into one of John's holding companies."

Les chuckled. "I understand he has a few. Investors are angry, sure, but often they're embarrassed, ashamed. They wonder how they could have made such a mistake, how they could have been so easily taken in. There might be some litigation, but John has the upper hand with all the wiles available to him in a self-policing industry. It's not called bankruptcy protection for nothing.

"The question victims always ask is why. 'Why would someone do this to me? Why would they hurt me like this? Why do I feel guilty and that it's somehow my own fault and I deserved it?' All I can do in my job, Paul, is let you know that it's not your fault, or your mother's fault, or any of his victims' fault. It's nobody's fault but your brother's. He's a textbook psychopath, someone who has no empathy for other people, no conscience. No feelings or emotions. He's intelligent about people, very. He's obsessive, compulsive—psychopaths always are—and when *the beast needs to be fed,* as he says, he loses behavioural control and goes on a spree. He doesn't feel it, he can't, as I said, but the guilt is fully his and, mark my words, it will catch up with him someday. Even though you won't read about it in the news, one way or another, he will pay for what he's done."

It was my turn to be impressed: such an accurate profile of John, Les, with such passion for his job that he would cut right to the bare-bones of what we were dealing with and honestly explain, with respect to the legal process, justice inevitably gets done in ways and in places other than court rooms.

I rode the elevator downstairs with him, thanked him for his frankness, for his insights, his reassurance. "That's the hard part in this whole business," I said. "You experience these things with John that I have over so many years, yet you can't talk to anyone about them and the effect they've had on you and your siblings. People don't take you seriously; the stories are so incredible. It's hard to outsell John's version of events. There's not much empathy when what you want to tell people about someone is so hard to believe."

"I hear you. And John knows that, and works to isolate you and your brother and sister from each other. Like I say, he knows lies will outsell truth every time. He's a master manipulator with no conscience who will always keep himself several steps ahead of you. For the police or the courts to pursue him is problematic. Your brother knows exactly how to turn the finer points of law to his advantage. My advice is to limit your contact with him or avoid him altogether. He's a toxic personality in free fall. People could get hurt more than they have been already. We'll see if we can get him into court, but I can't promise anything."

We left it at that. Les would keep me in the loop on any developments in my mother's case and told me not to hesitate to call him if I ever had questions. As to the *will-say*, the more the better from the prosecutor's point of view, though sticking to the facts was important, of course. I could email the finished product to him at the address on his card. We shook hands. I watched him show his badge at security, turn and throw me a wave just as he went out the revolving doors . . .

The second week of April, John called Judith and gave her a list of things he wanted immediately removed from Beinn Tighe and taken to the garage-workshop she had in her backyard. She would need to rent a truck to move the paintings, furniture, the wine fridge, the ATVs (which had mysteriously reappeared), and the Yamaha dirt bike. Apparently Gerry Gurdler and an asset-retrieval team were paying a visit to the farm the following morning.

He showed up at my house a week later with Byron, the Oakville Movers truck and the same two guys who had moved him in. Apparently he was storing everything, then heading off to live in Ottawa. He and Tammy were getting married as soon as his divorce came through, although it could be a while: Ellen's lawyer, Phil Epstein, a total prick, was demanding *fantasy millions* that John didn't have. He said he'd be in touch and we could reconvene when he got his new project off the ground in Ottawa—an association to promote Canadian business and industry associations—a typical John segue to his latest delusion: imaginary ideas for new businesses that were *guaranteed* to bring in imaginary millions.

"—Associations join our association and we promote their association and its members."

"Kind of a super-association."

"Exactly."

"Do you have a name?"

"We're working on it."

"We?"

"Some guys I used to work with from Montreal. Do you know how many associations there are in North America?"

"Haven't a clue."

"Nearly twenty-thousand, research shows. And some of these associations have five, ten thousand members. Did you know that?"

"I didn't."

"People want to be part of an association to give their organization credibility. They take the association seriously because they have to pay to join. It confers status. Status you have to pay for, right? We're talking millions in annual dues to be part of our association—"

I made no comment and let him go on, his hyperactive disorder on full display as he ran upstairs and down, supervising the moving operation.

A rush job, Byron and his crew were done and climbing into the loaded truck in just under twenty-minutes, ready for the getaway to Tammy's place in Ottawa. On the lam, John was *taking to the mattresses* until things cooled down. He drove off behind the Oakville Movers truck in the black Mercedes, which, now that the Porsche had been repossessed, was sporting the *RSKY BZNS* plates.

When Nicky and Carson came home from school that afternoon, I had them help me return our furniture, carpets, lamps and artwork to the living room and dining room. Except for the framed photograph on the wall in his bedroom that I'd given him of our two families and my parents beside the swimming pool at the 40th wedding anniversary party Jill and I held for them twelve years earlier at our old house, you would never know John had ever been there.

I would miss Tammy. I liked her. I hated seeing how John used and controlled her. It seemed abusive to me. In a drunken rant one night before he bolted to her place, he recounted again the story of having picked Tammy and groomed her. The details, with a few exceptions, were more or less the same. I got the distinct impression that he was keeping her in the picture only as long as he had a use for her. Like all the other women in his life, she would end up getting hurt badly. I knew Tammy loved John and wanted desperately to marry him, but his money (the millions she thought he had) clouded the picture, making her blind to his faults.

I leapt at the opportunity to help Ellen when I received the email she sent out to family and friends celebrating her divorce. John was continuing to avoid the subject with Tammy. If it ever came up when I was present, he ranted about Ellen's divorce lawyer, Phil Epstein, sabotaging things by trying to *extract* even more money from him. Any final agreement looked like it was going to drag on. His hands were tied. He was afraid to say it, but marriage would just have to wait.

*No it won't!* I wrote in the subject line of the email I sent to Tammy from a third-party email address I sometimes used, copying and pasting Ellen's celebratory email, what she called her "emancipation proclamation:" *The years of John refusing to agree to a settlement are over. I'm finally free of him and still in one piece. Though just barely. There are days . . . but he's Tammy Doodle's problem now!!*

According to Ellen, by way of the girls, Tammy exploded. She confronted John with the email. No more excuses!

Unable to put it off any longer, John arranged for them to be married at the exclusive Rideau Club in Ottawa, a club of which he told me he had been a long-time member. Just a small family wedding, Ellen said: as in Tammy's family, and John's three girls so as not to humiliate Tammy entirely, whom they felt sorry for.

June 3rd, a Monday, Honda Credit called to let me know as the lease-holder that they'd be repossessing the CR-V Crossover that I'd bought five months previously. A payment had been made February 1st, but there had been nothing in the three months since. Adam from the collections department wanted to know what I intended to do.

The phone numbers on the lease for Tammy Young and John Illidge didn't exist as far as he or anyone in his office could tell. As well, there had been no response to any of the overdue notices that had been sent in the mail to Tammy Young's address in Ottawa. Consequently I was on the hook for $2,900, four payments plus penalties, due at Toronto Honda within twenty-four hours, along with the CR-V of course, which they were repossessing.

I asked him how that could be. The lease had been transferred to Tammy Young. I didn't see how it could be my problem.

"—I'll stop you right there," Adam cut in. "You signed for the transfer of payments, not the lease itself. It remains in your name. We need a plan for those overdue payments before we get off the phone."

The only thing I could do was tell him this was the first that I'd heard of the missed payments; that I'd look into the matter and get back to him. I asked him for the address John and Tammy had put down on the lease.

He gave it to me. I hung up before he could resume talking.

I checked with 411. The operator had no telephone number for T. or Tammy Young at that Ottawa address. I called Les Vuyk, explained the situation and asked if he could check to see if the address was a house or an apartment.

It turned out to be neither. Les couldn't suppress his amusement. "It's an adult video store. Do you want to know the name?"

"Does it matter?"

We laughed.

I called Adam back and explained the phony information on the lease.

"So what?" was his response. "You still owe me twenty-nine hundred and a forty thousand dollar CR-V."

"Hang on," I told him, putting the phone to my chest. Did Tammy and John even have the car still?

I got back on the line. "Send one of your people to Pfaff Motors in Newmarket, Ontario," I told Adam. "That's where my brother has leased his cars for the past fifteen years. I'm pretty sure that's where you'll find the CR-V."

He was sceptical. I didn't blame him.

I looked up the number for Pfaff Motors and gave it to him.

Forty minutes later he called back, saying he'd seen a lot at his job but he was incredulous after talking to the people at Pfaff. They knew John well. They knew the car. It was sitting in their lot for sale at $28,500. John had wheedled $20,000 out of Chris Pfaff for the nearly-new vehicle. Adam's repo men were on their way to pick it up.

"The missed payments?"

"Not to worry. We've got the vehicle. That's all that matters."

A happy ending for all, as they say in the adult film business . . .

# CHAPTER FOURTEEN

# THE GLASS CAGE

**M**OLLY HAVING ALERTED me the night before, I set the alarm for 6:30, drove over to the convenience store for copies of the morning newspapers and took them across the parking lot to *Mr. Beans*, where I bought a coffee and muffin, sat down and thumbed to the business section of the first newspaper:

### *Investment Dealers Association of Canada fines John James Illidge $425,000 Imposes Lifetime Ban*

Three-hundred thousand was the fine, one hundred and twenty-five thousand the cost of investigating him. A lifetime ban from stock trading as the result of by now familiar securities offences: documents regarding trades that appeared to be signed by his clients that turned out to be forgeries, opening accounts in the names of fictitious clients to conceal his own activities, operating client accounts after they'd been terminated, fixing share prices—

I called Molly.

"Well?"

"It's for what he did at St. James seven years ago. What took them so long? And no mention of Rampart? Will they take seven years to look into that?"

"Why would they bother? He's bankrupt. My guess is he'll still be bankrupt in seven years. Remember these are just disciplinary measures for breaking rules and regulations and conduct unbecoming. He can't be prosecuted now that there's a settlement agreement in place, and they've banned him for life so it won't happen again. Case closed. As I've told you before, it's *caveat emptor* in the investment business. What else can they do?"

"It seems inadequate somehow."

"Agreed. But it's not criminal."

"It's fraud."

"There's no such crime really. Well, there is, but as I've told you, you're required to establish clear intent in order to prove it beyond a reasonable doubt—like finding the step-by-step plan a murderer drew up before killing someone. How're you going to do that with someone like John who makes things up as he goes along? His life seems to be a series of almost random improvisations. It's hard to see the real intent of anything he does."

"Why did you want me to read it? There's something about it being made public like this, being *out there* that, I don't know, embarrasses me. Is that just my vanity talking? Family reputation and all that?"

"Not at all. A $425,000 fine isn't something anyone wants to be associated with, let alone have exposed in the media."

"I don't have anybody else to talk to about it, Molly."

"I know that. I thought seeing it in print might be cathartic. Place things in the real world where they belong. Know what's in the public domain, as they say. John living with you wasn't real-world. Someone as delusional as he is in your house for almost a year is crazy-making. When you saw the headline, all the toxic feelings you attach to him rushed to mind. The public shame. The family name. The sense of helplessness, powerlessness—"

"I wouldn't go that far—"

"Of course you wouldn't. But the truth is the headline did bring it all back. The IDA can't touch him, the police can't touch him. There's to be no consequences. He's bankrupt and his companies are bankrupt. John moves on, and you can't do anything about it, or get anyone else to. That's a lot of power to hold over someone, and he holds it over you for some reason that a shrink could probably figure out, but my assessment is there's a sense of fear you have when dealing with him, even though you're the older brother. It's like he's got a hold on you of some kind. It's been about a year now since he's moved out. I wanted to find out how you're doing with your recovery. Suggest you start looking at your brother John in a whole different way."

"What way are we talking about?"

"I think from now on you should forget he's your brother and just focus on him from the point of view of yourself as a journalist covering a story, objectively reporting on his words and actions. 'Third-Person-It' as we say in law. Emotional detachment. Don't react to everything he does. The facts, m'am, just the facts, that sort of thing. The truth is, he's out of your life. He's not your concern anymore. He never was, but you allowed him to become your concern by getting involved in the search for your mother's missing money."

"No one else was going to."

"Fair enough. But at this point there's pathology at work. I think his behaviour, the manic bender he's on if I can put it that way, I think it haunts you somehow going back to childhood, the psychotic times with your mother before her breakdown. Maybe you see something similar happening to John."

"He's never been the breakdown type. That would be giving up. John never gives up, even if he knows he should."

"But he's never been in this position before with no money to fall back on."

"That we know of . . ."

"True. Maybe that's what all the Oakville Moving cash he counted at your kitchen table was for. His rainy day fund."

"I'm sure he's got something lined up."

"Like what?"

"Something he said about a week before he left when I asked him what he was going to do for cash got me thinking. Seems Tammy's uncle, her mother's brother, a former cop, passed away from cancer and left Tammy, his favourite niece, a $1.2 million inheritance. Tammy wants John to manage it for her . . ."

\*\*\*

Two days later, Barbara Somers held a contract-signing lunch at her house with Kim McArthur, the publisher we'd found for the Crest Theatre book. Leonard and James, owners of the bookstore Theatrebooks near the university, would attend as well, ostensibly to talk about how they could promote *Glass Cage: The Crest Theatre Story* as the book was now titled, to their customers and the wider theatre community.

I didn't like the idea myself. I had my suspicions about Kim McArthur from things I'd heard about her from other writers and some publishing industry people I knew, but in deference to Barbara, who was jubilant we'd found a publisher after nearly two years of searching, I agreed to it. Tess, my agent, confirmed with me that indeed Leonard and James were attending at Kim's request for the purpose of checking me out as a matter of course, being John Illidge's brother. The John Illidge in the news being fined and kicked out of the securities business for stock fraud, the John Illidge who stole Barbara's money. Kim wanted their seal of approval before any contract signing or advance payment took place. Tess, who knew the situation, told me I wasn't to worry. She could handle Kim, and John and Leonard were very nice gentlemen.

Tess I had met through Barbara. She had been Barbara's husband Harry's agent (Harry Somers, one of the country's preeminent modern composers) for many years. She agreed to represent the book, and took the project to Kim for consideration. Kim expressing interest, Tess set up a meeting at her office.

Things started out well enough with a peppy, almost giddy Kim expressing enthusiasm for the book. She liked publishing titles where there was a historical element, especially to do with Canadian history, which the Crest story obviously had to it. Did I have a title yet? I did: *Glass Cage: The Crest Theatre Story.*

Not bad, not bad. After pondering for a moment she began talking in a way that, from long experience, seemed just this side of manic. She spoke fast, her conversation darting between a melange of topics so that it was hard to follow what she was saying. Imperious, vivacious, sarcastic, her mind wandering between various trains of thought unrelated to anything we were there to talk about, she blurted: *"Let's talk about how we got here,"* which left Tess and I exchanging apprehensive looks.

She spoke even faster, rambling about how she lost her job three years earlier at Little Brown publishing when it was taken over by the Time/ Warner conglomerate... end of the Canadian publishing division... out on her ass, but determined to be a phoenix and rise from the ashes doing her own thing—which now she could boast she very much was. Only three short years in what was a cut-throat business, and here she had been given an annual line of credit by the Canada Council for $500,000 and become a publishing success. A phenom before long, she kidded, though from the suddenly agitated look and firm set of her mouth, not really.

She name-dropped some of the authors in her stable (I was unfamiliar with all but one). Went on congratulating herself for all that she'd put into building the company, her brand, the relationships she had with her international authors, her table at the Frankfurt Book Fair every year. She played the Eminent Publisher role to the hilt, holding forth to the not-so-eminent Writer and his Agent, there on bended knee begging for a book contract—

I finally interrupted her to ask if we could return to the topic of the

Crest Theatre.

Her nose out of joint, she laughed, mock serious: *Of course we could, but there were questions to be answered first!* A bevy of them, as it turned out, some vague and unrelated to what we were supposed to be talking about, some pointedly personal and none of her business, some segueing back to my connection to Barbara. How long had I known her? (Not long, but I'd worked with her brother Donald on a play I'd written for him in the late 1980s). What was the play? (I told her). And you were teaching at Upper Canada College then? (I was). Did I know that she, Kim, was a good friend of Barbara's cousin Jamie, who was her lawyer? (I did). Did I know Jamie Davis? (No, but I knew about him through friends). Did I know he had gone to Upper Canada College (I did, I knew people who'd known him there, and in university I'd had several dates with the woman he eventually married). Yes, said Kim narrowing her eyes, weirdly fixing her gaze on me in a hostile glare that could have been accompanied by an ominous, silent-movie piano *tremolo,* making no secret of the fact she despised me.

Just like that, snapping her thumbs like she'd just remembered, she leapt to the topic of John and Leonard, owners of the *Theatrebooks* store on St. Thomas Street, they knew all about the Crest Theatre of course. Had I ever met them? (I had not). Did I know *Theatrebooks* the store? (I did). Kim said it surprised her that for someone writing a book about theatre I wouldn't know John and Leonard. Why would that be? (I said I had no idea). What was my theatre background? Did I have any background? Had I worked in theatre? What other books had I written—

I cut her off politely, pointing out that this information was all in my CV, which I saw she had in her lap. She held it up as though looking at it for the first time, set it back on her lap and started browsing it. "Tell me anyway," she said, leaving Tess and me to make confused faces at one another behind our hands while Kim had a word with one of her assistants. *What the fuck is going on?* I asked Tess in a note I passed to her. Kim continued to study my CV, biting down on her bottom lip, a bothered look coming into her face. I kept quiet.

The bothered look turning to a stare when she glanced up from the CV, she levelled her eyes at me: a penetrating, no nonsense, tough negotiator stare. "Let's talk money."

Tess stepped in. She was thinking an author advance of $15,000 would be appropriate, considering the book would be a piece of prestige Canadiana, that $6,000 for Robert Ragsdale's pictures (Ragsdale had been the Crest's photographer) had to come from the advance, as well as her commission.

None of this her particular problem, said Kim, she felt fifteen-thousand was too much for a book like this. Non-fiction books in general weren't doing well. She tended to publish mostly fiction for that reason.

Tess made the case for its Canadian history pedigree again, pointing out there stood to be healthy library and ongoing college and university drama department sales, plus I'd have worked on the book for three years. She said that she didn't think seventy-five hundred, which is what I'd be getting on the deal, was too much to ask.

Kim threw Tess and then me a stare that exuded hostility and aggression like something about me was eating at her and she could explode at any second.

But realizing she'd overstepped the mark, she quickly regained control of herself, assuring us that she wasn't necessarily saying no. She wasn't closing any doors. She just needed to see how this book would fit with her *list*, and her budget of course.

Evasive, noncommittal, she let us know she could only take on so many properties—in the meantime why didn't we arrange a meeting with John and Leonard, the *Theatrebooks* boys? Get *their* thoughts on a book about the Crest Theatre. Include Barbara. She should be there too. Would I arrange that? I said I would.

The meeting over, she walked us to the elevator. *"Did you know,"* she asked me once again as we shook hands, "that *my good friend* Jamie Davis is Barbara's cousin?" She caught herself, giddy, giggling. *"Did I tell you that already?"* she said more to herself than me.

She was drunk.

No mention of it as we rode the elevator down to the ground floor, I told Tess when we came outside that I couldn't see myself working with someone like Kim. "She's a flake. All that questioning that had nothing to do with the book. She isn't stable as far as I'm concerned. She's got a drinking problem. I don't think she'll be able to pull together a book like this, not with what's eating her about me. Did you pick up how paranoid and suspicious she was about me taking money from Barbara to write the book, asking for a fifteen-thousand dollar advance? Small change when John defrauded Barbara of half a million. I get the feeling she knows that through her friend Jamie, Barbara's cousin and lawyer, the one who's going after John. That's what Kim thinks I'm up to with the Crest book. She thinks it's another Illidge scam. She thinks John and I are in cahoots trying to soak Barbara for the mega-profits on a book about a theatre she and her brothers operated nearly fifty years ago. Not exactly bestseller material."

We laughed at the idea walking out to the street. I broached the topic of finding someone else to publish the book.

"Hard to say. A bird in the hand and all that. The priority is just to get the book out by the fall of 2004 isn't it, the fiftieth anniversary of the theatre's founding? If we don't go with Kim, there's no telling how long it could be before we'd find someone else willing to take it on. Why don't we set up that lunch with the Theatrebooks boys as she suggested. I'll impress on Kim that we need a commitment, and tell her to bring a contract along. We need to get moving on this. And don't worry. I'll run interference for you. She's clearly uneasy about you, I agree. But I doubt there's anything you can do about that except a good job on the book. Which Barbara and I both know you're going to do . . ."

The lunch with Kim and, as Tess called them, the *Theatrebooks* boys took place on a blistering hot day two weeks later at Barbara's house (she wouldn't hear of us going to a restaurant on such an auspicious occasion as a contract signing). After drinks and appetizers under the awning on her deck, we retreated indoors to the dining room.

A curried chicken salad on the menu, the Australian chardonnay flowing freely while we ate, conversation ranged from Barbara's house, its history, her composer-husband Harry, her career (my contribution the little known  fact that in 1957 she had played opposite Sean Connery in an award-winning version of Arthur Miller's *The Crucible* on BBC television), to what everyone was hoping to see in the upcoming summer theatre season: Noël Coward's *Present Laughter* at Stratford (Tess), Harold Pinter's *No Man's Land* at Soulpepper Theatre (John and Leonard), Beckett's *Happy Days* at the Fringe Festival (Barbara), Kim not sure, *Eros at Breakfast* for me, also at the Fringe.

"By Robertson Davies," I added, a propos of *Eros at Breakfast*. "Davies wrote three acclaimed plays for the Crest Theatre before accepting that he'd never make any money at playwriting in Canada and turned to writing novels instead. The Crest with Murray and Donald's nationalist bent produced numerous Canadian playwrights at a time when everything was by an American, a Brit or a European."

"Here, here!" said Barbara raising her wine glass, everyone toasting, Kim downing her wine in one go then pouring herself a refill by the time the rest of us had set our glasses down.

Tess asked me to explain the timeline on the book and the format I had come up with (history in the main part of the book, a list of the Crest's 160 productions at the back, compiled from the original programs). I'd spent nearly two years researching the book so I felt I was qualified on the subject and able to write an engaging story about a literal as well as a cultural pioneering family.

Based on their comments and reactions, my pitch seemed to satisfy John and Leonard, however Kim, who'd been enjoying the chardonnay and was becoming more voluble by the moment, decided to take me to task and demanded that I tell her why someone would want to buy a book on the Crest Theatre, who would be interested in it, what would make customers, even at *Theatrebooks*, interested in purchasing it when it was about a theatre that went bust nearly forty years ago—

"It didn't go bust," I corrected her. "It was costing Donald and Murray too much of their own money to keep it going."

"Just playing devil's advocate, not criticizing."

"I didn't say you were."

"Lighten up for heaven's sake."

"Get your facts straight."

Kim bristled. She went to move her chair back and stand up but lost her footing and fell into me, white wine sloshing out of her glass onto my face. No apology, she made a snide comment under her breath, stumbled away from the table, made her way through the living room and out to the front hall.

Barbara with her usual grace announced that she would be putting the coffee on and bringing dessert out in ten minutes. People were *free to roam* in the meantime.

Tess remained at the table, John and Leonard, after helping Barbara clear, went upstairs with her for a tour of the house so that Kim, Tess and I could talk business.

I stood up to stretch my legs, stepped away from the table with my wineglass and was about to move into the living-room when Kim returned from the front hall with her attaché case, which she set on the dining-room table, opened and from which she took out a file folder. She turned, stepped up and shot me the same cold, manic glare she'd bestowed on me several times during the meeting at her office. She was loaded.

"As far as the advance goes," she said confronting me, her S's slurred as she railed: "*Barbara's* the one who deserves it, not you, because *YOUR! BROTHER! STOLE! BARB'S! MONEY!*" each shouted word accompanied by a hard punch to my chest that drove me back against a large Harold Town oil painting so hard that it popped off its hooks and crashed to the floor behind me.

I regained my balance, glaring at her, my right fist clenched with every intention of punching her back, only in the face and harder, but in a desperation gesture I took my phone out, put it to my ear, in one motion stepped around Kim who hadn't given way and raced into the kitchen so I wouldn't follow through. I was that angry. Drunk or not, the woman was demented.

After a couple of minutes I went back to the dining-room, ignoring Kim, who was closing her attaché case, no sign of the file folder. I asked Tess to apologize to the others for me. There'd been an accident with one of my kids, I had to go home. Why didn't I call her later?

And I was gone.

Phone calls went back and forth the next day, Tess convincing me that I should accept the advance Kim was willing to pay, Barbara hoping the fragile peace would hold long enough to get the book out.

I submitted the manuscript along with fifty photographs from the theatre's production photographer Robert Ragsdale, and a dozen from Barbara's personal collection, toward the end of July. No word from Kim by the middle of September, Tess pressed her for an explanation.

At first she said the delay was because there were problems with the book: it wasn't what she thought it would be; the format I called for was all wrong. She thought it needed to be rewritten, she wasn't sure how, just rewritten. Then the excuse became that her senior editor had gone on indefinite maternity leave (that left us scratching our heads). The third cause for delay Kim ascribed to a recent revelation that her graphic designer had been diagnosed with operable cancer (more scratching of heads). There was nothing Kim could do but wait and see how that turned out.

By the beginning of November, it was clear she had no intention of publishing a book on the Crest Theatre, at least one written by someone named Illidge. Citing breach of contract, I formally withdrew the manuscript, and asked for the photographs to be returned.

I contacted the literature officer at the Canada Council, with a complaint that my publisher had breached contract; that Barbara Somers and I were hoping to receive money from McArthur & Company's annual Canada Council allotment so we could publish the book ourselves and, if possible, have it in stores by the beginning of January, the fiftieth anniversary of the Crest's opening night.

Kim must have been contacted by the Council. She had *her good friend,* Barbara's lawyer/cousin Jamie, send me a letter threatening to sue, though for how much and why, the letter never made clear.

I'd promised Barbara when I took on the commission that the book would come out. Whatever the obstacles, I meant to live up to that without asking her for more money. To do otherwise would have confirmed Barbara's family's, and now Kim's, suspicions that I was pilfering money just as my brother had.

From a publisher friend I got the name of a graphic designer who could create the book file. With him on board, working fast, a talented guy who understood the pressure I was under, we were ready to send the book to the printers. The only problem was that I didn't have the $15,000 it would cost. Barbara would have given the money gladly, however I had resolved after the lunch debacle that I wouldn't take another cent from her. We had come this far; I owed it to Barbara and her brothers to tell the history of their theatre.

Nobody I talked to about financing possibilities had that kind of money at their disposal. It seemed the project was going to die, at least for now, until I remembered my friend Don Robson, who had been in a car accident recently and was at home recuperating. A mutual friend had told me to go to Don in the first place. This was the kind of thing he'd be interested in supporting.

I called and arranged to go over and see him.

The good news: things weren't as bad after Don's accident as initially feared. He was up and about, looking forward to driving again soon.

He cracked a bottle of white wine, we talked about progress on the Crest Theatre book, which he'd heard through some friends was in trouble. I gave him a capsule version of the situation, and events leading up to it with our publisher Kim.

"How much do you need for the printing?"

"Fifteen thousand."

Don had made millions as CEO of several international gold-mining companies. Our friendship went back to university. He had always respected me for taking *the road less traveled*.

He mentioned that now, asked me to reach him the pen by the telephone, took a check book from the drawer under the counter, wrote the check, tore it off and handed it to me.

"*Done*. No paybacks. Just give me a copy of the book. Now, I need a few things at the store. Can you drive me over . . .?"

\*\*\*

When I handed Barbara the first printed copy of *Glass Cage: The Crest Theatre Story*, she asked if despite all the silliness, the run-around and the frustrations early on I was happy with the book.

"Very," I said. "I hope you are."

"*Very very,*" she said, opening a bottle of champagne . . .

My brother Peter phoned just before Christmas with the latest on John. My mother had apparently given Peter $10,000 to buy a new used car (the Buick she'd been forced to bequeath him needed repairs that he couldn't afford).

John found out somehow, told Peter to let him have the ten-thousand dollars and he'd set up a deal with Chris Pfaff Motors for a two year-old Toyota Camry, a twenty-five thousand dollar car for anyone else, a steal at ten, and exactly what Peter was looking for. John said he'd call when the car was ready for pickup.

Ever unsuspecting, Peter sent him the ten-thousand. The call took several months to come, John telling him when it finally did that the vehicle was all set to go.

Peter paid $135 for the taxi up to Pfaff Motors in Newmarket, forty minutes north of Toronto. He spoke to Chris Pfaff the owner about his Toyota Camry. John had told him his car was ready for pickup.

*"What car?"* Chris had asked.

Peter had an address for John in Toronto, in the Beach, the Cape Cod-style lakefront development overlooking Lake Ontario that had gone up two years before on the grounds of the old Greenwood Racetrack at Lakeshore and Woodbine Avenue. I put in a call to him just after New Year's on his birthday, not to wish him a happy one, but to confront him about the theft of Peter's $10,000.

There was no answer at any of his numbers. No point in leaving a message even if I'd been able to, I decided to drive down to the house he'd moved into for when he was in town, on a street called Winner's Circle in the Beach by Lake Ontario.

An attractive three-story semi-detached place (garage in a lane at the back), light blue, dark blue clapboard, white trim windows, easily worth $800,000 at the time, a *pied à terre*, or so he told Peter, that he was renting from a friend who bought it but couldn't afford to keep up the $4,200 monthly payments.

I went through the black iron gate at the sidewalk, up the flagstone walk onto the porch to the front door, my finger having barely pressed the bell when fierce barking erupted inside the house, grew louder fast, broken by snarling—I could see through the slats of the door-blind a brown-faced black Rotweiler bounding forward, leaping, teeth bared— paws and snout hitting the door with a heavy *Thwump!* that had me jumping back terrified.

The barking continued even after I left the porch and went out the gate. My car parked about five houses down, the Rottweiler was still barking when I drove off. Nothing like a rabid guard dog to keep duns and debt collectors at bay . . .

# CHAPTER FIFTEEN

# ARBITRATION SOLUTIONS

"YOU'RE LIKE A BAD SMELL that won't go away," I said to Gerry Gurdler when I called him back after a blitzkrieg of hostile voicemail messages.

"I need to depose you," he said, ignoring the cut.

"Is that so. What for?"

"The fifty-eight thousand, which is sixty-three now, by the way. Interest, expenses—"

"General aggravation?"

"If you'd been nicer and returned my calls—"

"The money goes straight to the creditors, I'm sure."

"Of course. Why wouldn't it?"

"I think I'll hold onto it for now."

"So you have the money?"

"I didn't say that."

"You're wasting your time."

"I've got plenty to waste."

"I've already set the deposition up."

Which is what I wanted to hear: he'd booked an out-of-court deposition room and a court reporter to transcribe the proceeding. He'd have laid out a thousand dollars.

"How long are you planning to take?"

"Two should do it."

"When and where?"

"Next Friday. The twelfth. Ten a.m. 330 Bay Street, Suite 800."

"Should I bring a lawyer?"

"No need. It's just your standard deposition."

"Nothing's standard with you, Gerry."

"I wouldn't worry."

"I'll think about it," I said, hung up quickly and turned off my phone knowing that he would already have pressed redial.

A few minutes before ten o'clock on the twelfth, I presented myself at 330 Bay Street, Suite 800, a company called *Arbitration Solutions*. The receptionist took my name and asked me to have a seat. No one else in the waiting room, unoccupied chairs lining the bare walls, the receptionist returned to the magazine she was leafing through when I came in.

Some brochures in a holder on the table beside my chair caught my eye. I took one and opened it:

> At *Arbitration Solutions* we have combined all the resources needed to make your next arbitration or other out-of-court proceeding run smoothly in one seamless operation.

> At *Arbitration Solutions*, no request is too large and no detail too small. Members of our team will arrange for couriers, try to find you event tickets, recommend restaurants and make your dinner reservations. Leave nothing to chance: we handle everything, leaving you free to focus on your case.

Leave nothing to chance? We handle everything? Seamless operation? Event tickets, restaurant recommendations and couriers? What were they talking about here? What exactly did any of that have to do with arbitration? Arbitration of what?

As always with Gerry Gurdler, things were not what they seemed. The place gave me the creeps. Up from my chair, I was contemplating a fast exit when the receptionist called my name, pointing to a door across the way, its handle-lock buzzing.

Pocketing the brochure for future use, I walked over, opened the buzzing door and entered a security room, bare except for a uniformed cop confronting me, one hand resting casually on the holstered handle of his gun, the other pointing to a second cop over beside a body scanner, a third cop next to him handing me a plastic bin in which to put the contents of my pockets, money, keys etc., which he then passed to a fourth cop on the other side of the scanner, who returned the bin once I'd stepped through it. He pointed me straight ahead through a door in a frosted-glass wall that led along a corridor with tall clear windows to my left overlooking Bay Street, a row of offices to my right, Gerry with a sour smile on his face standing in the door to one, pointing inside.

A small office, bare except for the table and chairs where we sat down across from each other, a female court reporter sat with her steno machine at a small table behind the one where Gerry was sitting, facing me.

He began with biographical information, family, provenance of the two promissory notes, dates, circumstances, after which he segued into more personal matters like employment, asking what I was presently working at, my current sources of income, what my teaching pension amounted to—questions I ignored. We sat silently for several minutes, Gerry growing anxious, riled—

*"Gerhard Gurdler is in on a bankruptcy fraud with my brother John!"* I blurted over Gerry's head to the court reporter—

Gerry glared. "What are you doing—"

"Did you get that?" I called to the reporter.

A confused stare.

*"Gerry Gurdler,"* I shouted to her, she began typing, *"is in on a fraud with my brother John Illidge and is pursuing me on a bogus promissory note claim to cover it up—"*

*"Stop!"* Gerry snapped at the reporter.

*"He takes a cut from my brother's Oakville Movers money!!"*

*"Turn the machine off!"*

*"Twenty thousand dollars a week—deposits it in a bank in Ottawa—"*

*"Turn the machine—"*

*"Leave it on!"*

Confused, visibly frightened, the reporter maintained her professionalism and kept typing.

*"Off!"* Gerry screamed at her. *"What do you think you're doing?"* at me.

*"John Illidge is sitting on more than a million dollars right now—"*

*"That's Tammy's money! Her uncle left it to her—"*

*"So John says!"* I stood up.

*"Sit down."*

*"Tammy says she hated dropping your cut off every week because GERRY KEPT ASKING FOR BLOW JOBS—"*

*"Shut up!"*

The reporter kept typing.

*"This won't work, you prick!"*

*"YOU'RE ON THE TAKE, GERRY!"* I yelled at the top of my voice. *"EVERYBODY KNOWS—"*

*"Sit down you asshole!"* to me, *"Shut the goddamn machine off!"* to the reporter.

*"Keep it on!"* I said, turning quickly for the door.

But not quickly enough. Gerry leaned across the table to grab me; missed, ran around to my side of the table, lunging for me on my way to the door, just catching my wrist from behind. I swung around, the elbow of my other arm cracking him in the jaw. He threw a punch that glanced off my shoulder. I punched back hitting his nose, knocking his glasses off, sending him stumbling backwards—into the arms of three cops that the court reporter must have called.

While one kept Gerry on his feet, the other two came for me, took me by the arms and walked me not just out of the office but down the hall to the elevator, holding me till it came. When the doors opened and they went to push me in, I stood my ground. I'd noticed Gerry holding a handkerchief to his bleeding nose watching from the door of *Arbitration Solutions*.

I shouted down the hall as the cops wrestled me aboard. *"You'd almost think I was the one who absconded with a hundred-million dollars, wouldn't you, Gerry?"*

The doors closing, time for the cops to give me the old heave ho . . .

# CHAPTER SIXTEEN

# WHAT'S IN A NAME?

PLANNING FOR THE wedding of John's eldest daughter Rebecca hit a foreseeable snag when he announced that Tammy, as his new wife, felt she should be present at both the ceremony and the reception.

There were discussions. Rebecca and Ellen didn't have anything against Tammy *per se*. It was just that the usual wedding tensions were being exacerbated by John having defrauded, in some cases for substantial amounts of money, a number of relatives and good friends who would be attending. On top of which, according to John's detractors, of whom there were many, parading around at his daughter's wedding a mere two months after his own with a woman most would see as a bimbo-slash-trophy wife, and you had a recipe for a toxic situation that could well lead to uncomfortable confrontations after a few cocktails.

Rebecca and Ellen decided they couldn't take the chance. Tammy would be welcome at the ceremony but not the reception, where people were free to do whatever they wanted in their interactions with John. Surely everyone could rise to the occasion and take the high road for a few hours on Rebecca's behalf.

Which they did. After the ceremony in the chapel of the college Rebecca attended at University of Toronto, guests *reconvened*, as John would say, at the Granite Club for cocktails, dinner and dancing. Rebecca opted out of a receiving line in what she felt would be everyone's best interest.

John was conspicuous by his presence; however, I didn't see that it caused any problems. Without Tammy and free to mingle, he was his old schmoozing self, winning people over (or trying to) with his joshing light-hearted quips, snappy patter and humorous banter, though I did notice three of his oldest friends and their wives stayed well clear of

155

him throughout the evening. He even made a father-of-the-bride speech during the toasts that went off well enough as I remember, and he was still there chatting people up when the kids and I left around eleven. I'd said hello at the chapel, avoided him throughout the evening; said only goodnight on our way out.

The kids and I talked about him in the car on the way home. I mentioned his latest venture, related to me by my cousin Heather's husband Alan, while we waited for a drink at the bar. John had apparently lined up a consortium of investors for the leveraged buyout of *a big computer software company in Dubai* whose stock price, according to John, was already rising fast—and the new company had only been in business for nine months—

"And will be out of business in nine more," Carson quipped, "when they find out someone has been *taking money out the back door.*" (I'd explained the phrase to the kids in connection with the sudden bankruptcy and John's hasty exit from our house.) "And get this," Carson added, he told me he and Tammy were either moving to the south of England and buying a house in the Cotswolds, whatever they are, or buying the president of Queens University's summer cottage on an island in the St. Lawrence River near Gananoqué."

"Both luxury properties, I'm sure."

"$695,000 for the island in the St. Lawrence."

"Must be some cottage."

Nicky piped up. "I thought he was bankrupt? Where's he getting all his money from?"

"According to John," said Carson with more than a hint of sarcasm, "another uncle of Tammy's died and left her close to a million."

"How many millionaire uncles does she have?"

"As many as John wants her to have, Nicky," I said.

We laughed.

Nicky said he noticed John was still driving the black Mercedes. "I spotted the *RSKY BZNS* plates in the parking garage."

"Do you think he'll end up in jail one day?" Hannah wondered.

"Good luck," said Nicky. "They have to catch him first."

I smiled to myself thinking of a line from Frank *"Catch Me If You Can"* Abagnale's memoir extolling his prowess at eluding authorities:

*"I was slipperier than a buttered escargot."*

That was John . . .

While he was reviving his fortune managing Tammy's millions, I was working hard to make mine with *The Shakespeare Novels.* Shakespeare's seven greatest plays in versions I wrote while I was teaching. Shakespeare was compulsory in English courses, yet school boards stopped buying new copies of the plays so the ones available were so old, covered with graffiti, missing so many pages, and in such bad physical condition they were virtually unusable. The plays are poetry, always difficult to understand. I knew them inside out after twenty-six years teaching and directing them in student productions, but reading Shakespeare in hard copy was only possible if I asked students to triple- or quadruple-up on the books, a recipe for squabbles, lots of chatting, and general horsing around.

It was at this point I would announce we would switch to using my versions of the plays and act them out in class (periods were 75 minutes, plenty of time to go through a scene and discuss it), with everyone playing a part, whether as director, actor, lighting person, dialogue coach or creator of sound effects that were, for the most part, rudimentary as they would have been in the 1590s: the most popular auditions (the kids organized these themselves) were for the role of thunder—six or seven of the biggest boys in the class usually winning the part since it involved standing on desks at the back of the room stomping noisily with their shoes (most preferred boots) to warn of gathering storms, of which there are many in Shakespeare.

I had wanted to publish my modern novel versions for years—turn *Hamlet, Romeo and Juliet, King Lear, Othello, Macbeth, Twelfth Night* and *Midsummer Night's Dream* into prose books so the stories could be read, discussed and enjoyed like any other book in English class. No footnotes. No academic analysis. No history of England at the time Shakespeare lived. Just fascinating, dramatic stories, entertainingly told. Why should the world's greatest writer be a pain?

A book distribution company in Chicago heard about the books, felt they were a break-through concept and picked the series up for world distribution. I wrote the novels out and published them through the company I had started in order to publish *Glass Cage: The Crest Theatre Story*. I introduced the series at the distributor's December sales meeting held at the Cornell Club in New York City. The first printing sold well. Kobo invited me to put the series on their site as e-books. I began novel versions of three more plays, all comedies, since the original seven novels had been tragedy-heavy.

There was good news and bad news from Jeff Freketych (manager of my Mulvihill Wealth Management locked-in investment account) at a meeting to find out what he thought of the new business ideas I'd given him to look at with a view to helping me find investors and get one or two projects off the ground: ideas that incorporated different aspects of my teaching experience such as communication training, dispute resolution, team building, relaxation therapy, concepts that I knew were in growing demand among corporate managers.

Jeff felt the ideas were excellent ones on the whole. Any good manager would want professional development sessions like I was proposing. But he levelled with me in delivering the bad news: it was next to impossible to break into that area of the corporate business world when you hadn't worked in it, when you were looked at as an outsider. Competition for contracts was fierce even among insiders, very often cutthroat. Plus companies switched service providers all the time, looking for lowball rates since the truth was neither senior management nor staff themselves took these human resources sponsored programs very seriously.

And, whether I liked it or not, "John's (let's call them *rogue*) activities are well enough known around the industry during the last seven or eight years that, I hate to say it, they've left a taint associated with the name Illidge when it comes to the investment industry—I heard two of his daughters had changed their names and taken their mother's maiden name."

"One of them did. The other got married."

"No," Jeff said with real encouragement returning to the subject at hand, "the good news is your Shakespeare books. They're a winning idea as books for the education market especially. But I think they can be successful audio books as well. Sales and rentals of audio books are exploding all over North America right now. I took the liberty of mentioning your *Shakespeare Novels* to a friend of mine named Don Parker, Chief Financial Officer at a company called *Simply Audio* in Oakville. They operate a subscription audio-book service in Canada, the eastern and southern United States and southern California. According to Don, their subscription base is growing fast, so Connie their head of content development is looking for new books to add to their catalogue. Could you see yourself recording some of the Shakespeare novels for her if she's interested? Don says she's sure to be. He is himself."

I'd never even thought of audio books. With music and sound effects, they were a perfect medium. Sure I could see myself recording the novels.

"When do I start?" I joked.

He gave me the number for Connie the content developer at *Simply Audio*, recommending I call her soon to talk about the series which Don, the CFO and also *Simply Audio's* marketing whiz, was already calling *Simply Shakespeare*. Jeff asked me what I thought of the title.

What else could I think?

"Simply great . . ."

Later that day I called Connie, left a message and heard back from her the next morning. She was very interested in the concept of recording my versions of Shakespeare's plays. Why didn't I come out to *Simply Audio*, learn about their service and discuss the possibilities for *Simply Shakespeare*, the name they liked, provided I approved.

Though she was aware there were seven novels in the series, Don Parker, the CFO, who had spoken to her about the project and was personally excited about it, felt that they should start with the four novels that I thought would best introduce *Simply Shakespeare* to their subscribers.

The meeting with Connie couldn't have gone better. *Simply Audio's* subscriber base was currently concentrated in the northeast U.S. and Florida, but they were expanding aggressively into central and western states. Subscribers selected and paid to rent an audio-book from the company website. A CD was shipped out, returned after five days, post paid by *Simply Audio*. Subscriptions were growing every week. Soon they would top 400,000. They needed more content to keep up with demand!

Connie said that if everything went as they were hoping it would, by the time all seven plays were recorded I could be making as much as three-hundred thousand a year in royalties—especially if I read the books myself and *Simply Audio* didn't have to pay talent fees. The amount was so unbelievable that I took it with a grain of salt. Still, it felt nice to hear Connie speak with such confident optimism about the Shakespeare books. It's always nice to hear people say, as Connie and Don both did, that your idea is the right one at the right time. Who was I to disagree?

A quick sound-test of me reading excerpts from the books established that my voice was listener-friendly, conveyed a sense of confidence in the characters and events of the story, captured the kind of emotion necessary to appeal to subscribers in the key demographic categories and, as far as Don and Connie were concerned, would make Shakespeare "Simply Entertaining."

On the business side, *Simply Audio* would pay $1,200 for rights to each of the first four novels, $1,200 each for the last three. I hesitated. Since I'd have to make the forty-five minute drive to Oakville and back each day in the two weeks we'd be recording each book, I told Connie that if she made it $1,500 per play we had a deal.

We shook on it. Connie and Don would have the CEO sign off on the budget, draw up a contract and book a series of recording sessions for *Simply Shakespeare* with Colin their sound engineer in about three weeks.

But as things turned out, it wasn't to be . . .

# CHAPTER SEVENTEEN

# LIKE A HURRICANE

"*S* TEP *AWAY FROM THE TREE*—*drop the garden shears and put your hands where I can see them!*"

This, the barked command of a short paunchy man with a brown handlebar moustache, wraparound black shades and a blue POLICE baseball cap pulled low on his forehead, as he came charging across my front lawn with his police-issue black Glock pistol pointing at my head. It was shortly before 7 p.m. on an otherwise quiet, warm summer evening in our east Toronto lakefront neighbourhood.

His beige cargo shorts, tight-fitting white T-shirt, ankle socks and running shoes were laughable, however the Glock wasn't. He came up fast, halting a few feet in front of me, still shouting, two-handing the gun which he now levelled at my chest, even though I'd done what he told me to and dropped the shears I'd been using to trim the drooping branches of the weeping mulberry tree in my front garden.

I was not about to argue the point—not with a dozen or so other officers storming out of four dark-blue, tinted-window SUVs that had squealed to a stop in front of my house. Guns on their hips, wearing the same wraparound shades, blue ball caps, white T-shirts, cargo shorts and running shoes as the guy pointing his gun at me, they snapped to it, raced over and joined two women who had positioned themselves at the foot of my driveway.

In blue jumpsuits, black boots, shades and blue ball caps—guns on their hips as well—one of the women, whose manner suggested she was in charge, had the squad fall in behind. She shouted something and the squad marched up the drive, the officer in charge shouting another order.

Two of the officers broke away from the squad, drawing their weapons as they rushed forward and converged on Nicky, who'd been busy in front of the garage vacuuming the inside of the beater Plymouth Voyager van he used for his summer landscaping business. He was listening, as I had been, to Neil Young's "Like A Hurricane," which Carson was playing on his electric guitar in his bedroom above the garage, the window open, the amplifier on medium-loud. Hannah had gone over to her friend Holly's house two blocks away.

The noise of his vacuum leaving him unaware of the cops until they grabbed him, Nicky jumped back into the arms of a third officer who had joined the others, wrestling the vacuum hose out of his hand, standing him up, holding him by the front of his T-shirt while a fourth and a fifth officer ran up, one of them yanking Nicky's arms behind his back and handcuffing him, shouting something to the guy with his gun on me, who promptly shouted at me to keep my hands in the air, turn around and make for the front porch.

I did so, but the second I started walking a pair of officers swept up from behind, pulled my arms down behind my back in a wrist-up stress-position (called the "Guantanamo," I later found out), and slapped the cuffs on.

Because of the Guantanamo the pain in my upper arms and shoulders was excruciating, worse than anything I'd ever felt. I shifted my weight from one leg to the other as we walked, contorting my body in a palsied effort to find relief from the pain burning in both my shoulders, only to have the officer with his gun on me jab the barrel in my spine and shout "Stand up straight!" I did, but turned in spite of the pain to see what was happening to Nicky in the driveway.

The rest of the squad hovering around the officer in charge, she said something to her female counterpart, a brunette with a ponytail sticking out the back of her blue ball cap—I have no idea why it would have caught my attention at such a tense moment.

The squad reforming, they marched Nicky quickly up the front walk to where I was standing.

Two officers with black steel battering rams raced past me onto the porch, positioning themselves in front of the door, readying their rams to smash it open.

The officer in charge stepped up to me.

"Paul David Illidge?" she asked, glaring hard . . .

While the dozen or so drug squad members methodically tore our house apart searching for the cocaine, crystal meth and guns we had already told them we didn't have—told them all they were going to find in the way of drugs were eight marijuana plants in a grow unit under a 500 watt light, along with a few trays of clone cuttings Nicky was growing, with my permission, in a spare room in the basement. Indoor gardening, he called it—we sat on the living-room couch under the glare of the officer in charge.

We were interrogated for close to two hours in our living-room, something that I knew should have taken place at the police station, not in a family home. But what was I going to do? This wasn't a TV cop show where I could declare my Miranda Rights to a phone call, a lawyer, silence. This was real life.

The officer in charge was the hyper-aggressive type, out to prove that just because she was a woman in a traditionally male profession, you couldn't mess with her. She spoke to Nicky, Carson and me, sitting in front of her on the living-room couch in handcuffs, the same way she talked to her officers: every statement a rigid, verging-on-hostile command meant to scare us into telling her what she wanted to know about our grow op— leaning down eye-to-eye for effect every so often, hesitating for a moment before she shrieked into our faces things like:

"YOU'LL NEVER LIVE IN THIS HOUSE AGAIN!! WE'RE CONFISCATING THIS HOUSE AS THE PROCEEDS OF CRIME FROM YOUR DRUG DEALS!! YOU'RE LOOKING AT *JAIL* TIME HERE, BOYS!! FIVE YEARS MINIMUM!! NO SIR, THIS LITTLE GROW SHOW IS *OVER*!!"

It was impossible to take seriously, especially with the smell of coffee and cigarettes on her breath when she zeroed in for nose-to-nose close ups, repeating the in-your-face ploy and the same threats every ten minutes or so between periods of stony silence during which, only moving her eyes, she continued waging psychological warfare with searing repeat glares and hard looks that could burst out suddenly into SHOUTED reminders of what other criminal offences she could charge us with if we didn't smarten up and PLAY BALL!! The woman seemed to think we were as dumb as she was.

We sat there listening to the general mayhem upstairs and down. With all the whooping, shouting, slamming, banging and crashing going on, the cops seemed to be having themselves a whale of a time.

At about the ninety-minute mark, Carson whispered to me that he had to go to the bathroom, a bowel movement.

I conveyed this to Officer Val (the other officers had been calling her that) but her answer was a shake of the head: *No.* More requests followed at two minute intervals, each one more insistent: *No.*

Carson's distress worsening, a male officer across the room filling out our information forms could see where things were headed. He asked Val if he could take the kid to the bathroom.

Val thought about it for a painful few minutes before saying okay. Carson jumped to his feet. The officer walked him out to the hall, Val shouting after them: But the cuffs stay on!

Unable to take any more, I screamed that she was *ONE SICK FUCK*, a repugnant human being. Fucking *REPUGNANT!!*

No response, down the hall Carson let out a moan. The officer warned Val that things could get messy. Carson cried out. Val appeared to pay no attention.

Out of my mind, I stood up, ready to leap across the coffee table and head-butt her or worse.

Anticipating my move, she clamped a hand on her gun.

I froze.

She shouted down the hall: *"The cuffs can come off, but the door stays open!"*

A look of strained relief on his ashen face, Carson returned from the bathroom about five minutes later, the cuffs back on, the officer waiting for him to sit down before taking his file folders back from Val and hurrying out to the hall.

Nicky asked Carson if everything was okay.

"Just barely," said Carson casting Val a cold look.

"So what happens now?" I asked.

She gave a casual shrug. "We'll take the three of you to the station. You and Curly here," nodding at Carson, "can make statements and come home. This one," she glanced at Nicky, "stays in jail to face charges."

Nicky let out a nervous breath, his face and neck turning red as they always did when he was scared or under stress, but he held his chin up, kept his eyes squarely on Val to let her see what he liked to call his *unde-terred* look. Twenty minutes earlier he had told her he was the one doing the growing, with his father's permission, his brother wasn't involved, he would take the rap.

Under my breath I told Nicky not to worry, he wouldn't be going to jail alone. "There's no way this woman will let me walk," I whispered to him when she wasn't looking.

An officer in the hall with Val told her that transport was on its way.

"I'd like to phone my daughter before we go," I said to Val. "She's over at a friend's, house and I don't want her coming home to find the house trashed and her father and brothers missing."

"Not my problem."

"I need to call my daughter."

"You need to keep your mouth shut is what you need to do." Turning her head, she shouted to an officer in the front hall. *"Tommy, what's going on for cryin' out loud?"*

"We're good to go anytime, Val," he said, mobilizing the T-shirt and cargo shorts crew, who had been standing around waiting. Apparently everybody had to leave at the same time. That's the way it worked.

Val assigned two officers to Nicky, who led him out of the living-room into the front hall. Two more took Carson by the arms and positioned him behind Nicky, while another pair held me back on Val's orders, emptying my pockets and putting the contents on the console table: about $80 in cash, loose change, the billfold with my drivers' licence, birth certificate, health and social insurance, credit and ATM cards.

I mentioned, when they were done, that I'd lost all feeling in my left arm; that the arm had a metal staple in it from an athletic injury and it was digging straight into the bone. I asked if they could move the handcuffs from their position up-behind to down in front, otherwise I could pass out from the pain.

"The guy wants his cuffs switched to the front," one cop called to Val who, surrounded by the cargo-shorts crew, was in the process of dialling a number on her cell.

"Too bad," she replied as she finished dialling and held the phone up to her ear.

No surprise. Again, I asked one of the cops holding me if he could let me use the phone in the computer room we were standing beside so I could call my daughter and at least let her know what had happened.

"You'll get your call later."

*"Time?"* Val shouted to the group.

*"Eight forty-five!"* somebody snapped out.

*"Okay, let's roll!"* Val announced, strode up to the front door and pulled it open. *"Go!"* she barked at the officers holding Nicky, closing the door immediately after they'd stepped out. She motioned the officers holding Carson to bring him forward, waited a minute or so and, after a glance at her watch pulled the door open shouting: *"Go!"* and pushed it shut the moment they hit the porch. I knew immediately what this was all about. She was choreographing the whole thing for what she knew awaited us outside.

The cops holding my arms rushed me forward, stopped maybe five feet from Val, with whom I resumed my request to call Hannah. *Why couldn't she do the decent thing and let me make the call? Why?*

Pretending she hadn't heard, Val stared at herself in the large mirror on the wall beside the front door. Neither vanity nor introspection, it was a dead stare lasting a good fifteen seconds or so before she turned away, glanced at the cops holding me and shouted:

"*GO!*"

Though the sun was starting to set, there was still plenty of golden light along our street as the Serve and Protect Show played out, a full-scale dramatization of the Toronto Police Department motto: six police cars with their red-and-blue roof-lights flashing lined the middle of the street, which had been closed off in both directions. Yellow police tape had been strung across the road, two uniformed officers in their bullet-proof vests standing beside each of the six cruisers, more officers at either end holding cars and a crowd of maybe a hundred neighbourhood people back behind the tape, all watching in stunned silence as the cops brought me across the front lawn to one of the flashing cruisers where a uniformed officer was opening the rear door.

"*Wait!*"

The moment the voice rang out the police on either side of me froze, their grips clamping down hard, the two of them turning their eyes, as everyone else in the street was, toward my next-door neighbour's house.

Mary-Ellen McCluskey, a notorious gossip, neighbourhood busybody and mean-spirited rumour-monger was rushing across her front lawn toward me.

Pulling her mild-mannered husband Quin by the hand after her, she stopped ten feet from the police cruiser and called to me in a voice loud enough for everyone in the street to hear: "*It wasn't us who called them, Paul! I swear, it wasn't us!*"

## CHAPTER EIGHTEEN

# BADA BING, BADA BOOM

I N MY EARS THERE WAS the roaring that seashells make. I felt on the verge of passing out from the Guantanamo handcuffs, the pain excruciating by the time we arrived at the police station and were booked for marijuana trafficking. I could no longer feel my arms or hands.

The roaring grew loader, my head started to spin as four cops, two for Carson and two for Nicky, headed them one way, while two other cops materialized heading me off in another, the roaring in my ears so high and hissing when they brought me into a room with a shower stall in it that I couldn't make out what they were saying until one cop put his face right up to mine and shouted *"STRIP SEARCH!!"*

They removed the handcuffs behind my back. My arms fell half way down then froze, cramped, trembling, circulation struggling to return as to add to the indignities of the evening I was instructed to take my clothes off and submit to a "cavity search," a flashlight investigation of my anus.

I ignored the crippling shoulder pain as I attempted to undress, joking with myself to distract from the feeble result of my efforts to remove my clothes, that my humiliation was nothing compared with what this pair had to say whenever someone asked them what they did for a living.

I choked on my inner smile when I realized there was no way that my limp arms and hands could remove my clothes. The officers were getting quite a kick out of watching my futile fumbling attempts to undo my shirt buttons, one laughing out loud when I asked for some assistance like it was the funniest thing he'd ever heard. *Too many drugs, pal? Betcha wish you were stoned right now!*

The laughs kept on coming for ten minutes or so as, sweating profusely, breathing to relax before every failed attempt, I decided to hell with it, skipped the damn buttons altogether and worked my still-buttoned shirt off over my head inch by tugging inch. To this day I have no idea how I accomplished the feat.

With no belt to worry about, pants a size too big that I only used for gardening, I slid my limp fingers down the side of my legs and kept sliding them down with my elbows angling out so that after some hula-dance wiggling I managed to slide the pants over my hips, down to my ankles where I kicked off my shoes (the drug team had taken out my laces back at the house so I couldn't flee), then pulled off the pants. Underwear, with its elastic band, came off with no problem. Arms at my side, still shaking, shoulder pain forcing me to hunch over for slight relief, I stood there nude staring over at them.

Eyeing my body up and down as though searching for I couldn't imagine what, they finally made satisfied sounds and told me to step into the shower stall, bend over, spread my legs and touch my toes. The torso pain seemed a bit less severe as I let my arms dangle, shaking spastically as my blocked nerves struggled to come back to life.

*"Hold still!"* one of the officers barked, he and his partner stepping behind me, squatting down, training their small flashlights up at my anus, me with my upside down eyes watching while they peered more closely before being *satisfied that no drugs or weapons were hidden there.*

That was the answer they gave with straight faces when I asked about the purpose of the search. If I hadn't been in such pain I would have roared and made some sarcastic comment such as: *You actually think I stuffed a pistol up my ass?*

They told me to speed it up getting dressed. Grew irritated when I couldn't. Told me to cut the crap and *Get a fucking move on, we haven't got all night.*

Mission finally accomplished, the cops fit to be tied, they fast-walked me down a floodlit grey corridor, opened a grey steel door, ordered me inside, slammed the door shut, and for the next three hours, I was alone.

Three hours by myself in a small holding room pacing around the walls, counting the floor tiles, whistling music from every genre and era I could think of to try relieving the tedium, the restlessness, the fear that comes with being trapped but not knowing when, or if, someone is going to release you. Music helped smooth out the uncertainties that had come flooding in as the shock wore off and anxiety set in.

The whistling I did with a kind of defiance, a personal act of protest against the miscarriage of justice that was under way over a few pot plants growing in a family's basement. I kept the whistle loud, bright, fun, and always directed up at the surveillance camera in one corner of the ceiling. I knew that somewhere in another part of the building, some cop was looking at a monitor and forced to listen to me warble crazily on without pause. It gave me some satisfaction to whistle my mad medley over and over to the point it would drive the cop on duty crazy listening to it—

A key rattled in the lock. In came a guy maybe in his mid-twenties, black hair almost to his shoulders, a goatee, wearing a soiled white T-shirt under a ratty red-and-black lumberjack shirt, a dirty white ball cap on his head that I remember had *REEM* written in orange over the bill, beaten up red Converse high-cut running shoes on his feet, one sole held on with a piece of twine. A plainclothes cop? How would I know? He showed no I.D.

He had a small notepad in one hand, a pen in the other. Opening the pad to a random blank page, he stared at it for several seconds. When asked, I gave him my name, birth date, home address. He wrote them down. Tapped his pen on the page, reflecting, no eye contact, none since entering the room—

"The arresting officer," he blurted, "is charging you and your two sons with trafficking in cocaine, marijuana and crystal meth. Because there are three of you, you're to be considered a criminal organization."

"A criminal organization?" I asked, incredulous, "like the Mafia and the Hell's Angels? Because there are three of us?"

"Pretty much," he said, studying the bit of information he'd written down for a second before closing the pad, putting it and the pen back in his shirt pocket, turning for the door and walking out.

Too stunned to swallow with shock having turned my throat desert-dry, the list of our offences knocked the whistling right out of me. Officer Val going after me for calling her *repugnant* in front of her squad, that had to be it. She had looked like the vicious type right from the start. This only confirmed it. I was mobster Tony Soprano and the boys were my soldiers. We were an insidious crime family. A danger and a threat to neighbourhood safety, who, thanks to good citizen Mary-Ellen McCluskey, had been exposed.

The boys would be all right. Val would be after them to say I was the ringleader, Fagin out of *Oliver Twist* who had forced them to grow the pot plants for me—warning them severely, as she had repeatedly back at the house, that they would be over their heads in trouble if they didn't co-operate and admit the truth about what was really going on at our house. Val wanted me, there was no question about it. Wanted to see that I got the mandatory five years in penitentiary. From what I'd heard and read about cases like these that the police trumped up when they wanted to really get someone, it would be a slam dunk guilty verdict for the prosecution. They controlled the process, so they held all the cards

Would the boys hang tough, or fall for Officer Val's threats? They had always been taught to stick to the truth (*When in doubt, let it out*, the maxim we used). I knew I could count on them to do so with contemptible Officer Val.

*"I have to pee!"* I called up to the surveillance camera then repeated the request every couple of minutes until about twenty had passed without the sound of a key in the door.

*"If you don't come in the next five minutes,"* I finally said, *"I'll just go on the floor!"*

It was closer to ten minutes by the time the door rattled, an officer opened up, stepped in and held the door open, motioning me to get moving.

He walked behind me down the fluorescent-lit hall, around a corner, along another hall that soon came out into an open area . . . where I started whistling on a hunch that if the boys were somewhere nearby they'd hear—the officer accompanying me pointed to a wall-mounted urinal across the way.

I turned my head as I stepped up to it, glancing back over my shoulder down the cell row, which I'd noticed. Whistling louder, it wasn't long before Carson's voice rang out from the cell row: *"Is that you, Dad?"*

I called back that it was. "How're you doing?"

"So far so good—"

Nicky joined in, saying he was in the cell next to Carson's. "Where are you?"

"In a holding room on the other side of the building."

Time up, the officer told me to get moving.

I started walking, slowly, the officer not seeming to mind.

"Get this," I called to them. "A plainclothes cop came in to tell me that because there were three of us we were now being charged with running an organized crime operation, of which I'm the boss. Call me Tony Soprano!"

"Move," said the officer.

"Gotta go!" I called to the boys.

*"Hang in there, Tony!"* Carson shouted.

*"Bada bing, bada boom!"* Nicky added: Bada Bing was the name of the club in New Jersey where *The Soprano* crime family liked to hang out . . .

My one phone call came at 3:30 a.m. The officer who had taken me to the bathroom brought me from my cell, walked me through a steel door at the end of the cell row that led into a better part of the jail, a small suite of glass-walled rooms around an open area where the officer brought me forward to a small wooden shelf attached to the wall with a rotary-dial black phone sitting on it, the dial removed so there was just a receiver. An older man wearing horn-rim glasses and a plaid cardigan who might have been in his late fifties sat in a glassed-in office across the way, a set of headphones hanging around his neck, an illuminated control board and several telephone extensions sitting on the desk in front of him.

The officer picked up the phone receiver for me, pointed to the gentleman in the control booth, handed me the phone and left.

I saw the man in the booth's lips move before I heard his voice: "What number do you want?"

"Could you connect me to Information?" I intended to call a longtime friend who was a criminal lawyer. His number was 9's, 6's and 0's but in my present state I couldn't remember the order—

"No information, no long distance. You give me a number, I dial it. Or you ask for duty counsel, the on-call lawyer that works for The Court."

No choice, I opted for duty counsel.

The man in the control booth slipped off his headphones, spoke into one of his telephones for a minute then looked over at me and nodded.

A man introducing himself as McDaniel or Nathaniel, I wasn't sure which, came on the line talking fast. "Forget lawyer-client confidentiality. They listen in on these calls. Be careful what you say. Be brief. They could cut us off at any time. So what happened?"

I did my brief best to describe the raid, the living-room interrogation, Val's ranting, her promise that if we told the truth things would go a lot easier for us. "So we told her the truth and—"

"Things went south."

"About as far as they could go."

"Any idea who called the cavalry on you?"

"My nosy next-door neighbour."

"Plants in your backyard?"

"Tomato plants in my son's garden."

"Nice neighbour. Why'd the cops come inside?"

"No idea. She probably made up a story."

"Must have been a whopper."

"She's got a vivid imagination."

He laughed. "Anything else?"

I mentioned the washroom standoff, the noise of destruction, laughter and glee, the *Law & Order* final scene culminating in the perp walk from the house to the cruisers in front of the whole neighbourhood.

"Pricks," McDaniel said like he meant it. "That's the drug squad. Bottom of the police-barrel. What did they book you for?"

"P for P. Whatever that is."

"Possession for the purpose of trafficking."

"We're not traffickers. It's my son's hobby."

"I know. It's just what they do. What did they put you down for?"

"I heard someone tell the arresting officer zero to three."

"That'll be pounds. How much did you have?"

"I don't know. Maybe ten, twelve ounces."

"So less than a pound then?"

"I would think so. Where do they get three pounds from?"

"It's irrelevant anyway. Everyone knows they put a foot on the scale when they weigh the stuff. Earth, roots, a boot on the scale can boost you to however seriously they want to charge you. Nobody ever checks the numbers. P-for-P on the pot then. Anything else?"

"Cocaine and crystal meth."

"Are you fucking kidding?"

"You'd think I was. They found traces of an alkaline powder in an aluminum saucepan under the sink in our basement bathroom. The pipe drips sometimes. The dried water leaves a small white ring."

"You see it in a lot of basement bathrooms. So they took that for crystal meth?"

"Stuffed it in an evidence bag. I don't know what they thought was cocaine."

"And because there were three of you they booked you as a criminal organization."

"Us and the Hell's Angels."

"Ridiculous."

Speaking more slowly, he went through what would transpire the next morning. Transport to Old City Hall court at Queen and Bay Street, jail in the basement, upstairs for arraignment in bail court.

"Just remember what I said. Not another word to the cops. You'll do fine. In six-months or so it should all be over. I know it probably doesn't seem like it right now, but it's not the end of the world. It's sound and fury signifying nothing, if you know your *Macbeth*. Cage-rattling mostly, but it can fuck your life up pretty badly if you take it too seriously. Just letting you know."

Back to my cell across from the boys' cells (I'd been moved there after my phone call), I lay down on the stone-hard ledge bed built into the wall. Because the stainless steel toilet had overflowed, the water on the cell floor was over my ankles and ice cold. I forced my eyes to stay open as my contact lenses were starting to dry out. I only lasted about five minutes before drifting off, exhausted.

# CHAPTER NINETEEN

# THE PIT

THE POLICE VAN WAS running late. They'd handcuffed and rushed us out of our cells at 7:30 by the station clock we passed on our way downstairs to the garage where the court van was waiting: Carson crammed into a four-foot by four-foot single compartment, Nicky and I put in a not marginally bigger double for the trip downtown to bail court.

But first we had to stop at finger-printing and mug shots then pick up prisoners at two other divisions, the ensuing ride downtown, one from hell. In handcuffs, our heads bent below the top of the compartment, we braced ourselves with each burst of speed by the enraged driver for the sudden hard slam of brakes that sent us head first into the galvanized steel wall. If the car sickness didn't get us, the broken neck surely would.

Out of the van somewhere underneath the building, the officers led us via an alternate route to the basement entrance due to construction in progress. Officers guarding us front and back, we were led through a labyrinth of damp, mouldy-smelling basement corridors of the Victorian-era building until we finally reached our destination, had our cuffs removed then were put in a holding cell with about two dozen other men and teenage boys, some standing on benches along the walls, some pacing, no one sitting, all waiting as we were to be called up to bail court. The boys and I were the only ones wearing orange coveralls. The others made way, gathered around curiously, someone in the crowd calling out: *"Welcome to The Pit!"*

Around eleven we were brought up to bail court for the first time, back in handcuffs for our appearance, hoping the people we'd had our duty counsel lawyers call earlier would have appeared to bail us out. As McDaniel had explained, we each needed someone who would post a

$5,000 surety bond with the court, with whom we'd have to live and who would be responsible for us 24/7 until the date of our trial in six to eight months, though McDaniel did warn there was no telling how long a case could go on.

Glancing around the courtroom, the boys and I exchanged disappointed looks. Except for the robed Crown prosecutors and court clerk, the three duty counsel, the stenographer and the Justice of the Peace on high in a grey three-piece suit with a green, scarlet and gold academic hood over his shoulders, there wasn't a familiar face to be—

A commotion at the prosecution table, the male prosecutor whom we could only see from behind approached the bench, spoke to the judge briefly, nodded to him then returned to the prosecution desk, put some files in his case and closed it. He spoke to the court clerk and to the female prosecutor, turned and started down the aisle for the door.

Nervous, slightly embarrassed as he approached, he shot us a sidelong glance as he walked past the prisoners' dock, held the glance as he gave us a half-smile and a short, hip-level wave.

Nicky whispered, "Is that who I think it is?"

It was: John's son-in-law Jim Cassels, his eldest daughter Rebecca's husband. We knew Jim was a Crown prosecutor. What were the odds that our case would have landed in his lap?

The female prosecutor approached the bench for a word with the judge, who announced that we were to appear later while the prosecution familiarized itself with the case, Jim Cassels having had to recuse himself due to the family connection.

Reassuring as it was to see a familiar face like Jim's under the circumstances, I had a sinking feeling in my stomach as the officers led us downstairs and back to The Pit. I knew exactly how things would play out. Jim would call Rebecca, who would call John, who would rejoice at the opportunity to put the word out to everyone he could think of about my drug-dealing ways, with the express purpose of having them forget about anything they might have heard about his own questionable activities, and be shocked to the core by the news about *the Paul they thought they knew.* The number one son who could do no wrong, the golden-boy, the *favourite*—in jail for drugs and, as John would be sure to tell it, bound for a lengthy stint in the penitentiary.

The day wore on. We were taken up to bail court again after lunch, the female prosecuting attorney in place now that Jim Cassels had recused himself . . . yet here at our second appearance, still no one that we had asked our duty counsel lawyers to phone had shown up to bail us out.

Back in The Pit, panic began to set in, the spectre of spending the night in the maximum security, 160 year-old rat- and bug-infested Don Jail if no one bailed us out.

With court closing at 3:00, we were brought upstairs for a final appearance at 2:20, Don Jail bound if no one showed—Carson and Nicky breathing sighs of relief to see Jill and her next-oldest sister and her husband sitting in a pew on the far side of the courtroom, about as far from the prisoners dock as you could get, mortified, arms crossed, staring straight ahead, no eye contact or acknowledgment of the boys, to whom it didn't matter: no one had shown up for me. I was spending a night in the Don.

I looked to my duty-counsel Laura in appeal. She hurried over to the prisoners' dock. I asked to see her notepad where she'd written down my publisher-friend Jeff's number earlier in the day. I'd given it to her because Jeff's office was only six blocks from Old City Hall courthouse. We'd been friends for forty years. I knew he'd drop what he was doing and get himself to court the moment he heard.

How could I not swear at Laura when I saw the reason Jeff hadn't shown up: she'd reversed a six and a nine. She'd been leaving voicemail messages at the wrong number all day.

It was 2:25. The JP reminded Laura court closed promptly at 3:00.

She apologized profusely as I wrote the correct number down on her pad in large bold letters. She took it and raced for the doors, the JP scowling at her breach of decorum as she flew out the door.

Carson and Nicky still in the Pit while their paperwork was being processed, I was brought up to bail court again at 2:40, twenty minutes till closing time, no sign of my friend Jeff.

Laura rushed to the prisoners' dock. She'd reached him. *He's on his way!* She turned and informed the JP, asking for patience, even though everyone in the room could see His Honour was itching to adjourn for the day.

At 2:50 he announced that ten minutes was plenty; he couldn't wait longer. Court would be adjourned for the—

*Wham!*

The double doors at the back of the courtroom crashed open and in sprinted my friend Jeff, gasping for breath, sweating profusely, calling to the judge that he was appearing for Paul Illidge.

He took the stand. After posting his car ownership with the court clerk as the $5,000 surety for me, the JP imposed the same bail conditions on me as he had on Carson and Nicky: I could not be on the premises of my residence on Friendship Avenue at any time or for any reason, other than to attend there immediately after my release to pick up personal belongings. I could have no contact or communication with my sons until after our trial, and I was required to live with Jeff until the case had concluded.

"Excuse me, Your Honour!" I called from the prisoners' dock. "I don't think that's right."

"What you think has no bearing here, Mr. Illidge," the JP said irascibly. "You and your sons have been identified as a criminal organization, and your house a crime scene subject to an ongoing investigation."

"It's a family home."

"Not for the time being, it isn't."

"This is ridiculous, Your Honour. If it's a crime scene, it's because the police turned it into one looking for drugs and guns we didn't have. *They're* the criminal organization, not us."

"You were running a marijuana grow-operation, Mr. Illidge."

"An *alleged* grow-operation," I reminded him.

"Object as you may," he said, his irritation mounting, "those are the provisions in law regarding grow-operations and criminal organizations."

"An *alleged* grow-operation, an *alleged* criminal organization," I reminded him.

"We'll let the court determine that."

"But you just told the court about provisions for grow ops and criminal organizations. That hasn't been established."

"You're getting into contempt territory, Mr. Illidge."

"I'm sure I am, but this is overkill, Your Honour."

"One more word . . ."

"Is the court prepared to pay my mortgage and my bills for me? I'm a writer. My office is in my house."

"That's not the court's problem," he shot back, his face reddening.

"My surety Jeff Miller lives in Casselsson, an hour's drive from Toronto."

"That's of no concern, Mr. Illidge, since you're not *living* at your house."

"—I wasn't aware that posting bail required Mr. Illidge to live with me, Your Honour," Jeff put in from the stand.

The JP looked over at him. "Are you saying you'd rather *not* post bail?"

"No, Your Honour. Only that it could be months before the case comes to trial. I have a wife and two children, and I travel a fair bit for my work."

"Again, that's not the court's problem. As his surety, you're expected to know of Mr. Illidge's whereabouts at all times—"

"With respect, Your Honour, I think it's asking a lot of Mr. Illidge, a man in his fifties and a single-father to live with me and have to be treated like one of my children."

"Perhaps Mr. Illidge should find someone else as surety then." He looked at his watch, closed the file folder in front of him.

"—No, Your Honour," Jeff shot back. "That won't be necessary. I'm sure we can work something out."

"Let's hope so," the JP said, ready to call it a day.

"Your Honour," I spoke up. "It seems to me by not letting me live in my house you're impeding me from keeping up my employment, which you made clear was a condition of my bail."

"I did, yes."

"As I told you, I'm a writer. I work at home. How am I to generate income and pay my bills if I can't be in my place of work?"

"Well," he said, "you'll just have to pull your computer out of there when you pick up your personal belongings, won't you?"

"It's professional belongings I'm concerned about, Your Honour. It'll take me more than one visit to remove the things I need—"

"In that case," he cut in, "you'd better make sure you have a brush and a can of paint handy when you're doing so."

"A can of paint and a paint brush?"

"That's right," he said, gathering his papers, darting his eyes up at the clock then fixing them on me. "If the police come by while you're moving these professional belongings as you call them, you can tell them you're just performing routine maintenance. Otherwise they'll take you to jail, where you'll remain until your trial." He peered at me above his reading classes. "Are we clear about that?"

"No, we're not," I said.

Floored by my defiance, the JP tilted his head forward and hardened his already threatening look that screamed: *Just try me buster!* Holding the glare for a few moments, he at last turned and consulted briefly with the Crown, the two of them, along with the court clerk and Laura, directing their gaze upwards and to the side of the room where a large Grand & Toy office calendar for the month of August had been sloppily fastened to the wall beside the clock with strips of grey duct tape. The tape on one of the top corners having come loose, the calendar tilted noticeably to one side. I felt like I was in a bad cartoon.

The consensus reached after a quick look at the lopsided calendar on high, was that I was to attend at court again in two weeks' time. No reason given for the hearing, the JP let me know that if I failed to appear I'd have breached a condition of my bail. A warrant would be issued for my arrest and I'd go to jail until the time of my trial.

No further business, he promptly adjourned the hearing, everyone in the court springing to their feet as His Honour, a good and peeved look on his face, stepped down from the bench and, the folds of his black gown flowing out behind him, made a hasty exit through a door to his right, my friend Jeff still on the stand, waiting to be dismissed.

It was 3:35.

# CHAPTER TWENTY

# JUST SAY NO

S O BEGAN OUR SIX-MONTH *interaction* with the criminal justice system, which consisted of court appearances by the boys and me once a month to set the date and time of next month's court appearance, decided upon after the judge, the court clerk and lawyers had all gazed up from their laptops at the lopsided Grand & Toy large-print office calendar duct-taped high on the courtroom wall. I appeared at my hearings in person, my long-time friend Trevor, who was defending me pro bono saying it wasn't worth his time to show up.

Trevor had offered to have two of his friends who had handled drug cases before act pro bono for Carson and Nicky. But their mother and her family wouldn't hear of it. Instead they paid $5,000 to a lawyer for Carson, who wasn't involved in the plant growing, and $15,000 for Nicky's lawyer because he was. How his lawyer, Lorne Schuster, could be charging such an exorbitant amount for a simple P-for-P summary offence prosecution was outrageous according to Molly and my other lawyer friends. Where had this guy come from? Nobody in the legal community had ever heard of him.

As it turned out, Nicky's aunt and her husband discovered Lorne's weekly cable television show *Legal Matters,* where he took phone calls from viewers with legal questions. I'd seen the show myself. It was an advertisement for his law practice. If your question wasn't answered on the show, or you had a legal problem you needed help with, you were urged to: *CALL LORNE AT THE NUMBER ON THE SCREEN TODAY— TOLL FREE!* Lorne had told Jill and her family incorrectly that ours could be a very complicated case going forward. He claimed he would have to put hours into it *just to be on the safe side*. There was no telling how

179

things could turn out in a trial, he warned Nicky's mother's family.

At the beginning of November, police disclosure (the evidence against us) came down. Charges against Carson had been dropped, so only Trevor and Lorne were to be at the case conference with the prosecutors to decide whether there would be plea bargains, or whether we would opt for a trial. Trevor showed up and told them on my behalf there would be no plea deal, I wanted a trial. He and the prosecutors waited for half an hour but Lorne never appeared, and couldn't be reached. One of the prosecutors called him to find out Nicky's position. He would plead guilty, something I know he didn't want to do.

As it turned out Lorne had gone to the family prior to the prosecutor's meeting to point out he would need to charge $35,000 if the case were to go the trial route. The family considered that they had already spent $15,000. Though they were well off, they didn't want to spend more than they already had. Lorne had made a mess of things for $15,000. Imagine what he could do with $35,000!

All Lorne needed to do was register a plea of not guilty, along with mine, and let the prosecutors decide whether they'd be able to prove in court that we were doing all that Officer Val said we were. Trafficking pot. Cocaine. Crystal meth. That we were a criminal organization.

There would have been no trial. There never is in these cases. Lorne let Nicky hang out to dry because he couldn't squeeze an extra $35,000 out of Jill and her family. He was off the case. He'd been a fraud all along.

The trial was a formality. Nicky entered his guilty plea and agreed to pay $3,000 to the court, and $3,000 to a drug treatment charity of his choice. He would attend meetings with a probation officer once a month for a year, and he would have a criminal record, no word as to how long, or when he would be eligible for a pardon. With so much going on at the time, and shifty Schuster having abandoned Nicky, this aspect of the plea bargain would prove to be the harshest punishment of all: with a criminal record for possessing marijuana he could never be hired for any job: at eighteen, he had become an ex-con . . .

John having woven one of his sensationalist tales about our criminal drug activities, voicemail messages I left with my sister Judith to explain the truth of the situation went unanswered. I wanted to give her the real version of events that I knew John with his hyperbole and lies deliberately would have neglected to tell her.

I waited almost three months to get in touch with him because I knew he would be expecting any call that I made to him to be a penitential one in which I offered contrition, guilt, maybe even an apology for having disgraced the family by being *busted for drugs*, something John abhorred with a degree of disdain that kept him from regarding people who used them as nothing but *worthless losers, scum, vermin*. Hence, in contacting him I opted for a surprise strategy which I hoped would leave him baffled: mentioning in my message that it was money I wanted to talk to him about.

*Not borrowing it, making it.*

Sure enough, I heard back from him in just under an hour. I got right to the point: I wanted to find out more about his and his friend Paul Posay's back-dated promissory note scheme (he'd described it to me one night after a few vodkas), and see if they were still doing that because Jill was insisting on putting our house on the market as soon as possible. I wanted to know what was involved with the promissory scheme; would I be able to use it on the sale?

A pregnant pause before replying, he said in a less-than-enthusiastic, couldn't-care-less tone that he'd be open to discussing my venture. "How 'bout the lounge café at the Granite Club, tomorrow, 11:30. Not lunch. I'm working out of the club these days. I have some appointments, I can squeeze you in."

*Squeeze me in?* I knew he was dying to talk to me.

Natty in navy-blue dress pants, black brogues and a white, fresh-from-the-cleaners button-down shirt, he was waiting for me outside the lounge. He greeted me with a handshake, put a hand to his glasses and adjusted them as we walked off to the café.

As it had just opened, we had our pick of tables. John directed me to one and we sat down. Signalling the server, who seemed to know him, he ordered his usual lunch, times two.

"You said there wasn't time for lunch."

"The club sandwiches here are to die for."

*Club sandwiches to die for?* I suppressed a smile.

The server returned with a vodka rocks she put down in front of him. She turned to me: "Did you want anything to drink, sir?"

"Just coffee, thanks."

He stirred his drink before taking a sip.

"How's life on Winner's Circle?" I asked, hoping to catch him off guard.

The question having its desired effect, he spilled a bit of the drink, threw me a frown. "Winner's Circle?"

"I was in the neighbourhood recently."

"I'm only there when I'm in Toronto."

"The Rottweiler isn't exactly Mr. Friendly."

"You met Bruno."

"In a manner of speaking."

"It's Tammy's dog. I wish she'd get rid of the thing. Sometimes I wish I could get rid of her. She's costing me too much. Anyway, Ellen's cancer resurfaced," he said, almost as an afterthought. "She's in Princess Margaret Hospital. The doctor decided against treatments. They're just keeping her comfortable." He paused while the server put my coffee on the table. "The girls are pretty upset of course. I've been talking to them. We've been through this before a couple of times. We know the drill. But the good news is Ellen has left them sitting pretty. A million-eight each."

"How do you know that?"

"The girls told me."

"You sat down with them and talked money?"

"Losing Ellen—"

"She's not dead yet."

"—it's brought the girls and me closer," he said with a complete lack of anything you'd call genuine emotion.

I asked him if he'd been to the hospital.

"I told the girls I might try to get in this weekend. I've been in Ottawa. Things are pretty busy with my latest venture."

"Tell her I'm thinking of her if you do end up going, will you?"

"Sure thing," he said, sipping his vodka rocks, something eating at him and I knew what it was.

"What's wrong?"

"*Drugs.*" He let the word hang in the air for a moment. "What were you thinking, Paul?"

"We had some marijuana, a neighbour ratted on us, so what?"

"You could do time, you know."

"Not for the little bit of marijuana we had."

"Jim said it was cocaine and crystal meth."

I looked him in the eye. "Jim's in a lot of trouble if he told you that."

"He told Rebecca."

"Doesn't matter. He recused himself from the case. He's not supposed to tell anyone. He could be disbarred."

"Were you pushing?"

"Were we *what?*"

"Pushing."

"What're you talking about? This isn't the 60s."

"*Dealing.* Selling the stuff."

"We weren't."

"Are you an addict?"

"What kind of question is that?"

"Well are you?"

"You think people who smoke marijuana are all drug addicts?" I nodded at his vodka rocks. "Are people who drink vodka all alcoholics?"

"Touché."

A surprise concession. "Can we talk about promissory notes?"

"We can—"

The server brought our club sandwiches then returned to the table a minute later with another vodka rocks for John, a coffee refill for me.

"As I said on the phone, Jill wants to sell the house. Fast. She's afraid the government will confiscate it."

"That's what they do with grow ops."

"If you're the Hell's Angels maybe. Back to the house: Jill and her sisters are dying to get their money out of the place. And mine too. Their lawyer is telling them they can screw me out of my share of the equity because of the raid, which they can't, but I've got better things to do than put up with that kind of bullshit right now. I was thinking of just saying fuck it and walking away from the whole situation. Let the money be paid into court so no one can touch it without the other person's agreement."

A look of alarm stormed his face. "—But then I remembered the promissory note business you mentioned a while back that you and your lawyer-friend, Paul Posay, were running. I thought maybe that was a better way to go. Is there some way I could utilize one of your back-dated promissory notes when it sells? Which it should pretty fast."

He was all ears. "Sure. We could put a promissory against your house—what's it likely to go for?"

"We're asking $480,000. It's one of the bigger houses on the street."

"Two-forty would be your share then. We'd probably do the back-date for two-hundred thousand, with a probability that we'd get around one fifty. Could we make it out to your publishing company for a business development loan that our people gave you a few years ago?"

"Would I need to show a receipt for the two-hundred thousand?"

"The promissory is your receipt."

"Have you done many of these?"

"A dozen and counting."

"So it should work."

"Nobody's complained so far."

"How is the deal set up?"

"Posay and I put a lien on you for the $200,000 we loaned your publishing company. We take fifty thousand on the way through for handling things. Deduct your mortgage from the $480,000 selling price. What's the mortgage at?"

"$160,000."

"Any back taxes?"

"About ten-thousand. Jill never paid her share."

He took out a pen, did some calculations on a napkin. "With that and closing costs make it $185,000. With the promissory yielding $150,000, which as I say would be realistic on a $200,000 claim, that's $335,000 off the $480,000 sale price, leaving $145,000 in equity, of which you receive about $70,000 on top of the $100,000 from the promissory. Jill and her sisters are left with $70,000 when they wanted the whole nut. They get fucked."

My head was spinning, he rhymed the numbers off (so fast).

"You make it sound like a walk in the park."

"It is. Just let me know and I'll get Posay working on it."

We finished our sandwiches, John letting me know that in the meantime there wasn't much he could do for me if I needed money, which he said he expected, from talking to Judith, I probably would. Unfortunately, all his funds were *tied up in one venture or another* at the moment.

"No worries about money," I said.

"Really?"

"With my drug connections, I'll get by," I said with a straight face.

A look of shock. *"What?"*

"I'm pulling your leg, John."

He scowled, not amused.

The server had left a pen with the bill. He wrote down his club membership number.

"Give the promissory venture some thought," he said. "It'll be the easiest money you ever made."

"And it's guaranteed?"

"I told you. No dissatisfied customers yet."

He ordered another vodka rocks, stayed seated when I stood up.

*"Just Say No,"* he quipped. The anti-drug slogan. Only half-kidding.

"You should give pot a try. It might lighten you up."

"Not in this lifetime."

"What're you afraid of?"

"Not afraid."

"Of course you are."

"They've connected pot to Alzheimers."

"That's ridiculous."

"It's a fact."

I was about to be sarcastic and say: *Maybe that's how Dad got it then. Slipping out to the garage all those years for a toke—*

But his phone rang.

A quick thank-you for the lunch, I turned for the door, reaching into my shirt pocket as I came out to the hall. The micro-recorder still running, I said the date, time and location into it, adding: "John explaining to me the promissory note back-dating scheme he and Paul Posay are operating," then clicked the recorder off, mission accomplished: I had him on tape showing intent to commit fraud.

Three weeks later an obituary appeared:

*Ellen Jane Fox, 54, passed away peacefully after a long and courageous struggle with cancer. Beloved mother, cherished sister, lovingly remembered by her nieces, Ellen will be greatly missed by her many cherished friends. She was a dedicated teacher who valued the role that education played in children's lives. She was always able to see the humour and magic in every child she taught.*

Just as his name was missing from the obituary, there was no sign of John at the funeral. As expected, the church Ellen, John and the girls had attended for twenty-five years, St. Georges United in North Toronto, was full. There was joy in the music her friend Karen played and sang (Karen had sung at her wedding); in the remembrances of her brother, her sister, a few old friends, and Emma and Rebecca, who was eight months pregnant with her first child: "A blessing on this sorrowful occasion if there's one to be had," the minister offered in his own fond tribute to Ellen.

During the singing of the final hymn, Carson, who was standing next to me, nudged me with his elbow, nodding above and behind him to his right. I turned and glanced up.

John was sitting by himself in the choir loft.

Nicky noticed us looking up. "What is it?"

"Check out the choir loft."

He did, then turned his head back to me. "What about it?"

I looked up.

John had left . . .

# CHAPTER TWENTY-ONE

# MR. ARULANADAM

A s I HADN'T EATEN breakfast, I stopped in at Mr. Beans, the local coffee shop before going to the house where Jill and her real estate agent, Lenny, who would handle the sale, were going to meet me to make sure the work I'd done readying the property for market had made it look like it was worth every penny of the $480,000 asking price. Lenny had ordered the For Sale sign to go up that afternoon.

After coffee and a cinnamon-raisin bagel, I came out of Mr. Beans, went across the plaza to the flower shop and picked out three colourful bouquets of cut flowers to put in vases in the living room, the dining room and the kitchen, a floral finishing touch that I knew Jill would appreciate.

I parked in front of the house, grabbed the flowers, ran across the lawn before nosy Mary-Ellen McCluskey could see me, ducked under the still untrimmed branches of the weeping mulberry tree then hopped onto the porch—only to stop dead when I spotted a notice that had been posted on the front door, on red 8 ½ by 11 inch cardboard, the printing in large, Bold-font black letters:

TOXIC WARNING!!
PREMISES UNDER QUARANTINE

I stood there reeling, blood pressure spiking, pain shooting down my neck and into my arms, fear and outrage churning my stomach after all I'd been through in the last few months. *How could this be?*

Had Mary-Ellen been tracking my comings and goings while I worked on the house?

*No*, I thought suddenly, stepping closer to read the notice: yet another twist of the revenge knife by Officer Val.

By order of the City of Toronto Public Health Department, the building has been quarantined due to the presence of *Bio-hazardous Materials*. No one is allowed on the premises at any time, for any reason, until further notice. Fines and imprisonment will result from violation of this order. The property is being monitored regularly by Health Department officials. It is a criminal offence to tamper in any way with, or remove, the order as posted.

The *Bio-hazard Warning* was repeated at the bottom. There was a phone number in the lower right-hand corner that I could call for further information.

*Toxic warning? Bio-hazardous materials?* What the hell could they mean by that? The raid had occurred eight months ago. The house was in pristine condition, the best shape it had ever been in. I'd washed, scrubbed, vacuumed, grouted, polished, painted, dusted, disinfected and deodorized for the last five days—*Mr. Clean* wouldn't have thought twice about moving into the place with the condition it was in now.

Lenny's real estate sign would be going up in a few hours. The listing would appear online. Within twenty-four hours prospective buyers would be driving past to have a look at the place. *Why,* they would wonder, *is there a red notice posted on the front door?* They would get out of their cars to have a look.

I stepped closer, checking the tape they'd used to put up the order, thinking maybe I could peal it off and take the poster down until things got sorted out. Call the information number and complain that a mistake had been made, the order had been posted on the wrong house—demand they come and inspect it for bio-hazardous materials ASAP.

Feeble fantasy, of course. Whoever had posted the order had taken no chances: all four edges were expertly tacked down with two-inch wide strips of heavy-duty clear scotch tape, a second series of strips overlapping the edges of the first. Any attempt at pealing or cutting the tape would prove fruitless.

The words *premises monitored regularly* leapt out at me. Though it had only been a few minutes, I'd been foolish to linger. I memorized the information number, turned casually, stepping down from the porch and, as if nothing was amiss—like I'd merely stopped by to drop off some flowers for whoever lived here and they weren't home—walked calmly across the lawn back to my car, scouting the street for a vehicle in which a Health Department official might be sitting staking the house out. It was only

10:30. The warning couldn't have gone up too long ago. Yet for all I knew their strategy in cases such as this might well have been to slap the notice up then hang around making sure people took it to heart.

From what I could see, the coast was clear up and down the street, the only cars in driveways. I opened my car door, casually set the fresh flower bouquets in the passenger seat, stepped in, started up and drove around the corner and part way down the street behind my house.

No one about, I sneaked into the backyard of the house kitty-corner to mine, climbed the wooden fence, made my way along the top rail thirty feet or so then jumped down into my backyard. I ran across the lawn and patio to the sliding-glass doors and slipped inside the house.

Fast across the kitchen, I cut through the dining room and stood next to one of the living room windows, looking through the half-open shutters to see if there was anything going on out front. For the first few seconds there wasn't—until a small white sedan came into view, driving slowly. . . but it was only a woman with a baby-seat in the back. When she'd gone past, I took out my phone and dialled the Health Department number.

Composing myself while it rang, resolved to stay calm, level-headed and matter of fact, I let the woman who answered know the situation, asking if there was someone from whom I could get more information about a quarantine order that had just been placed on my house.

It was nearly 11:00, half an hour until Jill and Lenny arrived.

She took my name and address, went off the line for a moment then came back on to say she was putting me through to the inspector handling the case.

A man picked up after several rings, identifying himself in a robust East Indian accent: "Dar Arulanadam."

Dar listened while I explained the reason for my call, gave me a suspicious and, I realized immediately, crafty response. He wondered *why I was calling from inside the quarantined house in defiance of the posted order*. I told him I wasn't defying anything, I was on my cell phone. "I read the order when I arrived at the house, but left without going inside."

The grilling continuing, he asked where I was calling from.

"A coffee shop nearby."

"What's the name of it?"

"Mr. Beans."

*"Beans?"* ·

"As in coffee beans."

Still not convinced, he warned me the premises were being monitored regularly to ensure the order was being upheld. In stern tones he informed me I could be arrested if I was calling *from inside the house*, which he went so far as to say, again, that he was sure I was. "Most people have a tendency to do exactly that when orders are posted. We have to be vigilant."

Playing along, as I knew I had to, I conceded that, although it might be the case with most people, I liked to think I was smarter than that—the kind of person who did his utmost to cooperate with the authorities in circumstances like this.

My cloying obsequiousness enough to mollify him concerning my whereabouts, he got down to business explaining the order. A police search of my house had turned up a marijuana grow operation, the report by the officer in charge of the search indicating that black mould, a toxic contaminant, had been found on the premises.

I kept my frustration in check and assured him that there had been no mould of any kind inside my house at the time of the search, and never had been in the ten years I'd lived there. "On what date?"

He paused while searching. "Last July, the 25th."

"That was eight months ago."

"It is what it is. The police sent it in. I'm required to follow up."

"Where exactly was the black mould found?"

He went off the phone, shuffled through some things on his desk then came back on. "According to the police report that I have in front of me, the officer leading the search identified patches of black mould about halfway down the main floor corridor . . ." I scooted from the living room into the hall, walked halfway down. "On the baseboard," he continued, "directly across from the basement door."

Crouching down for a look, there were indeed two brown spots each about the size of a dime about half an inch off the floor. I must have missed them when I was cleaning.

"On closer inspection, officers were able to determine that the two patches were of the black mould variety commonly present in buildings where marijuana is grown."

While he'd been talking, I'd kneeled down and rubbed the two spots away with my thumb: splashes of Coca Cola that probably spilt from a glass when someone was heading to the basement to watch TV. They were brown, not black, and they were definitely not mould. I didn't tell Mr. Arulanadam, but I'd cleaned up such spots before.

"Anywhere else?" I asked him.

Perhaps from the relieved tone in my voice, he pounced. *"Are you in the house, Mr. Id-leridge?"*

"For heaven's sake, *Mr. Aru-lana-dam*," I said patiently, enunciating the syllables clearly so as to emphasize the correct pronunciation of his name, "I'm in a coffee-shop. Do you want me to pass the phone to the owner and have him vouch for me? And by the way," I threw in without thinking, hoping it would put Mr. Arulanadam on his back foot, "My last name is pronounced *Illidge*, one D, no R's. Here's Alain who owns the coffee shop."

"—I don't think that will be necessary," he came right back, chastened by the sound of it.

"So what am I supposed to do now, Mr. Arulanadam? My house is set to go up for sale later today. How can I do that with a quarantine order on the front door?"

*"Well you can't!"* he said sharply. "No one is allowed on the premises until you've taken corrective measures and had the house tested."

"But as I told you, no corrective measures are necessary."

"Well according to the police they are."

"We'll let that go for now. How soon can you do the testing?"

"Oh, we don't do it. You have to call an approved environmental testing company, preferably one of those our department works with, listed on our website. They forward us the results, and if they meet our criteria we schedule an onsite inspection. If we determine that the quarantine order was observed in all respects—namely that no one has been on the premises since the time of the police search in violation of the order—"

"But the order just went up this morning."

"It's retroactive to the police search."

"Why would the police wait this long before notifying you?"

"That's not for me to say."

"How long does the testing process take?"

"That depends on the time required to repair the structural and water damage in your house."

"There *is* no structural or water damage. As I told you, we're putting our house up for sale this afternoon. How could we be doing that if there's structural or water damage?"

He was puzzled. "No water or structural damage?"

"None. It's a family residence, Mr. Arulanadam. One of my sons had some pot plants growing in a room in the basement."

Dar exploded. "Let me be clear, *Mr. Id-leridge!* No one, and I can't stress this enough, is to be in your house until corrective measures have been taken and we have verified that all hazardous substances have been eliminated."

"I quite understand, Mr. Arulanadam—"

"And you're calling from there now," he threw in again.

"No, I'm not," I said, trying not to sound impatient. "But tell me one thing, Mr. Arulanadam, out of curiosity more than anything else."

"Yes?"

"Since no one is allowed on the premises for any reason and under any circumstances, if I happened to be in a position where the house needed corrective measures for water and structural damage in order to pass environmental testing, how exactly could I have got people in to do that?"

A wily customer, he laughed. "Well, the house can't very well clean itself up now, can it?"

His idea of Health Department humour I guess, Mr. Arulanadam appeared to have missed the point of my question entirely . . .

Ten a.m. Wednesday of the following week, I met the technician from TH Harrison Environmental at the house. Dressed in street clothes, introducing himself as Dennis, he ignored the red notice, had no problem with me showing him around the house for the next half hour while he did his testing, most of which consisted of holding high-tech digital instruments in the air, or attaching probes and sensors to the walls.

When he was done, and we were standing at the foot of the basement stairs, I asked him if he could give me some idea of the results. He said the data had to be processed in their lab, and the health department never publicized what its acceptable levels were. As far as he could see, everything seemed normal, the readings in the basement slightly high, probably because some of the windows had been left open.

"Wait a minute," I said. "Mr. Arulanadam, the health inspector handling my case suggested a little fresh air wouldn't hurt the test readings."

Dennis made a face. "That's nonsense. It's just the opposite. The contaminants come in from outside, especially at this time of year. Mouldy leaves, pollen, dead plant-matter, that sort of thing. I have no idea why he would have told you something like that."

"I just assumed he knew what he was talking about."

"I wouldn't worry. I don't see it being an issue."

We went outside to the front porch. I handed him the $1,500 check, a friend having loaned me the money. He thanked me for the payment, said he hoped things worked out for the best and we shook hands. I watched him drive off down the street—past a small, silver-grey sedan parked four houses down on the other side of the street, no one behind the wheel, but there was a bald man in a trench coat sitting in the passenger seat, pen in hand, writing something on a clipboard.

Not waiting around to see if it was in connection with me, I pulled the door closed, locked up and hurried down the front walk and across the driveway, ducked around the side of the garage into the backyard. I climbed the fence, made my way along the railing, jumped down then ran for my car.

Before starting up, I called Lenny, told him the testing was done and all we could do now was hope the readings passed muster with Mr. Arulanadam. Lenny asked if I'd given any thought to what we'd do if for some reason they didn't.

"No I haven't, Lenny. Burning the place down might be a good start."

Jill would go Chernobyl when I told her about the quarantine order. Lenny would earn his full commission trying to convince her it wasn't the end of the world.

I started up, made a U-turn, headed back around the corner driving slowly toward the house to see how noticeable the red notice would be from the street.

I glanced over: it screamed *STAY AWAY!!*

The bald man, still sitting in the passenger seat of the silver sedan writing on his clipboard, looked up and over at a white panel van pulling up in front of the house. I slowed right down, watching in my rear view mirror as two guys hopped from the van, one positioning a FOR SALE sign on the lawn with Lenny's picture, name and phone number on it, the other pounding it in with a sledgehammer.

Not surprisingly, nosy Mary-Ellen had come out to stand on her porch, cell phone in hand, adjusting her glasses as she peered over at the real estate sign. Always the first to know what people were asking when their places went up for sale, she punched in what I knew was Lenny's number to find out.

Wouldn't she be thrilled, I thought to myself as I drove off, when she snooped over to the front door and saw the *TOXIC WARNING* notice— taking it in her community-minded way as further proof that she and her husband Quin had done exactly the right thing by turning us in to the police—

My hand shook so much when I saw that it was Mr. Arulanadam calling that I fumbled the phone. It took me a few seconds to accept his call.

"The readings are too high for my liking Mr. Id-leridge, especially those in the basement."

"You suggested I open the basement windows to let in some fresh air."

"You went into the house and opened them?"

"No," I came back, ready for his question. "I had one of my sons open them from the outside. More to the point, what am I supposed to do now?"

"There isn't much point in doing anything. You've had the house cleaned up, you've repaired the water and structural damage, and yet you have higher-than-normal readings."

"The house is in pristine condition. And as I told you initially, there was no water or structural damage. Except for the windows you suggested I open, the house is exactly the way it was the night the police raided it."

He pondered a moment. "Well, I suppose you *could* have the house tested again . . ."

Dennis reduced his fee to $750 for the retest. The results met with Mr. Arulanadam's approval, however in order to remove the order he was required to visit the house in person with one of his Health Department colleagues for one final test: the inspection.

Mr. Arulanadam and his colleague, a Ms. Hong, came to the house two days later. We went inside, Mr. Arulanadam and Inspector Hong (as she'd been introduced) removed their shoes, Ms. Hong taking off her suit-jacket, stepping into the living room and, after neatly folding and placing the jacket on the back of one of the armchairs, she peered inquisitively around with several probing looks into the dining room.

Announcing in an official voice that *the inspection* was now underway, Mr. Arulanadam had me walk the two of them through the house, starting with the second floor: the master bedroom, the kids' bedrooms, the spare room and the bathrooms, Ms. Hong methodically checking the contents of closets, cupboards and drawers, peeking under beds, behind shower curtains, into garbage cans and laundry baskets, snooping in every corner of every room with what seemed like a practiced forensic eye that could determine whether anyone had been living in the house, while Mr. Arula-nadam remained in the doorway of each room and made observations of his own, noting them down in his file folder with a pensive frown on his face yet saying nothing until Ms. Hong, her search of a room complete, nodded and we proceeded to the next location.

The search, invasive and irritating as it was, had me fuming, but I was powerless. I would have objected at my peril. If I thought things couldn't get more absurd (I felt like I was in a scene out of Franz Kafka's novel *The Trial*), I was wrong.

Down to the main floor we went, the inspecting duo conducting a meticulous search of all the kitchen cupboards, noting the *Best Before* dates on cereal boxes, the same with the milk and packaged foods in the fridge.

They had me open the dishwasher to see if there were dishes inside (there weren't), checked under the sink to see if there was anything in the garbage (there wasn't). Had me take them down the hall to the laundry room, where Ms. Hong peeked in the washer and dryer (both empty), noted the settings on the control dials for no reason I could think of, after which she instructed me to take her and Inspector Arulanadam downstairs so they could search the basement.

My nerves had had about as much as they could take. There was nothing to hide; I had no reason to be afraid, yet I was terrified, hoping I hadn't overlooked something they would pounce on. *Guilt written all over my face with a capital G* as Mickey Spillane used to say, I sat at the bottom of the basement stairs while they quietly proceeded with their inspection.

A clean slate, as far as I could judge from the expression on their faces when they returned in a few minutes, Mr. Arulanadam saying that was it, they, were through.

No hint of a verdict, upstairs we went, Ms. Hong ducking into the living room to pick up her jacket on our way out.

Mr. Arulanadam waited for me to lock up before delivering his decision.

"Despite a few reservations about clothes in the upstairs closets and the dates on some of the items in the fridge, Inspector Hong and I agree that the property meets with Public Health Department specifications. The quarantine will be lifted."

I thanked them. Mr. Arulanadam ceremoniously removed the order with a purpose-made tool, stepped down to the walk and headed for his car while Ms. Hong lingered beside me on the porch for some reason, a knowing smile spreading across her face as something dawned on her.

She stepped over to our large brass mailbox and with an *Ah-hah!!* look on her face, threw the lid open . . . only to find the mailbox stuffed tight with mail: the final proof that no one was living in the house.

Ms. Hong glared.

I gave her a thin smile, resisting the urge to gloat at the way I had outwitted the Sherlock Holmes of public health order compliance.

My first call was to Lenny. Overjoyed, he broke down in tears. His own marriage was falling apart. He'd already told Jill. He thought I should know. He needed this sale so badly. I assured him that we'd come this far, there was no doubt in my mind that everything was going to work out in the end.

I hated lying to him, but what else could I do when I knew Officer Val probably wasn't finished with us yet?

## CHAPTER TWENTY-TWO

# BUDDHA SAYS

"YOUR GOOD BROTHER informs me your house is up for sale and I can expect to collect my $73,000—oh that's right, I tacked on five-thousand on top of the sixty-eight thou for your little stunt at Fran's, and five more for the deposition suite and stenographer."

Gerry Gurdler, as aggravating as ever.

"We'll see, Gerry," I said. "He who laughs last and all that . . ."

"What's that supposed to mean? You think I'm joking?"

"I always think you're joking, Gerry."

"Is that a nice thing to say to the man you owe seventy-three large?"

"As to the house sale, John is registering a promissory note against my publishing company for two hundred thousand that you apparently don't know about. He and Paul Posay, his partner in the promissory sideline they're running, are expecting to settle for $150,000. He'll take fifty, I get a hundred. I've got him outlining the scheme on tape. The rest of the equity I'm having paid into court. That leaves you with nothing for your trouble, Gerry."

"That'll never work—what promissory sideline?—who's Paul Posay?"

"They're leaving you out of the loop, Gerry."

\*\*\*

Two days after the house went up for sale, we received an offer of $423,000, $57,000 below the asking price. Jill was incensed, wanted to tear it up. I said we should take it and move on. But she wasn't to be dissuaded. This was personal. The agent for the purchasers was a notorious low-ball manipulator named Janice Evanoff, whose sales strategy consisted of digging up dirt on a property or its owners (or hiding it on properties she was selling) and using the vulnerability to make the kinds of deals she wanted. Jill knew this more than anyone; her daughter, Kim, was a good friend of Jill's. Kim had heard about the drug raid when it happened, and, as her mother knew Jill, thought she'd mention the incident to her. However, Janice decided to betray the confidence and use it to her advantage. We would lose $50,000. Jill was livid and hurt. There was simply no way she could let the house go to the bitch Janice Evanoff.

Her spirits soared three days later, however, when an offer came in for $480,000, conditional only on financing. She and Lenny were elated. They went off to celebrate.

At ten-thirty the next morning, in a strained, hoarse voice shaking from a hangover or bad news, Lenny said it was the latter—the sellers weren't able to secure financing. None of the major financial institutions would put mortgages on properties used as marijuana grow-ops. Financing had to be arranged privately—

"—Jill said you'd worked on this kind of deal before, Lenny. That you knew all about grow-ops."

"I went to a workshop on it."

"Didn't they mention that particular detail?"

"They may have. It was a few years ago."

"Have you told Jill?"

"I'm afraid to."

"It's going to be the same with every offer. Private financing, or no sale. Can you call Janice Evanoff and see if she and her clients are still interested? Maybe under the circumstances agree to raise their offer a little?"

"Jill will go ballistic. Janice put in a low-ball to begin with because she knew."

"Of course she did, Lenny," I said. "What other choice is there?"

Blame fell on me, of course, and intensified with each passing day. But with word having spread among realtors, no offers were forthcoming. There was talk of suing me, of there being a legal basis for Jill receiving all the proceeds of the sale, nonsense in both cases.

I remained positive. Our house was one of the best on the street, six bedrooms, 3,300 square feet, hardwood floors, priced lower than it had to be for a quick sale, the community and the walk-to schools, ideal for families.

Janice Evanoff told Lenny her clients were still interested. They would up their offer by $7,000 to $430,000.

Poor Lenny had to break the news to Jill. It was a knockdown, drag out deliberation that went on for a full day before she agreed. The deal would close in three weeks. I would have to look after moving. Jill wouldn't help, she felt she had no reason to. And she wouldn't allow Nicky to either. That he was eighteen and had a mind of his own never occurred to her. With a Rastafarian mover named Junior that my lawyer-friend Trevor had set me up with (Junior was a former client), I would be handling moving day on my own . . .

After a packing frenzy that came to an abrupt halt just after 4 a.m. when I was seized by a full-body cramp that only a searing hot shower and two extra-strength ibuprofen loosened up enough for me to make it to my bed and pass out—until the cell phone alarm exploded in my head three hours later.

I inched over to the edge of the bed, dropped my hand on the phone several times until it shut off, slid off the bed, sank to my knees as the phone alarm resumed ringing.

Apprehensive about my legs holding out, I climbed to my feet, grabbed my phone off the bedside table, turned off the alarm and went looking for my shoes and clothes amid the warren of stacked, packed and half-packed boxes and green garbage bags cluttering the cold bedroom.

Dressing proved painful since I could barely bend my left knee, and the fingers of both my hands had a sort of Parkinson's shake that holding them under scalding water in the bathroom sink took care of enough so that I could pull on my clothes, brush my teeth and, with a couple of Egg McMuffins and coffee at *McDonald's* in mind, head out to my car just before 7:30, only to discover with a stray glance as I opened my door, that the front left tire was as flat as could be.

With Junior scheduled to arrive in about an hour, I hoped there was a chance he'd be late and put in a call to Dan at the neighbourhood car repair shop. He was just opening, he didn't have a portable "pig" air compressor at the moment, but said that Gord who ran the shop across the road did, and he'd probably let me borrow it if I asked him nicely.

I made it to Gord's in about twenty minutes, carried the pig back to the house and pumped up the tire. I drove to Dan's, let him plug the leak then stopped off at *McDonald's* for Egg McMuffins, coffee for me, a large orange juice for Nicky, who was possibly coming over to help—the result of a phone conversation with Jill around midnight in which she let me know she wouldn't give Nicky permission to help out.

"Fine with me," I told her. "I'll be long gone by morning. Good luck selling the house without me."

Apparently she decided I was serious. Nicky was waiting for me when I got back to the house at 9:15. No sign of Junior yet, we went inside and had breakfast.

Just after 9:30 the doorbell rang. I went and opened the door. A moving truck had backed up the front walk almost to the front door, a black man in his thirties and two helpers in their late twenties were standing behind what I presumed was Junior, about my height with shoulder-length dreadlocks, his helpers with Afros tucked under large green-and-yellow Jamaican toques. Junior apologized for the lateness; he had to get rid of some things in his truck along the way.

Nicky came out to meet the crew. We showed them inside so they could lay out their tarps and drop-sheets. Junior's eyes bugged when he saw how much still had to be packed.

Not as bad as it looked, I explained my system of coloured Post-It notes indicating the different destinations. That sounded good to Junior. He and his crew got underway.

Jill and her lawyer wanted a final separation agreement signed before the end of the day so they could claim all the equity when the deal closed. It had now been seven years since our separation. At the time, Jill and her family had given me six months going it alone with the house and the three children, having quit my full-time teaching job. With no child support coming in (Jill and her family refused to pay any), or help with the taxes or upkeep of the house, by selling it and claiming the full equity on the property to which they believed they were entitled, they were determined to ruin me at last, leaving me destitute so I would have to turn the children over to their alcoholic mother.

I had retained a former law partner of Trevor's named Stephen Sinukoff to represent me.

I called Stephen up to see how things stood.

"The excrement's hitting the whirling blade, my friend," he laughed into the phone. "The girls are losing it because they haven't received their final agreement yet, and they want one within the next three hours. Equally amusing, Skolnick, the lawyer representing your brother's bankruptcy trustee Gerry Gurdler, has upped the promissory nut to $88,000. Fifteen grand in a fuckin' week! What a prick . . ."

Our real estate lawyer, Bill Tatum, called half an hour later, irked, on edge, extremely disconcerted (his word) about the way things were looking. In his sternest warning yet, he said the deal was going to die on the table unless I resolved matters with Revenue Canada who, a week before, had been tipped off that I was selling my house. Unless they had my income tax return from two years ago, they would block the sale of the house.

John had been living with me two years ago. I remember he was going to the post office one day. I'd asked him to mail my return. There had never been a word from Revenue Canada; I took it for granted he had mailed it. My duplicate copy was buried somewhere in a suitcase, box or bag—how could I possibly track it down and get them a copy in six hours?

"I've been trying to resolve matters for the last week, Bill. But I was only given the name and phone number of the person who might be handling my file yesterday afternoon. The first name they gave me turned out to be someone in Indigenous Affairs. I've already left two messages for what's supposed to be the right person, a Mr. Archambault, but according to his phone greeting it could take up to twenty-four hours for him to return the call—"

"We don't have twenty-four hours."

"I told him that in my message, Bill."

"Well, you better hope he calls you back."

After I got off the phone I put in another call to Mr. Archambault at Revenue Canada, listened to the same greeting: It could take up to twenty-four hours . . .

Lenny phoned just before noon for an update, telling me the buyers were in a panic. Their movers were going to be finished loading the truck by one o'clock, the deal on their house having closed an hour ago. I told him the same thing I'd told Bill: I was waiting to hear back from a guy at Revenue Canada. "But things are going well over here," I said to console him. "I should have everything out and the place spic and span by six."

He groaned, disappointed. "They're pretty anxious to get in."

"Well I'm pretty anxious to get out," I said, and let him go.

In two full-load trips to the storage facility, Junior through some kind of packing voodoo managed to fit nearly the entire contents of my house into the ten by twenty-five foot unit I'd rented, not an inch to spare when we lowered the door and slapped on the padlock.

Back at the house by 1:30, Junior loaded up his truck with the lamps, chairs and couches he'd agreed to take off my hands. He said $1,050 would probably cover everything. I pointed out we'd agreed on $850.

"We did," he said, "but the extra two-hundred's for the furniture I'm taking to resell to people in need."

"Sounds good to me," I said, too tired to argue. We shook hands and I counted out his cash, twenties and fifties—noticing when I was turning to go back in the house that Mary-Ellen McCluskey had been watching the whole transaction between me and the Rastafarians through her storm door, telephone in hand.

I looked over, smiled and waved. A horrified look on her face, she stepped back quickly and slammed the inside door behind her. I suggested to Nicky that we take a trip to *McDonald's* for half an hour in case Mary-Ellen got another case of itchy police finger.

When we got home, Nicky's friend Chris and his girlfriend Melinda had shown up with his father's truck and trailer with a hydraulic lift in it that would make offloading things at the garbage transfer station a breeze.

In the meantime dozens of boxes and garbage bags had to be brought from the basement to the front hall, just over thirty boxes containing hundreds of books, my personal library, bound for the recycling depot shredder.

Catching my breath after bringing up a box full of heavy hard cover books, I was having a sip of bottled water out front when my phone rang. I pulled it out of my pocket, caller ID showing "Revenue Canada." Mr. Archambault?

It was. He verified my social security number, went quiet for a few seconds, looking over my file no doubt. When he came back on he informed me that he couldn't do anything about lifting the lien against me, I'd have to file my income tax for the previous year again, this time with the inclusion of a check for $18,800 dollars which was the amount of the lien.

"What lien? I have no idea what you're talking about, Mr. Archambault."

"The one the tax department placed on you nineteen-months ago and for which you should have accounted in your last year's return."

"I was never notified about any lien."

"I'm sure you would have been."

"Honestly, this is the first I've ever heard of it. What was it in connection with?"

"We need last year's return to determine that."

"To determine what?"

"What income went untaxed."

"None of my income went untaxed."

"So you say, but apparently it did."

My throat had gone dry. In a panic I struggled to speak. "You're saying you want me to file last year's income tax return and include a check for $18,800 or you won't allow the deal on my house to close?"

"That's the idea. The lien is against your house."

"But I'm right in the middle of moving. I'm packing as we speak."

"Without that return there's nothing I can do."

"I don't understand, sir. Everything I own is packed away. I can't retrieve anything now. I certainly can't get my hands on eighteen-thousand dollars."

"Eighteen-thousand, eight-hundred."

"Surely we can deal with—"

The phone blipped, the line cut out, the battery had died.

I asked Nicky for his phone. His battery was low too. Not worth risking.

2:45. Bill Tatum, in his last call, had said the Registry Office closed at 4:30. If he didn't have a waiver from Revenue Canada by 3:30 at the latest—and even that was cutting it close because Jill and I still had to come in and sign the papers—he wasn't going to be able to proceed.

Chris and Melinda had taken a run to the transfer station. I rounded up all the loose change I could find, got in my car and drove up to the Black Dog, the neighbourhood pub, where I knew there was a payphone in the hall by the washrooms.

No one using it, I'd remembered Archambault's number but in my anxiety had forgotten that it was a toll-free call.

Mr. Archambault answered after the fifth ring, took my security information once again and resumed our conversation where he had left off: the matter of last year's return and $18,800.

Putting on the most obsequious voice possible, I promised I'd send him a revised tax return by the following Thursday if he would just let the deal on my house close. I said there were children involved, and a contentious divorce proceeding. I explained that I was up against a wall and begging him to let the deal go through.

"I'm sorry, Mr. Illidge. My hands are tied."

"Please, Mr. Archambault! I'm down on my knees here and I'm begging you to please let our deal go through . . ."

At that moment a man came out of the washroom off to my right. I put the receiver to my chest and called over, asking if he could do me a big favour.

"I'm down on my knees, Mr. Archambault," I pleaded again into the phone and sank to my knees. "There's a man standing right here beside the phone. You can talk to him if you like—he can tell you,

I'M DOWN ON MY KNEES HERE!!" I passed him the phone.

"He's down on his knees all right!" the man confirmed, handing the receiver back to me, still on my knees as I waited for Mr. Archambault's decision.

Silence for a moment, then for another, Archambault came back on the line and, after getting the contact information for two people who could ensure that the matter was being taken care of, agreed to send Bill Tatum a legal waiver by fax in the next half hour.

When I hadn't heard back from Bill by 3:40, I decided I'd better get over to his office and find out if the waiver had come through.

It had, but Bill was fuming. He'd been trying to phone me for the last twenty minutes. I explained that my phone had died.

He slapped the legal papers down in front of me, handed me his pen and I signed in the appointed places.

I followed him outside to his car. There was no guarantee he'd make the Registry Office by 4:30 when it closed, but he said he'd give it a shot. He opened his car door, threw his briefcase into the passenger seat and zoomed out of the parking lot at what, for someone as law-abiding as Bill, seemed an excessively high speed.

Too busy to worry, fending off the fatigue that was setting in with two Mr. Beans espressos (the cafe was across the plaza from Bill's office), I drove home and, now that the house was empty, went into clean up mode, Chris and Melinda busy taking care of the garage, Nicky loading clothes and personal items into his van.

I was sliding a box of tools into the open area at the bottom of the basement stairs when Nicky appeared on the landing half way up, a worried look on his face: the new owners and their father had just arrived and were waiting in the front hall.

"What's the time?"

"6:05. They were told the house would be available as of six-o'clock."

"I told Lenny eight-o'clock at the earliest. How do they seem?"

"Not happy."

A couple in their mid-thirties, the woman petite and thin, with short blond hair, her husband dark-haired, a lanky six-foot six. She broke away from him and the elderly gentleman, came across the hall and introduced herself as Carina, her husband Joe, her father-in-law Hector.

"Sorry about this," I said. "Today has been a complete comedy of errors."

Joe's father laughed. "Everything's too much of a runaround these days. It's not good for us." This lightened the mood.

"It's just been my son and I and his two friends. We've gone as fast as we could. I can promise I'll be out by ten. But that's the best I can do."

They were visibly disappointed, for which I could hardly blame them. However, I think from my dishevelled appearance and Nicky, Chris and Melinda working fast lugging boxes out the front door, they got the picture. We shook hands all round, and they went on their way.

By 9:30 everything was out of the house and I was finishing the floors in the front hall. Chris and Melinda were done in the garage, sweeping up, chatting and laughing with Nicky while he loaded his tools and equipment into his van.

I did one last circuit from top to bottom, turning lights off, closing doors behind me as I went. I put our coats and boots, a suitcase with some clothes I was taking back to the friend's with whom I was staying, the last bag of garbage, the vacuum and all the cleaning supplies on the front porch.

Stepping back in for a final look around, I thought bitterly of how right Officer Val had been in saying that we'd never live in this house again. I closed the door, leaving the keys in the lock.

Nicky was meeting Chris and Melinda at Swiss Chalet for dinner to celebrate. Chris was buying. Did I feel like joining them? I did, however there was a piece of business I had to take care of first.

It was 9:50 by my dashboard clock when I pulled out of the drive behind Nicky, the headlights of two cars parked a few houses down on the other side of the street blinking on. They came past me and in my rear-view mirror, I saw them turn into the driveway: Joe and Carina.

Continuing down the street, I pulled over to the curb and parked. I grabbed a small yellow plastic grocery bag on the passenger seat, ran nine doors up the street to the McCluskey house, the lights on upstairs, the main floor dark as it usually was by this time of night.

I took the ten-inch green glazed clay Buddha a student had brought me back from Japan years ago out of the plastic bag. I'd always kept it as a talisman. Nicky set it in an honoured place beside a small fountain in his plant garden. Broken open by the police looking for drugs the night of the raid, I had managed to reincarnate the pieces with Scotch tape and Krazy Glue so that Buddha looked more or less like his old self, just a little patchy in places.

No one about in the street, I scooted up the hedge side of the McCluskey's drive, crossed in front of their garage, hustled up the walk and hopped onto their front porch where I took Buddha quickly out of the grocery bag and set him down on the front door mat. I pushed the doorbell ten or eleven times as fast as I could, like there was an emergency, then turned, jumped from the porch and beat it down the street.

I started the car, did a fast U-turn and drove up the street, slowing right down as I passed the McCluskey house. The porch light on, in her housecoat, telephone in hand, Mary-Ellen stood inside the storm door watching Quin who had come outside and picked up the statue. He was holding it above his head in the porch light so he could make out the one-word message I'd printed in dark blue capital letters on the neon-yellow Post-It note I'd taped to Buddha's chest:

PEACE!

CHAPTER TWENTY-THREE

# GHOSTWRITER

**M**OLLY PHONED ONE morning when Nicky and I were having breakfast in our favourite diner.

"Can you find a copy of today's *Toronto Star*?"

"Hang on." I went over to the counter beside the cash register where customers left the complimentary newspapers. I found a *STAR* and took it back to the table.

"Open to the financial section. I'll call you back in five."

## OSC bans stock manipulator for life
By James Daw

John Illidge, a bankrupt former executive and securities dealer, has been banned for life from public markets in Ontario. The Ontario Securities Commission approved a negotiated settlement and issued the ban yesterday.

Illidge admitted he had allowed bogus press releases and secret trading to manipulate share prices of Hucamp Mines Ltd. in 2000 and 2001 while he was the president and later chair.

OSC vice-chair James Turner said it was clear the founder of the former St. James Securities Inc. and one-time director of the parent company of the former Rampart Securities Inc. was the directing mind in the stock manipulation scheme.

He said the executive had been disciplined in the past, and should have known better. Turner called the multiple infractions of securities law extremely serious and detrimental to the public.

The OSC order does not estimate losses suffered by the public, but does say one pair of lottery winners had $2.5 million of Hucamp shares and debentures put into their Rampart account without their knowledge.

The commission would have insisted on a financial penalty if Illidge was not an undischarged bankrupt, said Turner.

Illidge has reported losing more than $4 million when trading in Hucamp was halted and Rampart closed several years ago.

Earlier this week Stafford Kelley, 76, of Oakville, a former officer of Medallion Capital Corp., was ordered to pay $10,000 in costs for having a part in the Hucamp deception. He was banned from trading securities for five years and from being an officer of a public company for 10 years.

Before Kelley and Illidge negotiated their settlements there was to be a four-week hearing starting next week.

Now a hearing into allegations against three others is to be held in September if settlements are not negotiated sooner. Illidge said he would appear at that hearing if called as a witness. He would not say how he earns his living now.

"I am just a private businessman," he said.

I passed the paper to Nicky.

Molly called back. "I like that: private businessman. So private nobody knows what the business is. Who does he think he is, Howard Hughes?"

"He was always talking about a guy named Bernie Madoff."

"Of course," said Molly, "Ponzi schemer extraordinaire. Makes sense John would be interested in him."

"It was more than interest. He was obsessed with the man, not so much by the money amounts involved as how Madoff managed to pull it all off. Even with the FBI investigating him six ways from Sunday they still couldn't get anything on him until his sons turned him in."

"John can still use his surrogates."

"He's been banned, Molly. Why would they want to put their careers at risk like that?"

"They believe in him. He's always come through for them in the past. Besides, I know some of these people. I worked with them. Because of their association with John they can't get jobs anywhere else. Your brother has a soft spot for the underdog, at least that's what he always claimed."

"Don't believe it. Was he thinking of the underdog when he took $2.5 million from the elderly lottery winners?"

"Sure he was. He left them with $1.5 million, didn't he . . .?"

I rented a basement apartment five minutes away from the house Jill's sister had bought for her, around the corner from our old one so the kids would have somewhere to live. My place was beside Highland Creek ravine, a scenic walk through the forest down to Lake Ontario, a bungalow with a renovated basement apartment, the middle-aged owners and their daughter living upstairs, chain-smokers and heavy drinkers all, who might wander into my apartment at any time and want to talk. It was bearable only because of the proximity to the ravine where I went for long walks in the early morning and late at night, and because I was out helping Nicky with the lawn-cutting/landscaping business that he had decided to revive after a surprise letter was forwarded to me by the Toronto Police Department, *Evidence Division*.

My heart pounding at the sight or sound of the word *POLICE* as a result of our recent experiences, I asked Nicky to open the letter.

His jaw dropped. "You won't believe it," he said and passed it to me.

The police were returning $1,000 in cash taken from our house the night of the raid as evidence in a *case now resolved*. If interested in the return of this evidence, I was to present myself at the police evidence unit in west Toronto within ten days.

Nicky's grandfather, a retired engineer, ran a small home security business. He installed *Secret Service*© wall safes in people's homes to protect their valuables. As an eighteenth birthday present three weeks before the raid, his grandfather installed a wall safe in Nicky's bedroom behind an innocuous-looking white board covered with photos of his bird, pictures of guitars, motorcycles, a calendar. The police found the safe, had Nicky give them the combination. The thousand dollars was bagged to be used as evidence that we were trafficking drugs. Nicky's explanation about the birthday-present safe and the cash being payments from his summer lawn-cutting business (he offered to show them his business card) fell on deaf ears.

With the thousand dollars and a loan of two-thousand more from one of his aunts, he bought two commercial lawnmowers and related landscaping tools. He put *Montclair Lawn Care* flyers out in several nearby communities at the beginning of March and within two weeks had contracts that would begin May 1st and run until the end of September. Twenty- to twenty-five lawns for us to cut each day, including weekends.

I did my writing at night, a good time in that the landlord Andy played casino poker until four or five in the morning, and Jean his wife and their daughter usually passed out in front of the television around ten o'clock, at which point Andy had instructed me to go upstairs when all was quiet and make sure no cigarettes had been left burning.

Besides money from working with Nicky, I managed to make some with a ghost writing commission from a publisher-friend on the history of the "M'Naughten Rules," the principles used in the insanity defence at criminal trials (chiefly, did the perpetrator at the time of the crime know the difference between right and wrong).

The Rules were created following the assassination of the personal secretary to British Prime Minister Sir Robert Peel in London, 1842. The assassin, a Scottish woodturner named Daniel M'Naughten, who alternately yawned and slept through his trial before the Chief Justice of England, was judged of unsound mind at the time he fired the pistol killing Peel's secretary Sir Edward Drummond, and thus was found innocent.

Queen Victoria was outraged, demanded the House of Lords meet and establish rules by which, in future, a person's sanity could be concretely determined so that what she saw as a travesty of justice in the M'Naughten case could never happen again.

For his part, M'Naughten spent the rest of his life in a new mental asylum built as part of the deinstitutionalization movement in Britain to improve conditions for mental illness sufferers. For the next twenty years he enjoyed concerts, outings, an extensive library, dining with other patients and dancing with them at the socials held every Saturday night where it was said he *glided across the floor in three-quarter time with the best of them.*

Had he fooled everyone in the end? Many, including Queen Victoria, thought so.

My publisher-friend had called me up one morning to say he had a problem with the manuscript a federal justice had written on the history of the M'Naughten Rules. A fascinating subject and potentially a great story, however (and this wasn't for public consumption), despite having five degrees, four of them post-graduate, two in law and two in psychology, it turned out that His Honour didn't know how to write a proper paragraph much less an authoritative book on the history of one of the most contentious issues in law.

He had gone to London during a sabbatical year and copied microfiche records of proceedings at the Old Bailey, London's central criminal court, from Daniel M'Naughten's 1842 murder trial. He had cobbled together a manuscript containing some of his writing on the Criminal Code of Canada and current mental health laws in Canada, photocopies of internet articles about the M'Naughten trial and the creation of the Rules, plus Wikipedia pages on significant historical events in England and around the world at the time of the trial, along with references to articles he had apparently written for scholarly psychology journals, which turned out to be plagiarized from papers by other people, in two cases former colleagues of the judge.

It was a disorganized amalgamation of material, but in no way a book. My job was to make it one, smoothing over the Wikipedia and plagiarizing issues and, it was to be hoped, keeping quiet about them. After all, I was just the ghostwriter . . .

After a fire in the electric panel in my apartment at Jean and Andy's (the 1940s metal wiring had finally given out), I moved into an apartment on the main floor of the house several blocks away that Nicky had just rented. He and his friend, Chris, who had helped us move, were starting a metal recycling business so I was on my own during the day. I wrote on my computer in the morning, went to the public library in the early afternoon to check email then headed down to the lake for a walk along the shore, hoping to come up with ideas for books I could write. The commission market was petering out. Following the M'Naughten book, I made several deals to write personal histories, but the people commissioning me turned out to be kooks.

In the aftermath of the police raid  and after ghostwriting the judge's book, crime became my chief interest as a subject to write about. For years, as my brother's criminal proclivities intensified, I had thought of writing a story about him, but I knew there needed to be a balancing counterplot along with it. I couldn't write exclusively about John in every chapter. There had to be another storyline into which his could be woven. John takes control of every situation he finds himself in, as sociopaths do. What person could be strong enough to compete with him for attention on the page?

*I could,* I decided out of nowhere one day on my way to the library.

Excitement like I hadn't felt about a story idea in a long time overflowed to the point that I began to run, rejoicing to find a library computer open. I searched for the email of a moderately well-known Toronto publisher whom I'd met a few years earlier and wrote this outline for him:

> A book that opens *Like a Hurricane* on the night police vehicles pull up in front of my house and conduct a gunpoint raid. It continues with the aftermath as my children's lives and mine are turned upside down. This compelling trip down criminal lane of cops, court and lawyers will alternate with compelling scenes showing my brother the psychopathic fraud at work as police close in on him.

I reminded the publisher that we'd talked about the idea in La Guardia Airport after our mutual distributor's sales conference in New York several years earlier. Of course he might not remember. But he had said to be sure and send something to him about the story whenever I was ready.

I felt that afternoon I was ready. I pressed *SEND*.

Someone else waiting to use the computer, I went outside, over to the

7-Eleven on the corner, walked in the park for a bit, then headed back to the library to wait for a computer. In my excitement over sending the story outline I'd forgotten to check my email.

"I'll publish that book!!" the publisher had written in his reply to my query.

In the next week I had my outline and sample chapter approved, a contract signed, a $3,000 advance, a recommendation to the provincial arts' council for a $5,000 grant. The only decision left to make was where to write, or at least start writing the book. I knew I couldn't do so in Toronto. I had to go someplace and live with someone who would appreciate that, as much as my purpose was to write a book, it was also to be in a place and in an environment where I could recover from the sticks and stones and slings and arrows that had been hurled my way. They'd left their mark.

"*—Healing time! Come to Cape Breton, b'y!* That's all there is to it!!" my friend Don said when I asked his advice. A friend from childhood, Don was thoroughly easy-going, light-hearted, peaceful and, best of all, a wise *enjoyer of life* who had helped me in the immediate aftermath of the raid by introducing me to the writings of Chögyam Trunga Rinpoche and Pema Chödron, his long-time Buddhist teachers whose advice to go toward what scares you rather than run from it helped me find my way back to clarity, courage and self-confidence after having been criminalized, and seen my sons criminalized, by the police, family, even friends, who, in some cases, had smoked marijuana regularly for years.

Don made the arrangements as soon as he got off the phone: a plane ticket the second week of January on Porter Airlines, Toronto Island terminal to Halifax, Nova Scotia, then shuttle-van north to East Margaree, the fishing village on the northwest side of Cape Breton on the Cabot Trail where Don had lived and worked for thirty-two years . . .

The flight departing at 6:30 a.m., I'd need to be at the downtown terminal by 5:30 a.m. With Nicky and I living in the far east-end of the city, even with no traffic at that hour of the morning we'd have to leave by 4:30, as I would if I took a taxi, not the best idea when the cab companies in our area were notoriously unreliable. It seemed to me there was no harm in trying John, his house on Winner's Circle was just off Lakeshore only twenty minutes from the Porter terminal.

I gave him a call.

# CHAPTER TWENTY-FOUR

# MR. JOHN

AS EXPECTED, JOHN took three days to reply to my message, leaving directions to an Italian restaurant named *Campanelle* on Queen Street East in the Beach about four blocks from his house. We met there the night before my flight to Cape Breton.

Nicky drove me to the restaurant at 6:30, parked beside *RSKY BZNS*, John's newest black Mercedes glistening under the parking lot lights in the light snow that was falling. "I guess the bankruptcy business is booming," Nicky joked as we got out of the car.

I ran inside the restaurant to get the keys from John, came out and helped Nicky transfer my packed-within-an-inch-of-their-lives suitcases into the trunk of the Mercedes. Nicky and I agreed it was going to be strange being separated after seeing each other practically every day for so many years. He promised to have a new place lined up for us by the time I came back from Cape Breton. Sales were on the rise in his metal business; we could step up to renting a house, he was sure he could find one. We hugged, he drove off. I stayed in the parking-lot for a minute, closed my eyes, put my head back and let the snowflakes land on my face.

The restaurant was a quaint little place with low lighting, dark Old World Italian decor with prints of Renaissance painters on the walls, red globe candles glowing on the mostly unoccupied tables (it was still early), and black-tasselled red lampshades hanging above.

John was sitting at a table near the back nibbling on his perennial appetizer: garlic bread topped with a tomato slice, a slice of bocconcini cheese and fresh basil. The owner, Clementi, whom John introduced me to when I came in for the keys, escorted me to his table, took a bottle of white wine from the ice bucket beside the table and poured me a glass.

John ordered two Osso Buco for dinner—veal shanks, the house specialty.

"To die for?" I beat him to the punch.

No comment, he set the bocconcini platter on the table in front of me. "So how's Nick?"

"Good," I said. "He's just taking *RSKY BZNS* for a spin around the block."

John's eyebrows shot up. He stopped chewing.

"Just kidding," I said, passed him his keys and reached for a piece of tomato bocconcini. "No vodka rocks?"

"I'm back on the grape."

Dressed casually in a powder-blue, quarter-zipper cashmere sweater, his wavy black hair cut shorter than when I'd last seen him, after asking about *the kiddies* he launched into an encomium on how excellent things were between him and *the girls*, the three of them and their husbands one big happy family to hear him tell it, especially now that he was a grandfather, Rebecca having given birth to a boy two months after Ellen died, who was now three years old—and Rebecca was expecting again.

Following his usual dinner script, he brought up the names of mutual friends from high school, several of whose obituaries he said he'd noticed in the paper recently and whom he wondered if I remembered, segueing next to the names and latest news about various other people, some of whom I knew, some I'd never heard of—a kind of gossip roundup which, as far as I ever knew, he only engaged in with me. John loved his gossip and, like my mother, made a point of being the first one "in the know" with "the breaking news," as he liked to call it, often recycling the juicier items with the excuse that either I might not have remembered them, or he hadn't remembered telling me before.

At this point, Clementi arrived with our Osso Buco, accompanied by one of his servers with a fresh bottle of chardonnay, and we started eating.

I knew the conversation would soon shift to Bernie Madoff; his arrest in mid-December for running a $55 billion Ponzi scheme was still headline news with names of his high-profile clients popping up every day. I teased him for the latest on his buddy Bernie.

"Buddy? No thanks."

"What's he facing?"

"He won't be out of prison till he's 220."

"How do you figure that?"

"He's 70 now, and he's looking at 150 years, minimum. Restitution to his clients over twenty years would top $170 billion if he had the money to pay it, which he doesn't." After a sip of wine he continued. "I predicted this would happen years ago. Remember? At *Centro?*"

I did, but humoured him. "Vaguely. I forget how you said you knew."

"I know my Ponzi schemes."

I choked on the mouthful of Osso Buco I was chewing at the irony of the statement, to which he seemed oblivious. "So you would know," I blurted to cover the food malfunction, "about what they call *front-running*" (a term in the securities business also known as *tail-gating*: buying or selling securities based on private information not known to the public, highly illegal, like insider trading).

He shot me a look. "Where did you hear that?"

"I was reading about Madoff's case."

"Where?"

"*The Economist.* Front-running and I think *strike price* in derivative trading (a practise prone to fraud) were mentioned as key parts to Madoff's scheme."

"Nah," said John, "it was all marketing. Madoff's a modern master. He set things up so his operation was an exclusive club, blue-chip, where it was a privilege to let him handle your money for you. People wanted to buy in. You didn't deal with underlings, you dealt with Bernie personally. He'd check you out like you were being vetted for membership in his club. He promised twenty-five percent returns when the best anyone else could offer was eight. He had billions under management. Everybody fell for it. The more his fund went up, the more clients invested for a payday in the future that would be colossal. It became a general thing around the late nineties."

"Joining Ponzi schemes?"

"Joining Ponzi schemes." He put down his knife and fork, had a sip of wine. "Remember that time you called me when Jill's friend Evelyn wanted her to pay five-thousand into an 'investment club' she had joined? The hook being that she couldn't say anything to anyone about it except for five friends who would be able to put in five-thousand themselves, and in a year they'd get back a hundred-thousand?"

"A pyramid scheme."

"Pyramid, Ponzi, the same thing. Like I said, it was all the rage in the 90s. I told Jill not to do it, didn't I?"

"You did."

"Did Evelyn ever get her hundred G's?"

"Not that I heard." At which point I took the bull by the horns. "Were you ever part of a Ponzi scheme yourself?"

"Nah," he said. "Not my style." He'd finished eating. "You want some dessert? The tiramisu here is the best you'll ever have."

There was no telling when I'd be seeing him again, probably not before my book was published, so I explained that it was non-fiction, a true story, that he would be in it, warts and all, and waited for his reaction. The news not appearing to register with him one way or another, he waved Clementi over and told him to make up the bill.

"Why the hell are you going to Cape Breton to write it?"

"Toronto's just not conducive. Plus I need to clear my head of, let's just say, recent interactions of the police kind before I'll be in a frame of mind to get any writing done. Don invited me down."

"What the hell is he doing manufacturing cutting-boards in a place like Cape Breton? How can you make money doing something like that?"

"Don just manages the company. It's owned by a wealthy young guy originally from Toronto named Ben Webster—"

The Websters were an Old Money Toronto family. At mention of the name, John jumped in and let me know of his dealings with the Websters over the years until Rosalina, a plump, black-haired woman in her early sixties with 1950s teardrop glasses, brought our check. The smile that lit up her face when she saw the three $100 bills he peeled off his wad and placed on the change-tray (our tab was $135) told me all I needed to know about her and Clementi's affection for Mr. John.

# CHAPTER TWENTY-FIVE

# THE LIGHT IN THE HALL

**N**OT QUITE 8:30 WHEN we left the restaurant, I had John stop at a Dunkin' Donuts on the short drive to his house, ordering a regular rather than a decaf coffee even though we had to be up at five a.m. My nerves needed more steadying than usual after the last two hours with him and maybe another two to go.

We drove down his street, Winner's Circle, past the three-storey, Cape Cod-style townhouse that I'd visited the day I met Bruno the Vicious. We made a right onto Northern Dancer Boulevard. (The development had been built on the grounds of a former racetrack, so employed a horseracing theme. Northern Dancer was a famous Triple Crown winner.) We made a right and then an immediate right into a lane lined on both sides with double-garages.

John hit the remote when we came to *#48*, backing the Mercedes into the garage beside his "other car," a new-looking, white Ford Explorer. "Deluxe Edition," John let me know as he got out of the car.

I managed, after some strenuous manoeuvring (the Mercedes parked too close to the Explorer on my side) to wrangle my suitcase out of the back seat, John watching my spastic acrobatics with a smile that turned into a laugh as I strained to hoist the tightly-packed, sixty-pound suitcase over my head and squeeze myself sideways in the narrow gap between cars up to the garage door.

"You look like Mr. Bean," he joked, holding the door open for me.

"Don't I?" I said setting the suitcase down in the tiny backyard. I wheeled it across the grass, hefted it up a small set of stairs and, memories of my earlier encounter with the canine of the house sounding the alarm, brought the case from behind me and stood it in front of me in the doorway.

Not a growl or a bark to be heard. "Where's Bruno the Wonder Dog?"

"Tammy took him. We split up about a year ago."

"You and Bruno?"

"Tammy. I'm suing her for spousal support."

News of the split not surprising, it was the *suing for support* that took a second to register. "You really think that'll fly?"

"She doesn't stand a chance with my lawyers."

"Who's that?"

"Gowlings." Gowlings was one of Toronto's top litigation firms. Whenever John threatened to go legal on someone he always mentioned Gowlings as his lawyers.

"I didn't know they handled family law."

"They do for me," he said.

Pushing the suitcase inside, I closed the door, took my coat off and set it on the back of a chair at the kitchen table where John had left my coffee. I opened it and had a sip. They'd forgotten the sugar.

"You have any sugar?"

"Check the cupboards."

I had another couple of sips as I walked over: the room lit by pot lights in the high ceiling, black marble countertops, stainless steel appliances, touch-to-open cabinets . . . with nothing in them. No dishes, no food, no sugar. I checked the drawers. Same thing.

I would have mentioned it to him, but John was standing at the stove, a little drunk after two bottles of wine (most of it consumed by him), lighting a cigarette with a wooden match from a small *Campanelle* pack Clementi had given each of us when we left.

"I have one occasionally," said John when he noticed me looking. "You want one?"

"Why not?"

He handed me a *Rothmans* (the brand our father had smoked), lit it for me then turned on the hood-fan over the stove, the two of us dipping our heads under it when exhaling, tamping the ash from our cigarettes into the drain in the kitchen sink, John running the water each time to wash the ashes down. It was like we were twelve years old again, our parents out for the evening and we were sneaking smokes John had cadged from my father's pack earlier in the day.

Looking around the sleek, designer kitchen which showed few signs that anyone was living here, I commented that he was running a pretty lean operation.

He chuckled. "With Tammy out of the picture I've been spending a lot of time at my new girlfriend's place. Karen. She's fifty-three, two years younger than me, makes a hefty $220,000 per annum in the planning department for the City of Milton. She has a large house in West Mississauga, which she got in her divorce settlement seven years ago. The stickler is her son and his girl friend, both in their late twenties with good jobs—supposedly saving up to buy a house—live in the basement. It's frustrating the hell out of Karen because they don't seem interested in going anywhere in the near future when they have it so good. She's trying her hardest—with my encouragement of course—to get rid of them. They seem to be doing a lot of other things with their money besides saving for a house, so she's not having much luck persuading them to hit the road. I'm telling her to take a hard line and sell the place out from under them. She'd get eight-hundred thousand for it easily, the kids can fend for themselves, Karen and I can buy a place of our own. The rent on this place is killing me. I don't know why I'm even hanging on to it except the owner, Richie, is a business associate from way back who's fallen on hard times and needs the rent."

How much of the story was fact, I couldn't say, but there were enough elements that gave it the ring of truth based on his modus operandi in the past: hunt down a single, middle-aged woman with a high-paying job easily smitten by his charms and sweep her off her feet in the rapture of later-in-life romance. John the wealthy businessman, the charming, fun-loving boyfriend persuading her bit by bit that she'd be smart to let him turn a few hundred thousand of what she'd get out of selling her house, into a few million by investing the money with him, a proposal which I could see him making to this new flame, Karen . . . if he hadn't already.

I knew then that I needed to get in touch with her somehow and as soon as possible. Warn her about continuing the relationship with John because she would end up getting hurt badly. Explain, with the evidence to prove it, that he was a serial fraud, a predator, interested only in putting his hands on as much of her money as he could before moving on to *happier hunting grounds*.

Would she believe me? It was none of my business and she didn't know me from Adam. She wouldn't even know that John had a brother. And if she'd already taken a bite of the forbidden apple, so to speak, and fallen in love with him. There was no way she'd believe me when I told her that the Eden she thought John was taking her to with his exciting, big-spender ways, wasn't the paradise it seemed. Ellen used to say: *There's a lot of glitter in John's world, which is what the women fall for, only to find out later that little of it turns out to be gold.*

We each had another cigarette while I finished my coffee, John reminiscing away about some of the characters we'd worked with at our Aunt Eunice Denby's flower shop in Forest Hill on weekends and holidays when we were teenagers. An accomplished mimic, John had always done riotously funny imitations of the eccentric cast of characters we worked with: Sean the Irish leprechaun delivery dispatcher whose lazy eye and thick glasses led some to mistake him for the philosopher Jean-Paul Sartre. His passions were Seagram's VO whisky at any time of the day, and telling ribald jokes, often about Catholics, of which he was one . . . Wally his assistant, a former fireman who'd lost his larynx to cancer but still liked to tell jokes, his voice a permanent, rough guttural rasp after the operation so he was hard to understand unless your ear was right in front of his mouth when he delivered his punch lines . . . See-Through Charlie, the most flagrantly gay of the flower designers. Charlie wore expensive see-through hosiery with his equally expensive shoes, and always showed us his latest purchase, wondering if he could *tempt* us into visiting the walk-in fridge with him for a little *bouchie-bouchie*. It was a term coined by Jacques, one of the other gay designers: affectionately known as Jacques-the-Cock because, according to Charlie, he stuffed a sock in his crotch to *attract trade.*

"—Remember those times when the two of them would corner us in the walk-in fridge?"

"How 'bout some *bouchie-bouchie*, boys?"

"We'd whack them with gladiolas."

"Whip them with thorny giant Bacarra roses."

"Then the four of us laughing at the stupidity of it all."

"Jacques would always be the last one out of the fridge so he could grab a squeeze of butt as we went out the door. *Bouchie-bouchie?*" John simpered, prancing away from the stove on tiptoes exactly as Jacques used to in his Cuban heels, spinning around as he took a final haul on his cigarette over at the sink, exhaled, held the butt under the tap then set it down with the others that he'd arranged in a meticulously neat row beside the stainless-steel sink.

"We better hit the sack if we want to be at the terminal by 5:30," he announced as he walked over to a leather-topped side table under the window, picked up a telephone bill and payment envelope, and waited for me to lug my suitcase from the back door. Flicking off the kitchen lights, the stove clock showing 9:45, we headed upstairs.

He led me along the hall to a guest bedroom on the second floor, pointing out the bathroom across the way. I happened to glance down the hall to what looked like the master bedroom, the door open a crack, a light on inside.

"There're towels and a face cloth in the bathroom. I'll set the alarm for five so you can grab a quick shower before we leave. Do you have everything?"

"I'm good to go, thanks. You might have to come in and shake me in the morning. With the packing, I didn't sleep much last night."

"No problem. Night." He started up the stairs to the third floor, a den with a fireplace which doubled as his office, so he told me when we first came in.

I wheeled my suitcase into the bedroom. It was a girl's room, pastel pink, a twin bed, frilly skirt, maybe a dozen cushions and sham pillows; just as many fluffy teddy bears and stuffed animals of the type a girl of four or five might have. I took note of their placement before I removed them and set them on the floor.

After using the bathroom, I peered down the hall on my way back to the bedroom, the door to the master still open a crack, the light off now.

I shut off the bedside light, 10:05 showing on the clock radio as I hopped under the covers, yawned, made myself comfortable and closed my eyes, slowed my breathing, listening to the quiet, hoping it would help me get to sleep . . . yet after a few drowsy minutes I made out the sound of John moving around upstairs in his den. Erratic, muffled footsteps: walking half a dozen paces, halting, walking some more, walking longer, stopping longer. There was a certain rhythm to the muffled pacing which, after a few minutes, lulled me to sleep . . .

*"Paul!"* John was shouting, shaking me awake from a nightmare, the light on in the hall behind him.

"*Something's wrong!*" a boyhood shout.

"Wrong?" I asked fuzzily, coming out of the dream.

"You were screaming in your sleep. I could hear it from upstairs."

I looked up at him, at the light on in the hall behind him. "I must have been talking in my sleep."

"This wasn't talking."

"Sorry."

"You all right?"

"Fine."

"Sure?"

"Yes. Thanks."

He apologized for waking me and went out to the hall, turned out the light and, from the sounds of it, headed back upstairs to the den, *3:20* showing on the clock radio beside the bed. . .

I'd been dreaming of my ninth birthday, the third of September, late afternoon. I was practising the piano in the living-room, my mother pointing out my mistakes from the kitchen where she had just finished making my birthday cake.

She went upstairs to get something, calling out a mistake on the way, leaving John, who was seven, sitting alone at the kitchen table with the birthday cake, a box of wooden matches on the table beside it.

Back in the kitchen on *mistake patrol* (at this point I was throwing them in on purpose just to make her mad), out of my peripheral vision I noticed my mother suddenly tear across the kitchen toward the basement stairs. I stopped playing, got up from the piano and went to stand at the dining-room door looking into the kitchen.

I heard my mother's shouts in the basement, John screaming as though he'd been struck, pleading innocence, apologizing, crying for her to let him go as she brought him upstairs, squirming frantically to get out of her grip as she dragged him screaming over to the stove, turned the element on and after waiting for it to heat up pressed the fingers of his left hand down on the element.

*"That'll teach you to play with matches!"* she screamed, letting him go, a look on her face as she rushed out of the kitchen like she was going to be sick to her stomach.

I ran to John, helped him to his feet, hugged him to stop his sobs and told him through tears that everything was going to be all right.

I heard the toilet flush upstairs . . .

Two nights later, just after 3:00 in the morning, she attempted to kill herself using one of my father's *Wilkinson Sword* razor blades on her wrists and neck.

The light on in the hall behind him, John woke me up whispering: *Something's wrong!*

We found her lying in a pool of blood on the basement floor, raced upstairs to wake our father, stayed in our room listening to him wail into the phone downstairs in the kitchen that he needed to report a suicide . . .

Grandma Illidge came to live with us. Life went on unchanged except it was much quieter around the house. I suppose we must have missed her. I can't be sure, though.

No one explained to my brothers and me what had gone on. We never asked. John and Peter wondered if she was dead. I said she couldn't be, or there would have been a funeral.

One Saturday in July almost two years later, Grandfather Shea, my mother's father, drove my brothers and me to Niagara Falls for the day. We saw the sights, visited Tussaud's Wax Museum, rode the *Maid of the Mist* then finished up with a trip under the Falls, riding the elevator down to an underground dressing room where we were outfitted with rubber boots, yellow raincoats and sou'westers for the walk out to the observation deck.

There, with a thundering curtain of water as a backdrop, my grandfather gathered my brothers and me together, put his face close to ours so we could hear him shouting over the roar of the falling water: *"You'll have to behave yourselves from now on, boys, or you'll make your mother sick again!! Especially you, John. No more nonsense!! Is that understood?!"*

We nodded that it was.

*"Is that understood?!"*

Again we nodded . . .

When we arrived home late in the afternoon, my father had taken my grandmother home, and my mother was standing in the kitchen making dinner. I have no recollection of anything being said, or of hugging her or telling her how happy we were to see her.

Other than my grandfather's angry warning at Niagara Falls, the incident was never spoken of again by anyone. It was as if it never happened, when John and I knew full well that it had because of the scars on her neck and wrists, which, after that, she always covered with turtle-necks and scarves, her wrists with large bracelets, long-sleeved blouses . . .

The white Ford Explorer that had been in the garage the night before was gone in the morning. On the drive to the Porter terminal, I tried to find out Karen, the City of Milton town planner's last name, but was unsuccessful. John could spot a ruse a mile away.

I thanked him for the lift, the dinner at *Campanelle* and the live entertainment by the stove, and wished him good luck with the spousal support case, going easy on the irony.

Passing me the handle of my suitcase which he'd taken out of the trunk for me, he walked to his car door, opened it and turned.

"Morris."

"What?"

He winked. "Karen's last name."

# CHAPTER TWENTY-SIX

# A CRUEL MISTRESS

A MICABLY SEPARATED FROM his wife for seven months as they worked through settlement details, while she remained in their home on the east side of the Margaree River, my friend, Don, moved with their golden retriever, Lily, to the main floor of a recently built split-level house on the west side of the river. His landlord, Paul, a former schoolteacher, lived downstairs. The house sat at the top of a curving drive on the southern slope of the fir-covered Cape Breton Highland Mountains, about a hundred and fifty feet up a curving gravel lane overlooking the river valley west toward the ocean.

Don spent the first few weeks introducing me to village life, the neighbours, the Margaree Co-Op grocery and liquor store, the social hub of the area where we bumped into people who knew Don and were happy to meet his friend *from away*. I also got to know his twelve-year old golden retriever, Lily, on practise walks while Don was at work. He was leaving to do company trade and sales shows in the U.S. for the month of February with the end-grain cutting boards he'd created using local larch evergreen trees. He'd built the company up from nothing into a going concern, a major tourist stop on Cape Breton's famous Cabot Trail.

I'm about as far from a dog person as you can get, twice shy from having once been bitten when I was young. It's not that I don't like dogs. I'm just wary of them. By the time we'd taken our second walk, I adored Lily. She was mild-mannered, fun-loving, and best of all, as I teased Don: like her owner, she wasn't a barker.

Don's Buddhist *sangha* (community) embraced me with their friendship, included me in their weekly *dharma* teaching sessions and made me a full-fledged member of their social circle. They were an eclectic and close-knit group who had known each other for many years, of varying ages and backgrounds, interesting, peaceful, life-enjoying individuals like my friend Don. There were regular gatherings for spiritual and social purposes, sometimes both at the same time. Within a week of arriving, I felt more relaxed, centered, and happier with myself and my life than I had been in the last few years. By the beginning of my third week, I had a good feeling about starting to write.

Showered, dressed, caffeined up and raring to go at seven o'clock one Monday morning after Don had left for work, I took out and set up my desktop . . . only to have it sputter, spark, release a tiny puff of electrical smoke and die, not to be revived unless I wanted to drive two hours to North Sydney and leave it with a technician at one of the three electronics repair shops in town that, chances were, would pronounce it D.O.A. and recommend purchasing a new machine, which I couldn't afford to do.

Don saved the day digging out a decade-old Dell laptop in the bottom of one of his closets. Right from the start the machine seemed to have a mind of its own and a voracious appetite for computer files, mine disappearing with troubling frequency, without a trace and unrecoverable. Don thought the problem—and the reason that he recalled sidelining the machine originally—was the jumpy finger-cursor that sometimes did the opposite of what it was supposed to, a problem that sent me into a panic every time I hit *Save.*

After my all-important opening chapter that I'd recreated from scratch for a third time was devoured, Don took me into North Sydney where I bought a mouse and a USB key, and went to work taming the ravenous "Dell from Hell."

Back on track, Don's deck gave a panoramic view of the pastoral Margaree Valley west almost as far as the Gulf of St. Lawrence. I took my coffee out there first thing every morning, inspiration for what I was hoping to write that day coming to me like never before. I started bringing a notepad and pen outside with me, my coffee sometimes growing cold before the flourish of ideas let up and I went inside to thaw my nearly frostbitten fingers under warm water at the kitchen sink.

I managed to rewrite the first chapter for a fourth time, this version finding the words I was looking for—so happy with it after all I'd gone through creating it that I was sure the publisher would have no reason to change a single word during editing.

Inspiration flowed. For the first time the book began to take concrete shape in my new outline. It appeared that my gamble to write at least the first section of the manuscript there in Cape Breton was paying off.

And it was, until the evening I met Jim Duggan, former chief inspector with the Metropolitan Police Service in London, England. Several nights before he headed to the U. S. for a month of trade shows, Don invited his next door neighbour Jim and his wife Carol over for dinner. In case I bumped into them walking Lily while he was away, Don thought he should introduce us. He warned me at the last minute that Jim took getting used to. "People sometimes find him a tad overbearing."

A *tad?*

The man's grip wrenched my hand while we were shaking like he was trying to wring a confession out of me. I couldn't get what was left of my fingers out of his hand fast enough. A tall man in his mid-sixties with an arrogant, supercilious, domineering manner, he had retired from the Metropolitan Police Service three years ago, heard good things about this part of Nova Scotia and found a house he could afford in East Margaree. His wife Carol, a slim, pretty, quiet woman in her early forties (a painter, Don had told me) let Jim do most of the talking.

While we were having drinks, Jim asked what had brought me to Cape Breton.

"A publisher's contract to write a book. I felt I needed the peace and quiet of a place like Cape Breton. Don invited me to come down and start the book here."

"What kind of book?" he snapped.

Startled by his aggression, I recalled Don's warning about his overbearing manner. "Nonfiction. A memoir I guess you'd call it."

"Who would be interested in a memoir about *you?*" he scoffed in belligerent condescension which, in deference to Don, I let pass.

"It's about my family, one of my brothers, as well as—"

"Why would I want to read a book about *your* family?"

"It's an interesting story."

"What makes it interesting?"

"The way I'm writing it, plus the people and events involved."

"Such as?"

Not a chance I'd mention the police raid to him. "Such as a younger brother of mine embezzling $100 million and getting away with it."

"Getting away with it?" A mocking smile. "He couldn't have got away with it."

"He did."

"Not something on that scale."

"A bit here and a bit there over the years."

"Somebody would have been onto him."

"Nobody was."

"Where was this?"

"Toronto."

"I was with the Metropolitan Police Service of London for thirty-six years. I can tell you with certainty that he couldn't have got away with a fraud of that size. You must have the facts wrong."

"He's my brother, Jim. I think I would know the facts."

"Not necessarily."

"It's been nine years and they still haven't nabbed him."

"Nine years? It couldn't have been nine years. They would have got him by now."

"Has it been nine years, Don?" I asked.

"It's been nine years," he replied.

Jim was unrelenting in his obstinacy. During dinner he took every opportunity when conversation lagged—and even when it didn't—to knock me, knock my book, my pretensions and the *preposterous story* (as he termed it) that I was *purporting* to tell. At one point he stunned me by saying that I was getting carried away with my imagination, the whole crime, as he saw it with a career's worth of experience, sounded contrived, made up and indeed I was the one who came across with a *reek* of fraud about him.

A few drinks and he appeared to have travelled back to his days in the interrogation room at the Metropolitan Police headquarters and I was a suspect who needed working over. His train of denigrating insults made it hard on numerous occasions not to lean across the table and stick a fork in his eye—

"That's the trouble with lay-people trying to write books about crime."

"Really? Who should write them, Jim?"

"People who know how the law works and doesn't."

"And police officers know?"

"Policemen, lawyers and judges."

"Really?"

"It goes without saying."

"Not always. My brother ran Ponzi schemes inside and outside the securities industry for ten years, Jim. He got caught by his regulatory body, admitted his guilt, negotiated a settlement that precluded police prosecution, then declared bankruptcy so he wouldn't have to pay the half-million dollars in fines the regulators levied. Most people would see that as getting away with it, Jim. At no point were any police, lawyers or judges involved and, from the looks of it, they never will be. In the meantime a bunch of people are out $100 million."

*"So you say!"* he exploded, *"but I just don't believe it! How could the police not have been involved?"*

"Fraud's a cruel mistress, Jim," I said obliquely, hoping to cut off his hysteria at the knees.

Carol, who hadn't said anything for most of the night, smiled as though she understood the deliberately obscure comment.

Jim glared at me. "What's *that* supposed to mean?"

I wasn't sure whether he was asking about the quotation, or about his wife's flirting smile.

Maybe, in an effort to redeem himself as he was leaving, Jim admitted that my story had taken him back to his days as an interrogator, something he had been very good at, the thing he missed most about being a police detective: "Getting people in that room and having a go at them."

All I could think of after they left was what Carol's life must have been like living with an abusive prick like Jim.

. . . *He had me in a jail cell, his left arm around my neck choking me, his right hand gripping my wrist tight as a steel clamp as he forced it out in front of me toward the open cell door that Officer Val was holding, Jim thrusting the hand into the opening so Val could slam it—*

I sat up in bed, short of breath, sweating, my right arm tingling with pins and needles. I went out to the living-room, sat in the darkness looking over the moonlit valley for an hour or so until Jim Duggan's imperious, taunting voice: *Your brother COULDN'T have got away with a $100 million fraud!!* faded away and I went back to bed; lay there staring at the moon-light on the ceiling for some time, asking myself if maybe, deep down, I was the real fraud.

In the morning, for the first time since I'd come to Cape Breton, not one thought about the book came to mind to put in my notepad while I had my coffee on the deck. The distraction continued during breakfast, waves of doubt, of guilt and shame washing over me as I sat there, to the point that I felt I was drowning in them—Jim Duggan with his hand on my head holding me under as I struggled to breathe, my throat filling—I jumped up from the table, ran to the bathroom and vomited.

All I could think to do after cleaning myself up was defiantly run to the computer, go into my book file, format a new chapter . . . but I could only stare and stare at the blank white screen, stare some more and con-tinue staring as if something would surely come to mind if I just willed it to hard enough.

Minutes passed on the clock at the bottom of the screen; frightened, agitated minutes passing until my breaths came faster and I started gasping—the sign a panic attack was imminent, thanks, I finally realized, to Jim's malignant mind-games.

I rushed outside for fresh air in an effort to slow my breathing. Letting go of any thoughts about the book, I looked across the valley and up to the sky hoping the eagles were soaring above the Highlands that morning.

They were.

Reassured, I watched them circling, smiling to myself at still being so damned vulnerable to mood disordered people like Jim Duggan, even though I'd been dealing with mood-disordered people all my life. How easily I fell into the traps laid by such types who, for one reason or another never made clear to me, had to feel they'd won against me, that they'd defeated me, out-performed or out-accomplished me, or, in Jim's case, shamed me into believing my book was not worth writing, even when I knew unshakeably that it was.

Knew as well, and took solace in the fact, as I had at the hands of Officer Val, that in the end you want to be careful how you treat a writer because they're the ones who end up having the final word.

As a rule, I went past Jim and Carol's house twice a day walking Lily down the road and back. I decided when I set out the morning after our dinner dust-up that it would be wrong to change routes out of a fear of encountering Jim Duggan.

Since his two big dogs were rabid barkers, I usually waited till I was almost past the house, an attractive, three-story white-clapboard place on a small hill back from the road, before turning to watch the spectacle of his snarling animals hurling themselves at the porch windows in vicious attack-mode until Lily and I were out of view.

In six weeks of walking by I'd never once seen Carol or Jim about, nor a vehicle of any kind in the door-less garage at the side of their house. I'd never met them on the road walking their dogs either, which was fine with me, except it intrigued me that the only sign of life I ever saw was their two large, ferociously barking canines launching themselves at the windows.

That changed, however, on Valentine's Day. The dogs foaming at the mouth as usual when Lily and I went by on our way home from our afternoon walk, I happened to glance up at the house earlier than usual for I'd spotted something: there gazing down at me from the third floor bay window where the night of the dinner she'd told me she had her studio, was Carol, smiling and with her hand raised, waving.

She was there the following day too. And the one after that. Standing at her studio window with what, perhaps fancifully, I saw as a captive smile, which I returned and held while waving back to her, the two of us with our eyes locked, heedless of the vicious cacophony down below that only abated when Lily disappeared around a bend in the road. I had no idea what to make, if anything, of the smile and wave, as Carol might have wondered the same thing about mine, or so I was vain enough to think. I often wished I could go to the door and say hello. Maybe strike up a friendly chat, the two of us, about art, writing, music. But there was no chance of that; no, not with those dogs, not with Jim . . .

Don and I had a few days together when he returned from his trade show junket at the end of February, but the second week of March, I moved down to Albert Bridge on the Mira River, cottage country thirty minutes southeast of North Sydney, to do a dog-sitting assignment for friends of Don's landlord, Paul—Brenda and Jim, who were driving to the other end of Nova Scotia to deal with a family medical emergency and would be gone for five weeks.

Having heard from Paul that I was writing a book, they thought it might be ideal for me to take care of their rescue dogs Whisky (a hyperactive, light-brown, short-coat hound who with his small head and pointed snout looked exactly like Man's Best Friend, Bart's dog on *The Simpsons*) and Luther (a large, long-haired white with brown spots, droopy-eyed *Disney* dog) at their cottage on the Mira River that Jim had just about finished renovating as a year-round home.

After talking to Brenda on the phone, I confessed that I wasn't much of a dog person, but realized they were in a jam and so would be happy to help out.

While at the cottage, I had use of a Jeep Cherokee to drive into North Sydney for groceries, or down to the beach at the Mira Gut where the river flowed into the Atlantic. When it came to groceries, I didn't need to buy many. Brenda had stocked her freezer with roasts, steak, chicken, freezer bags of vegetables, pasta, bread and an assortment of fruit, pies and cakes.

I set my computer up at the head of the long, glass-topped dining table across from the kitchen island, my back to the row of windows that gave onto the river so that I wouldn't get distracted while writing, a pointless concern since I had enough to do dealing with Whisky's frightened howling any time the wind rattled the eavestroughs or blew leaves against the door. Luther, chorusing along with a slow, throaty bellow, the combined racket hard on the ears, subsided only after I went over, sat down with them, patted and reassured them that everything was all right, they could calm down. At which point, I'd return to my computer for a few minutes of speed typing that in the end proved fruitless, since my nerves were so jangled, and I was in such a state of restless anxiety on windy days (most days were windy), that anything I did manage to write was such illiterate jumble when I read it over later, that I had no choice but to delete it.

Brenda phoned twice a week to see how everything was going (just fine), how The Boys were doing (just fine as well), and whether I was making sure they were on leashes when I took them outside for their last pee at night (I was). Her concern was justified. A female jogger had been killed by a pack of coyotes just a few months before on a hiking trail in the Highlands north of Margaree. The alarm went out across Cape Breton.

The eleven o'clock pee was a tense occasion. Even with the windows and doors closed, you could hear the coyote packs yipping and yapping in the woods along the road to lure the dogs into coming after them. Once outside in the darkness, the howling sometimes rose to such a cacophony I felt an attack was imminent and rushed The Boys back inside whether they were finished peeing or not.

One night, Whisky and Luther took the bait and ran off down the dark, dead-end road while I was putting on their leashes. I grabbed a flashlight, went streaking after them down the road, things turning dire when the coyotes suddenly went silent. I pictured Whisky and Luther having been dragged into the woods. I sprinted faster, came around a bend and, in my flashlight beam, saw Whisky and Luther sitting obediently in front of a large timber wolf whose yellow eyes shone at me in the light: Hector, owned by the family at the end of the road who kept him as a pet. I chuckled in relief at the cute scene, grabbed the leashes, fastened them on, warned the boys against anymore mischief then turned to thank Hector, but he was gone.

John called at 6:30 a.m. on April Fool's Day. Not a prank, he was quick to say.

"You know those new glasses I was trying out at *Campanelle* the night before you left?"

"I didn't know you were trying them out."

"Anyway, something's wrong with them. They're not right. I had the optician make me a new pair, but the guy wants another twelve-hundred dollars. I want to sue him. What's Trevor's number?"

"Gowlings won't handle the case?"

"Not something like this."

I knew exactly what had happened: he just didn't want to pay for the glasses and was forcing the issue with his claim that the glasses had been improperly made. There was more to the story. "Trevor's a criminal lawyer, John. He doesn't do civil suits."

"Give it to me anyway, just in case."

I gave it to him.

Trevor phoned a week later and explained: it was a criminal suit. Charges had been brought, not by John, but by the optician for fraud. John had paid for the glasses with a personal check on an account that had been closed (his supply of check books from the back of the Jaguar obviously hadn't run out). He maintained the glasses didn't fit properly, was sticking with that even though he couldn't describe what exactly made them not right. In any case, he wanted another pair. The optician wanted his twelve-hundred first, otherwise he was calling the police and, with no money forthcoming from John, he did.

"The cops asked John to come in so they could lay fraud charges for paperhanging, as it's known in the trade. Check kiting. I told him he wasn't going to beat it; he'd have to pay for the glasses in the end. He remained adamant that the glasses were faulty but couldn't explain how."

Three weeks later the case was withdrawn by the Crown, something to do with the optician. "Maybe," said Trevor, "John's contention that the glasses weren't right would present a reasonable doubt at trial. Hard to say. It was a complicated prescription. He could have been playing on that."

"Did he pay you your thousand dollars?"

"He did."

"Cash?"

He paused. "Check unfortunately."

*"How many times have I told you, Trevor!"*

"I know, I know. All I can say is your brother has his ways. Have you got his address by chance?"

Trevor reported back in a few days. When he arrived at Winner's Circle the front door was wide open. Stepping inside, he heard voices in the kitchen. The next thing he knew two heavies who looked like they might be packing appeared and confronted him about what he was doing there.

"Looking for John Illidge," Trevor said. "He owes me money."

The heavies eased up apparently: *You too?*

Back in Margaree briefly after my dog-sitting stint to say farewell to Nova Scotia, Don and I made the four-hour drive south to Halifax on a Wednesday afternoon to set up for the Atlantic Craft Trade Show starting the next day, where we were selling his Larchwood cutting boards. A busy show, I would help him in the booth over the weekend. He would drop me off at the airport Monday morning on his way home to Margaree.

Late Saturday afternoon while I was on a break, Nicky phoned to say he'd been talking with one of his clients who was in a jam, heading back to Fort McMurray, Alberta, where he worked in the oil sands; however, he'd had to evict his previous tenant and couldn't find anyone suitable to rent his house. It was a clean, well-kept two storey, four bedroom Tudor-style house on a cul-de-sac, nicely furnished, with a fully finished basement and recreation room, a large garage, a well-treed backyard, five blocks from the lake and only two minutes from our old house. Nicky felt it would be a mistake not to take it.

"Mistake? It would be a crime."

"The only issue is first and last month's rent."

"Not to worry," I told him. "The distributor of my Shakespeare novels called last week. She sold off the last of them to a book chain and is sending me a check for $3,500 that should arrive by the end of the week. We're in business!"

As things turned out, Monday morning, along with breakfast at the hotel before Don drove me to the airport, I received a serendipitous bon voyage present: a front-page story in the *Halifax Chronicle-Herald* newspaper. Jason, the manager of the Margaree Co-Op grocery and liquor outlet in town, had absconded with $380,000 sometime over the weekend and disappeared without a trace. Evidently he'd been perpetrating his fraud for the past year, almost from the time he was hired by the CEO of the Co-Op board of directors, former Metropolitan Police chief inspector Jim Duggan, who said that with all his years of police experience, he *"simply couldn't believe that something like this had been going on right under his nose."*

I could . . .

# CHAPTER TWENTY-SEVEN

# MORE JOHN

AFTER SHOWING HIM a first draft of my manuscript, on which I'd worked hard all summer so that I could write the final version over the fall and winter, Jack David, my publisher, said his only request would be to consider putting "more John" into the story.

*More John?*

I told him that while I could do that easily—there was no shortage of material and new developments were coming to light all the time—doing so would become problematic in that whether he tries to or not (and he usually does), for better or worse, people are compelled to give John their attention. As one of his best friends expressed it years ago, John tends to hijack situations.

"He'll take readers hostage and they'll forget all about me."

"Is that such a bad thing? I mean the taking readers hostage."

"It is when the story's supposed to be mine, John merely a minor character in it. More John means he becomes a major one. I don't know if I want to risk that."

"It's up to you, of course," Jack said, backing off, though he couldn't resist putting in a final more John plug: "He's an engrossing character who would definitely promote sales."

I kidded him. "And I'm not."

"Don't be silly. Of course you are. If you're worried about revealing personal or legal details about unprosecuted crimes—"

"That doesn't worry me. It's just that when you drop a big rock like John into the story pond, so to speak, it creates waves. Big ones. It throws the other elements off balance. I'd have to reduce or eliminate certain events, mostly involving myself, in order to accommodate *'More John.'"*

No comment, Jack pressed on, having missed my point. "We'll put the standard rejoinder on the copyright page: *To the best of his abilities the author has related experiences, places, people and organizations from his memory of them.* Something like that. Besides, if anybody wants to sue for defamation, you'll see in your contract that they can only sue you, not us. *We don't have anything to be afraid of.* Stick to the truth and you won't either."

Thus, the rewriting of the book to give it "More John" got underway.

Just before Halloween, Trevor phoned with news.

"Your *miscreant brother* called and asked if I would defend him for forging the signatures on two $10,000 checks from the account of his partner, slash, sidekick, Vince Philips. You ever heard of him?"

"Somebody mentioned to me that John was living at the condo of a Vince somebody and his wife in Richmond Hill."

"That would be the guy then. Anyway, I appeared for him at the bail hearing, which was contested by the Crown because the person posting bail for John was this Vince Philips, whose signature he'd forged on two of Vince's checks. Vince maintained the whole thing was a communications mix up: John gave the checks to a third party on Vince's behalf. They both bounced because of the communication mix up."

"The judge was certainly mixed up. He went ahead and let Vince sign for the bail and John got out. He'll live with Vince till the time of his trial."

"Where he was already living . . ."

"Pulled a fast one on the judge there," Trevor chuckled. "The poor wife. At any rate, after supposedly hiring another lawyer who wouldn't be available for this hearing today, John asked me to appear at Old City Hall with him on his trial date. He was looking to have the proceedings delayed till his *other lawyer* was available."

"Who's the other lawyer?"

"I didn't ask."

"There is no other lawyer, Trevor."

"No?"

"He doesn't pay you, yet you continue to act for him. Why would he go with somebody he has to pay?"

"Good point."

"Buying time is John's game. He's mastered the art."

"He's sure good at it, I'll give him that. As things turned out, it was only a pre-trial. Pre-trial is where the Crown establishes whether there's enough evidence to send him to trial, the Crown's preferred option since the trial would be a quick and fast conviction. John knew that apparently, and so in his pre-trial he waived his right to have a pre-trial (which had heads spinning, I can tell you), and asked to be remanded straight to trial in the Superior Court of Justice, where serious cases like murder, manslaughter and human trafficking are tried. Complicated, expensive cases that take up a great amount of time. Your brother knows the wheels of justice grind slowest of all in Superior Court, even in a relatively piddling case like his."

"What did Vince have to say about the forging?"

"That John was acting on his behalf. You can tell he looks up to John, the wheeler dealer who's told him he has many millions stowed away in the Cayman Islands which one day he'll use to pay Vince back whatever money he owes him. Or better yet, if Vince is willing to let the debt ride, John will cut him in for a percentage of any future investment projects they work on together. He lied to the judge when he said John signing the checks was just a communications mix up. The way I see it, they're a team. Buying themselves time, playing the system."

"How long can he put the trial off?"

"At the going rate? Five, six months, maybe more with his skills. He's got the prosecutor over a barrel. He needs a lawyer, but he can't or won't pay for one, and the court's reluctant to appoint one because of his demonstrated ability to manipulate the process in previous offences. He's got them stalemated."

I didn't have the heart to ask if John paid him for doing the hearing. What would have been the point . . .?

Molly, who continued monitoring all things John, let me know shortly afterwards that there was to be a Superior Court of Justice hearing on the $20,000 forgery charges in two weeks over the issue of John's search for a lawyer.

This was John's modus operandi: keep changing counsel without explanation. The names of new counsel never appeared on the record since, according to John, when pressed to explain why, he always had trouble finding a lawyer who would be *the right fit*. I decided to attend the hearing.

I arrived at Old City Hall court about 8:45, went through security and upstairs to the second-floor Superior Court room where the hearing was to be held. It surprised me that I was the only one in the hall outside the courtroom until, at nine-o'clock sharp, the court clerk, in black robe and white collar-tabs, opened up, the two of us entering the large trial courtroom. She busied herself with some files while I sat quietly for a few minutes in a front row pew before John walked in, accompanied by a short, stout man with high-prescription glasses I assumed to be his bail surety, Vince Philips.

Floored to see me, John recovered his composure enough to mutter an introduction to his friend Vince then asked belligerently what I was doing there.

"Picking up material for my book. The one I went to Cape Breton to write—"

He had turned away to confer over a piece of paper from a file folder Vince had with him.

My brother looked a shambles in a size too small, pill-covered grey and burgundy-striped wool sweater that did no favours for his prominent belly. The grey flannels he was wearing had lost both their shape and their crease long ago, and his salt-stained black loafers were splitting at the soles. Except for his expensive-looking glasses, he could have been mistaken for an indigent who had stumbled into Superior Court by accident.

Ignoring me, an expression of pure relief crossed his face when the courtroom door opened and, black robe streaming behind her, the Crown prosecutor rushed in. On her way to the clerk's station, she called over to John.

"What's this about a new lawyer?"

"I have to bring him up to speed."

The prosecutor let out a frustrated breath. "This will be the third one, John."

"I'm getting different opinions."

"Well," the prosecutor said, glancing at the clock, "we'll have to see."

She and the clerk conferred.

When John sat down in the front row I noticed a patch of white underwear poking through a small rip in the crotch of his grey flannels. I couldn't remember ever seeing him look like such a down and out poverty case. Had he really fallen so low?

Not a chance. He was putting his *smoke them out* strategy to good use. Neither the prosecutors nor the judges (all dedicated to progressive ideas about social justice for the poor) would have afforded him nearly the same tolerance and latitude in finding a lawyer sympathetic to his reduced circumstances if he'd been wearing one of his $2,500 Savile Row suits.

The situation too depressing to watch, there seemed no point in hanging around until the judge arrived and haggled with John over whether to grant him a fourth and probably far from final extension while he vetted imaginary lawyers, so I left . . .

Molly, Trevor and I heard nothing more about the forgery case, or about John for that matter, until the New Year, January 5th, the day after his birthday. Trevor received a frantic early morning phone call from a woman introducing herself as Karen, with whom John had apparently been living. Her voice shaking, she said she was phoning from the Brampton Provincial Offences courthouse waiting to bail John out of jail. He had given her Trevor's number to call about acting for him at the bail hearing. She confessed that she had no idea what was going on. They had gone out to dinner the night before to celebrate John's birthday. They went through a police spot check on the way to the restaurant, the police ordering John to step out of the car before they even asked to see his license and insurance. They handcuffed him, put him in the back of a police cruiser and drove off.

He called Karen from jail at three a.m. to say it was all a big mix up. He would be out first thing in the morning. Could she come to the courthouse and bail him out? John was hoping Trevor could handle the hearing for him.

Feeling sorry for the woman, Trevor made the forty-five minute drive west to Brampton and took stock of the situation. Vince Philips was there consoling Karen over the big mix-up.

The big mix-up for Trevor was that John was supposed to be living with Vince on bail pending his forgery trial, yet here was a woman with whom he was apparently also living, paying to bail him out.

"A judicial Catch-22," Trevor laughed. "Out of curiosity, I went off to get the lowdown from the prosecutor."

John had been driving the Audi A4 Turbo he'd given Karen six months ago as a birthday present. He'd leased the car, but never made the payments on it. The dealership where he bought it reported it stolen. He was being charged with theft and possession of stolen property over $5,000, an indictable offence, punishable by up to ten years in prison on conviction (contingent on his criminal record)—the same charges that John would have faced for stealing Tammy's CR-V if Honda hadn't decided it wasn't worth their while to prosecute him.

It was too early in the case to forecast an outcome, and because he had no intention of taking the case, Trevor didn't relate any of this to Karen, who was prepared to put up the $5,000 bail. John was already living with her, so becoming his surety wouldn't present any problems. That John already had a different surety for the forgery charges didn't seem to make a difference. There was nothing on the books as far as the Crown prosecutor knew that precluded such arrangements.

Nor did Trevor explain to Karen that he wouldn't represent John at his bail hearing because he had yet to receive payment for his previous legal services. He fibbed and told her that he had too heavy a case load just then to take on a new one in west Brampton when he was living in east Toronto. Duty counsel would be fine for a bail hearing. Trevor assured her bail proceedings were pretty straight forward, there shouldn't be any problem.

I asked him if at any point he happened to catch Karen's last name.

Trevor thought about it for a second. "Morris. Karen Morris."

So John had told me the truth at the Porter terminal the morning I left for Cape Breton. Had he managed to get the son and his girlfriend out from underfoot? Persuaded Karen to sell her house and let him invest a chunk of the proceeds so he could build her a *substantial investment portfolio?*

Hard to say, but my hunch was yes. Still, the urge to contact the woman was as strong as it had been originally. I felt I had to let Karen Morris know the broader background picture on John—warn her that more trouble was coming and the only way she could protect herself was if she reneged on his bail at the first opportunity, and for her own good, ditched John.

A little hysterical-sounding, I know. I would tone things down if I was able to speak to her in person. What was the worst she could do besides tell me to fuck off? Tell me that she was a big girl, that her relationship with John was none of my business.

I remembered that she worked in the planning department for the City of Milton, thirty minutes west of Toronto. A quick search of the city's website provided email addresses for planning department staff. I copied Karen's, wrote her an email explaining that I wasn't stalking her, but wanted to talk to her about my brother John—how I had wanted to before I left for Cape Breton after John had told me about his relationship with her . . . but never knew her last name until now, through my lawyer-friend Trevor, whom she had met at the Brampton courthouse before John's bail hearing, and who would be happy to vouch for me. Would it be possible, I wondered, for us to meet for coffee sometime to help me with some facts for an important part of the book I was writing on John's relationship frauds? I only asked that if she wasn't going to meet me, could she let me know sooner rather than later, as I had to carry on with my writing.

Trevor heard nothing more about the two pending cases, Molly nothing about where he was living or what he was up to, me not a word through any of my friends in the investment business except that John had people *looking for him.* I reminded Molly of what an FBI agent had once said about Frank "Catch Me If You Can" Abagnale Jr.'s elusiveness: *He was slippery as a buttered escargot.*

For the next several months, as was his pattern, John appeared to have *gone to the mattresses*, as he would have said, until Molly, who monitored these things for clients, noticed that he had changed his LinkedIn page so that it was even more bizarre than its previous iteration, which suggested to Molly that he and Karen Morris had broken up as a result of the stolen Audi, and that he was back trolling the dating sites again.

Molly sent me the link, called me up and went through it with me, the two of us laughing at the ludicrous contents: CEO or Managing Partner of this international corporation or that, plus managing partner of a bank *in the Geneva area*, a merchant banker with Lazarus Rothchilds Investments in London (there was no such firm, Rothschilds is spelled with two S's), one of Europe's banking dynasties going back to the early 1800s. What he'd done is mix the names of prominent investment banking corporations together so to the uninitiated they'd sound legitimate, when, in fact, they were complete fabrications.

"What's scary to me," said Molly, "isn't so much that John would try to pass off what's laughable as legitimate, but that smart, professional women out there would so readily believe it."

"He only needs to catch one."

"True."

"Then at some point he throws her back . . ."

Maybe after the Audi fiasco, Karen Morris had turned the tables and thrown John back.

Three days later we had our answer.

*"Where and when would you like to meet?* —Karen."

# CHAPTER TWENTY-EIGHT

# BIG DADDY

WE MET IN A small downtown cafe across from the St. Lawrence Market. In her mid-fifties, Karen was shorter than I expected (John had always liked women on the taller side), burgundy loafers, khaki pants, Hunter green cardigan sweater over a yellow blouse. Her hair short and dark, salt-and-pepper flecked, she would have been prettier without the gold aviator-frame glasses she wore, which gave her an undeserved mousy look.

To put her at ease I joked, as we walked to the table, that I had two pieces of photo I.D. with me if she wanted to check. She thanked me for the courteous offer in what was certainly a strange situation, but it wasn't at all necessary: she had done her due diligence through Google, as I'd suggested, and found me to be on the level—surprised that we could actually meet, she added wryly, when John, in the few fragments of information he'd shared about his family, had made a point of mentioning that his older brother had disgraced them all with his arrest for running a marijuana grow-op and was serving a five-year sentence in Kingston Penitentiary for drug trafficking. Amused, I joked that they'd let me out early for good behaviour. "Drugs are anathema to John. He doesn't see the contradiction in his binge alcoholism."

"No," she said. "Irony is not one of John's strong suits."

The ice pleasantly broken, after we ordered, to keep things as comfortable as possible I suggested that she just tell me what she wanted to about her dealings with John from the time they met to the day she ended up in the Brampton Courthouse bailing him out on a possession-of-stolen-property charge. I reminded her that, as I'd said in my email, I was writing about relationship fraud, known otherwise as affinity fraud—theft

240

from people one know.s—what serial fraudsters like John resort to when they're cut off from all other income avenues.

A little nervous, self-conscious and I think embarrassed, Karen explained that the urge to be candid and forthcoming with me, even about some of the more personal details of their relationship, such as it was, came from not having had anyone in whom she could confide about what she had been through in the relationship with John, until she'd begun seeing a psychologist, coincidentally just before I had emailed. She'd put off doing so for a long time, such were the effects on her of John's web of lies. It seemed to her that virtually everything he'd ever said to her was a fabrication of some sort, or what her father, a lawyer, used to call *paltering with the truth*. Now that it's over, it felt to her as if the affair had never really happened; that the relationship hadn't been real in any normal sense of the word—except that her bank account showed close to three-hundred thousand dollars missing.

She and John had met online, on a popular dating site her friends had recommended. John had contacted her almost immediately, which startled her, but there really did seem to be a spark, so they had started dating. Before she knew it, they were living together in the new house that she'd bought, at John's urging, after she evicted her son and his girlfriend from her previous one. Again at John's urging, she gave him $200,000 to invest in a new fund he was putting together, a leveraged buyout deal that would allow early investors like her to double their money when it was completed in a few months.

It seemed like a good idea at the time. She was in love with John, the prospect of marriage, she had to admit, one that was definitely on her mind after being single for seven years. She admitted as well to being dazzled that at fifty-three she could attract a man with the looks, personality and money John had. Or at the time seemed to have. He treated her better than she'd ever been treated in her life. By anyone. He was tender, thoughtful, kind, and, even though it was an old-fashioned word, attentive. She hadn't the least reason in the world to think that everything wasn't what it seemed.

Until the day she gave John the two-hundred thousand dollars to invest for her, took a taxi home from work in the early afternoon because she wasn't feeling well, and thought she noticed her Mercedes parked in the driveway of the house for sale five doors down the street. It had been for sale for a while. The owners were asking too much. Karen had grown used to seeing the real estate agent's white Lexus in the driveway. But that was definitely her silver Mercedes parked behind it. Only it had *RSKY*

*BZNS* license plates on it.

A female agent answered the door, John stepping out from behind her as if he was just leaving the open house. A sales brochure in hand, he thanked the agent for showing him the place, said he'd get back to her if he was interested.

As to the *RSKY BZNS* license plates, when they got home, John explained that he'd put them on for sentimental reasons. Before he'd met her he'd sold all his vehicles pending a move to London, England to run a new international investment fund he'd been recruited for. However, now that he'd met Karen, he was having second thoughts. Maybe it was time to buy a new vehicle and put the *RSKY BZNS* plates on it? That's probably what trying the plates on her Mercedes was telling him. It was time. He apologized if she thought anything different. What he would do then, he said, is what he should have done right off the bat in their relationship. He grabbed a plastic grocery bag and asked her to come to the garage with him, where he ceremoniously dropped the license plates in a garbage can.

She admitted not being completely with it at that point because she was feeling ill. John said he felt badly for the confusion, made her some lemon and honey, gave her Tylenol and sat with her until she fell asleep.

She was sick with the flu for the next two days. John didn't leave the house, at least as far as Karen knew, until the third day, when she started feeling better. After lunch he went out to buy groceries. While cleaning up the kitchen she remembered something she forgot to put on the list. She called him. A phone rang beside the toaster. The one she'd bought for John when his was "stolen." He'd forgotten it.

Not proud of herself for doing so, but in retrospect glad she did, there were calls and texts from Melanie the real estate agent, as well as three other women he'd probably met on dating sites. She admitted that she should have asked him about the calls when he came back from the store, but she was afraid to, afraid he'd blow up at her for snooping, afraid he'd leave her.

Then last July, for her fifty-third birthday, along came the Audi. She didn't need a new car. Her Mercedes was only three years old. She knew the car wasn't for her. It was for John to drive: a *Quattro Turbo-Matic* or some such thing that he'd been raving about.

Karen appreciated the gesture, but happily went back to driving her Mercedes Benz to work, John insisting that any time she wanted to drive the Quattro she could.

One day after picking up some things at the cleaners, she was driving out of the plaza near her house and was sure she saw an Audi the same color as John's, the *RSKY BZNS* plates on it, parked in front of the convenience store.

She came home and the Audi, with its normal plates, was already in the driveway. Karen mentioned to John, harmlessly enough, or so she thought, having seen his car at the plaza when she was on her way out, kidding him that he must have broken some laws getting home first.

*Wasn't me,* John said. He'd been home for twenty minutes. She pointed out that the car had *RSKY BZNS* plates. John told her she must have been mistaken, his explanation that there was another Audi 4 the same year and color as his in the neighbourhood. He said he'd seen it around. Besides, she watched him throw the *RSKY BZNS* plates in the garbage, didn't she?

Maybe, she remembered thinking at the time, it was all in her mind. Did she *really* see the *RSKY BZNS* plates in the lot, or was it just the power of suggestion because the cars looked identical? Feeling it served no purpose taking things further, she let the matter drop.

That was so her! Being self-assertive, particularly to men, was something she'd always had problems with. Calling John to account was out of the question, even if she was right and it had been him. She couldn't risk jeopardizing all the good things he'd brought into her life, and she certainly didn't want to lose her two-hundred thousand dollars, which was *fait accompli* if he walked out on her. In the meantime, her life became a series of rationalizations and excuses for what she saw now was clearly abnormal behaviour.

Despite her concerns that something wasn't right in the relationship, she hung in there, feeling that the solution to her doubts about the stress between them, strange as it sounded, was to become more accommodating. She'd always preferred taking the path of least resistance, the easy way out. Why start making exceptions now?

Pausing here and there to collect her thoughts, she ate her quiche Lorraine, spring salad and tea—admitting as an aside with guilt in her voice that she must sound incredibly foolish to have fallen for John's stunts. For someone in her professional position, she had found it humiliating. She bore a load of shame, for which, as she said, she was seeing a psychologist. To deal with the anger as well. More of a passive personality, she wasn't one who felt much anger generally, but with John, she got to the point she could rage with the best of them for what he'd done to her. Or rather, as her psychologist explained, what Karen had let him do to her. She had somehow never really learned the difference. That's the thing: all her anger had been directed at herself. John got off scot-free!

He quickly returned to being his attentive self after any future confrontations, and thankfully there were few. Karen said she experienced a kind of normality in her relationship with John after the Audi incident, never asking him about the status of the leveraged buyout, never questioning him about his comings and goings or absences of several days. They would do things together, go to movies, have dinner, see her friends and family. Talk about where they were going to buy a country place when the leveraged buyout deal closed. John mentioned the Cotswolds. Asked Karen if she'd ever been there. In fact, she had, as a teenager. Now that she thought about it, that ended the discussion.

The most distinguishing thing about John for her? He was the most private person she'd ever known. Karen didn't mind a certain amount of privacy, because she liked hers, however secrecy was another matter. She had always been shy and introverted, not secretive by any means, just one who kept to herself and respected that right in others. But one thing began adding to another. John would tell her he was going golfing with Vince, for example, only to find his golf bag sitting in the garage. One day, out of curiosity, she looked through it. There were *Absolut* vodka bottles of various sizes stuffed in the pockets, some empty, some not. Combined with the vodka drinking he did before dinner, three or four vodka on the rocks, after which he could turn extremely cranky, she felt he was, or was becoming an alcoholic.

Though he was never violent, his temper could explode when he was drinking. Karen was putting some presents in the trunk of the Audi for a Christmas party she and John were going to. She had to move a number of empty and half-empty *Absolut* bottles and a few other things out of the way first, including a plastic grocery bag that she opened, in which she found the *RSKY BZNS* license plates, which he'd made a show of throwing in the garbage after the incident with Melanie the real estate agent.

*Never mind!* he exploded at her like Mr. Hyde, snatching the grocery bag violently out of her hands. *Don't be so nosey! Mind your own business!* At which point he suddenly paused and reverted to being a pleasant Dr. Jekyll, calmly explaining that they were a second set of plates, old ones from his Porsche which he had forgotten all about. He kept them so no one else could register the personalized name while he looked around for a new car. He was thinking Ferrari. They'd never been on a Ferrari . . .

The arrest on their way to dinner in the Audi at New Year's, left her shocked and confused, never knowing what had really gone on. John going to court hearings for the next six months with his friend Vince to fight the wrongful arrest charge, yet never saying a word to Karen about it except that he was going to beat the case. The police had messed up. She wasn't to worry. How dumb she had been to buy his nonsense . . .

Thinking back over events in their past, she found little insights and not so little revelations coming to mind which she described as like finding missing pieces of a complicated puzzle she'd been trying to put together about John since shortly after they'd met. She acknowledged that a kind of trusting naiveté caused her to take things people said at face value. John always sounded so believable. If she hadn't been so emotional, had listened more closely and let herself put two-and-two together, she knew she would have realized the mistakes she was making. For example, Tanya, a good friend of hers, asked if she'd ever checked John's LinkedIn page when she first met him. Looked at his business background to see whether it was compatible with hers. Or even true.

No, she hadn't. She'd taken his dating site profile at face value—too good to be true in retrospect, but, well, she could admit it. She was desperate: seven years after her divorce and she didn't have one relationship to show for it. Not even many dates. If only she'd checked his LinkedIn page. When Tanya showed it to her the two of them went into hysterics at the thought of anyone taking its clearly contrived contents seriously.

With the Audi gone, they were down to one car again, mileage was piling up on Karen's Mercedes and she couldn't figure out why. Among the revelations that came to light later, was the fact that John was back driving the car to Toronto most days, sometimes returning to the city at night *shepherding the leveraged buyout along.* That was his word: *shepherding.*

Drinking vodka on the rocks, more empty bottles in the garage, in his golf bag, and then neighbours started reporting that he was knocking on their doors with a story about some emergency, he'd lost his keys, asking if they'd be good enough to loan him twenty or thirty dollars to *tide him over.*

Karen said she knew for the sake of her own mental health, but also for John's, she had to do something. She accepted that there was no leveraged buyout in the offing. And more than likely never had been. John was a fraud, and had been all along. He didn't have any money. There were no homes in Florida, New York, the Caribbean, not even in Toronto. He was a homeless con artist preying on her.

She asked him to leave, overcoming her utmost reluctance to do so because it meant kissing her two-hundred thousand dollars goodbye. But she was resigned to the loss as the cost of having him out of her life.

He fought it hard, hurt and angry that she would treat him like this after all he'd done for her: *She'd had the best lovin' of her life from* Big Daddy *and she knew it. How could she do this to him?* If this was about the two-hundred thousand, which he thought it was, she'd be sorry. The deal was ready to be consummated, a strange word for him to use Karen thought, *consummated.*

He was out with Vince the night she had the locks changed. She packed his few things in boxes and set them in front of the garage, leaving him a voice message explaining that if he didn't pick them up in the next twenty-four hours, she intended to put them in the garbage. If he tried to enter the house, she was calling the police. They'd been alerted. If he came to the door she would call them.

His things were gone in the morning.

She knew she should have gone to the police right away about the two-hundred thousand, however she felt stupid, ashamed, embarrassed that she hadn't seen what John was up to from the beginning. In retrospect, the red flags were all there. She'd just made the mistake of ignoring them. Plus, how seriously would the police take her complaint anyway? Her lawyer had told her they'd probably see it as a domestic dispute; proving he stole her money would be next to impossible without a rock-solid paper trail proving intent.

Karen did have the paper, lots of it. She'd been smart enough to insist on that. But first she just wanted to make sure he really was gone. Get him out of her mind. Calm down and return to reality, hoping he wouldn't turn up in the middle of the night and—

She went quiet, glanced out the window we were sitting beside.

It took her six months before she could bring herself to file a police complaint against him. They said they'd be in touch with her if other complainants came forward in the future. Her lawyer asked the officer taking the report if John was known to the police. Well known, they said.

Talk about victim shaming. How easily she had fallen for his lies. How do you tell your family and friends about something like that? What it says about you . . .

I told her it didn't say anything about her. Everything with John was a sociopathic delusion, a fantasy, a manipulation of one sort or another where he was in control without appearing to be. Sociopaths construct and control reality, so in John's case he could make it look like the breakdown of the relationship was all her fault—that he was somehow the victim. In his mind, Karen was guilty for whatever it was she'd done to him. In John's real or imagined thoughts, behaviour had consequences for everyone but him. She was the one to apologize. He was the victim.

He was the same way, I explained to Karen, with his first wife, Ellen, and with Tammy. *Sorry* and *I was wrong* weren't words in his vocabulary.

Karen laughed. "I never heard about a second wife. And now that you mention it, I don't think I ever heard him apologize, or if he did, that he meant it."

"John's an abuser, Karen. Not physically maybe, but mentally and emotionally. Sociopaths like him don't have empathy, sympathy, nothing in the way of personal connection with others. When John's through getting what he wants, *you're left traumatized, emotionally drained inside like you've lost the ability to feel anything.* That's how Ellen, his first wife, put it. You got out of his clutches just in time, Karen. I know it's hard to imagine after what you've been through, but things would only have gotten a lot worse if you hadn't removed him from your life when you did."

Karen said she realized that now, and despite the emotional blow of having been betrayed by him so often, she felt fortunate to have finally escaped from him. She still couldn't understand about the Audi, him thinking she'd be fooled by him passing it off as a birthday present.

I explained that he used the Audi to launder his stolen money. It was nothing personal. "He knew you had a car you liked, so he would end up driving the Audi by default. He wanted a hot new high-performance car to drive around in for a while before selling it to get the cash—cash is always the end goal. He did the same with his wife Tammy's Honda CR-V which, without my knowing it, he leased for her in my name. The Honda people retrieved the vehicle in the nick of time, sitting for sale on a car dealership lot. If they hadn't, I would have been charged with theft and fraud and ended up doing five years in prison thanks to John.

I told her I was sorry, that she wasn't to feel badly for falling into his trap and needing *emotional rescue* like dozens of us have over the years. Reporting her stolen two-hundred thousand to the police would be a good place to start the healing. "It would also add to the evidence file next time he's picked up, which won't be long in coming. John is an addict. Money is his drug. He gets high on the rush of a payday. He'll go to any length to get that rush. *The beast has to be fed* as he used to say."

Karen felt the drug analogy was a good one. She had seen it in his behaviour. "The drinking especially. With his upbeat, outgoing personality he seemed to me like the last person who would have a drinking problem, but hearing you talk, it makes so much sense. He probably drank to kill the pain. I can't see him doing some of the things he did to me without feeling some pain."

We were winding up. Karen was due to meet a friend while she was in the city.

"The thing to understand about John," I said, trying to sum up, "is that there are no accidents with him. Everything is deliberate, intentional, calculated according to what he calls his *smoke them out* strategy: times when it's to John's advantage to say he's in one place when he's in another, to say he's doing one thing when he's really doing another, to appear rich at times then at others, when it's to his advantage, to appear poor.

"John has masterful powers of deception. His secret for getting people to give him their money is making them think that he's good at making it, and as a result he has lots of it. His secret to not returning his clients' hefty profits is is leading people to believe his wizardry will bring them even more lucrative returns down the road. Having a relationship while he was defrauding you, it was just a question of time before you, your accountant or lawyer demanded the two hundred thousand back or you'd report his theft to the police. In his skewed way of looking at such things, it's conceivable that he forced you to give him the heave-ho so you wouldn't do that."

Karen conceded that was a lot to absorb. The idea that he might have planned both the beginning and the end of their relationship . . . Karen wondered why in the end he just wouldn't have taken off and, as he liked to say, moved on to happier hunting grounds. Why go to all the trouble of playing the situation out as elaborately as he had?

"Were there times when you were genuinely happy with John?"

"There were."

"Times when you felt he really did love you?"

"There were."

"Maybe for a time, and in his own way, he did love you, and wanted to let you down gently in breaking off the relationship by making it his fault, not yours. Let you feel that you were justified in ending things."

"I would never have thought of him doing that."

"It's possible, that's all I'm saying. As you said, you must have meant something to him Karen, because he actually mended his ways for a time after his, let's call them stunts, rather than walking out on you, as is his usual practice when ending a relationship." Her face brightened. She smiled.

We split the bill. I walked her to her car. Karen said she had something she wanted to give me: a yellow plastic grocery bag with a set of *RSKY BZNS* licence plates inside.

I told her I didn't want them any more than she did. We walked along the Esplanade until we found a garbage can. She gave me one of the plates and I took the other.

We tossed them in.

# CHAPTER TWENTY-NINE

# HELL HATH NO FURY

*Y*OU'RE DEAD!!!!!!!
This, including exclamation points, was the subject line of an early Christmas morning email from John, the first email that I'd ever received from him, the first I'd heard from him in nearly two years. What followed was a disturbing, illiterate, profanity-laced toxic rant letting me know, in graphically violent detail, that I was finished as a writer. He was in the process of *destroying my career*. I was *DEAD! DEAD! DEAD!* By the time he finished with me I would be reduced to writing on wet naps. Nobody would be interested in publishing anything I wrote. *Nobody!!!*

*The Bleaks*, my memoir of the police raid and its aftermath had been published October 15th to modest acclaim. An excerpt from the opening chapter had appeared in *Toronto Life* magazine a month before publication. In the two weeks after it came out, I did three radio interviews and an online interview with *Open Book Toronto*. The book received favourable reviews on the industry sites *Booklist* and *Publisher's Weekly*. It was profiled in the *Toronto Star*, a month later named a *Best Book for 2014* by Canada's national newspaper the *Globe & Mail*.

Numerous readers writing online thought the book was fiction: that what happened to me couldn't have happened in real life. One person went so far as to say authoritatively that things simply couldn't have taken place as I described them because there was no way police would have handled the raid the way I depicted it. It just doesn't happen that way in reality was her contention. Police, she said, would have read me my rights and followed a strictly legal process so as not to prejudice their case when it came to trial. I wrote back to her pointing out that she lived in the United States, not Canada, where there is no such thing as a Miranda Warning (the right to remain silent; the right to an attorney; if you can't afford an attorney, one will be appointed for you; anything you say can be used against you in court).

I added that most people derive their ideas about what police can and cannot do from fictional American crime shows and movies, when in real life, cases don't conveniently tie up all their story lines in one hour. And I mentioned that most Canadians (a number of whom had contacted me with this same concern), similarly assumed from television and movies that police in Canada, like their U.S. counterparts, are supposed to give Miranda Warnings.

They're not.

One of the more meaningful reviews for me was the one that appeared in the *Vancouver Sun* by columnist Ian Mulgrew, who had written a book called *Bud Inc.* several years before about the history of the marijuana industry in Canada:

> It is difficult to write a memoir at any time, more so when your life has been transformed into a Catch-22 tragedy. Black humour may be the only defence against mental collapse, but it is hard to sustain those ironic guffaws and see the bright side as the bills roll in and one's social world implodes. Paul Illidge does a remarkable job maintaining his perspective. The Bleaks is a *cri de coeur* in the face of the absurd personal destruction wrought by the century-old, ineffective criminal prohibition against cannabis. It would be truly funny, if it weren't true.

As to the title (taken from a chapter in my book, *The Bleaks*: my mother's name for her bouts of depression), I didn't mind it, though it framed the book as one about depression and mental illness when in fact, as one reviewer picked up, the story was meant to come across as a "wild, Kafkaesque black-comedy, teeming with grimly humorous and in many cases tragic ironies about the fallacies inherent in our justice system." It had been nearly five years since I'd signed my publishing contract with Jack David at ECW Press. Fulfilling his request for "More John" had seen the manuscript grow to 110,000 words, 415 published hardcover pages. I was burnt-out, debilitated and looking for closure. I wasn't about to quibble with "The Bleaks."

Shaken by the fury behind the Christmas morning email rather than its deranged contents, I realized when five more email dumps came between Christmas and New Years that John had read the less than flattering portrait of himself in the *More John* chapters that I'd added to the book.

After the fuck you, fuck everything about you tirades, he got down to business, claiming to have met with his lawyers at Gowlings LLP and directed them to sue me for $15 million on grounds of defamation and injury to reputation. He also demanded a **$250,000 cash payment** (Bold font his) from me within thirty days of receipt of his email; my publishers were to have bookstores recall sold copies of *The Bleaks* from customers, and prove to his lawyers that there were none left out there. Unsold copies of the book were to be pulped, full-page retractions were to be published in the major Canadian newspapers, and last but not least, my website was to be taken down.

"Hell hath no fury," said Molly after she read the nutty demands, predicting there would be more malign missives coming from his vodka-addled mind. And there were. Five on New Year's Eve alone, the last one reaching me just as the ball was falling in Time's Square.

Each delivered the same obscenity-laced gush about what he was going to *do to me*, the words *criminal, grow-op, drug dealer, addict, thief* and *fraud* tossed in wherever possible. As well as phrases like "parental favourite," "number one child," "the smart one," "everything handed to you on a platter," "never had to work for anything," "the rest of us living in your shadow." Sibling jealousy on steroids.

But I wasn't to worry about any of that now. He had been spreading the TRUTH to EVERYONE that in reality I wasn't the person they thought they knew. I couldn't hide it anymore. I was a *liar, an addict, a thief, all to pay for my drug habit.* I had shamed the family name. Our parents would have had cardiac arrest reading the SHIT in my so-called book if they were still alive—A DRUG KINGPIN USING YOUR OWN SON AS A FRONT!!! He had reported me to the Chief of Toronto Police, Bill Blair, who owed him a personal favour. *If you thought the raid was bad,* he wrote, *this'll be the wrath of God like you've never seen—and I'll come along and watch the cops haul you off, you crack-head druggie. FUCK YOU! By the time my lawyers and I get finished with you, let's just say YOUR FUCKED!! No, YOUR DEAD!!!*

Molly said she felt as if she'd had a bad, out-of-body experience reading his spew of invective. "Sick puppy hardly covers it."

I put John on my spam list and, *The Bleaks* finally out, moved on with a new book that I'd started, a mystery novel set in eastern Lake Huron cottage-country in early autumn about identical-twin sisters, one of whom is alleged to be a psychopathic killer, but nobody knows which one . . .

January 6th, 2015, the Tuesday after New Years,' I received a phone call from Jack David, my publisher at ECW Press. He'd received a call from *your brother John* to say he was coming in to see Jack and ECW's co-publisher David Caron the next morning. Jack assumed it had to do with *The Bleaks*. I explained about the barrage of crazed, abusive emails John had been sending me starting Christmas Day. I asked that Jack or David take notes of the meeting for legal purposes. I wanted to see whether what John told them corresponded to what his emails were threatening to do to me and my book: kill both me and *The Bleaks*.

As well, in case Jack had forgotten, I reminded him of the rejoinder in the book designed to pre-empt defamation claims, and the provision in my contract that ECW Press couldn't be sued, only I could as author, so they had nothing to worry about, adding what Molly had pointed out: the issue of John suing for loss of reputation was ludicrous since John, as a fraud known to police, had no reputation to lose. And more important, as an undischarged bankrupt he wasn't entitled to sue anyone. *There were people lined up to sue him!*

No word from Jack or David after their meeting, I assumed they'd brought these points to John's attention and thought no more about it. . .

John, using a new email address, recommenced his email onslaught mocking me for how destitute I was and *couldn't afford the price of crack,* while there he was with *bags of money* and new deals closing every week. In fact, he'd given our brother Peter *a chunk of cash* to help him out. At least he cared about Peter, which was more than I could say. He made some jokes about me puffing away on reefers all day long, shooting up with heroin, stoned and out of it all the time NOW THAT YOU'RE WRITING CAREER IS DEAD!! HA-HA!!!

In May, he organized a family get-together at one of his old haunts, an Italian restaurant on Avenue Road south of the 401 Expressway named *Rossini's*. His eldest and youngest daughters were present (their sister having changed her name and moved to England) with their husbands and children, Carson, Nicky and Hannah, my sister Judith, my cousin Heather and her husband, everyone in the "family" present and accounted for, except me, the drug-dealing criminal mastermind who had been ostracized by everyone, thanks to Uncle John.

According to Nicky, who was seated at John's table, he bragged during dinner about how well he was doing, the deals he was putting together *like never before,* strictly leveraged buyouts now because *that's* where the big money was.

Nicky said he was the same old John, no new tricks, the smooth-talking big spender shtick (he reminded people several times that he was picking up the tab for dinner—people should order whatever they wanted). At one point Nicky said John spoke to the waiter in Italian like they were pals from the Old Country. The waiter, an older man, smiling indulgently with an answer in Italian, winking at Nicky as he did so.

In June, I started preparing for a book tour that I had arranged that would take me through upper New York state during July, appearances at bookstores where I'd do a reading from *The Bleaks*, answer questions and sign copies of the memoir. I emailed Jack David my publisher about arrangements for having the U.S. distributor ship fifty copies of the book to each of the six venues where I'd be appearing.

Jack wrote back saying that unfortunately he couldn't do that. ECW had discontinued selling *The Bleaks* at the beginning of January, after my brother had come in to tell them he was suing them for defamation. Jack and his co-publisher, David, had decided, based on their conversation with John, that he was serious, was to be believed, and therefore stopped selling the memoir, asking bookstores to return copies to the distributor. Unless I could prove the things I'd written about John in the book were true, the book would remain discontinued. Or, I could rewrite the offending sections where John felt he had been defamed, in which case they could reprint the book with the corrected text—with costs borne by me of course— but they would at least be able to distribute the book again.

Jack claimed he had sent me an email to that effect in January.

I told him I never received such an email.

He maintained that he'd sent it.

I maintained that it couldn't have been sent: wouldn't any author have replied to his publisher if he received word that his book had been cancelled? Wouldn't a publisher have found it strange *not* to have heard back from an author under such circumstances?

*You told me you had nothing to fear,* I blasted Jack. *Now you're running scared from a person known to police and the courts as a criminal fraud, rather than standing up for the honesty and integrity of your author.*

Hadn't they bothered to check, as I'd asked them to, with their own lawyer about bankruptcy law, which prevents bankrupts from filing such lawsuits? Hadn't they gone on the internet and googled John's name, as I'd told them to? Hadn't they asked their lawyer to check on his record with the police, the attorney-general's office, his bankruptcy trustee, as I'd told them to? Hadn't they even called Gowlings LLP to verify that this person who had effectively strolled in off the street and announced a multi-million dollar lawsuit was actually a Gowlings client? Why, rather than believe the author they'd worked with for five years, and in whom they and government arts councils had invested nearly $30,000 in publishing grants, had they chosen to accede to the demands of a convicted fraud and undischarged bankrupt and so readily betray their author's interests, rights, efforts and achievement in writing the book, just to protect themselves from the taint of a lawsuit that could never take place?

I was outraged as much by their unprofessionalism and legal incompetence as by their cowardice. John had hit them in the jugular, their area of maximum vulnerability, scaring them into submission by reminding Jack and David (John would have done his due diligence) that ECW Press was government-funded, and, like all subsidized publishers, lived or died by their various levels of government grants. John knew that with the merest whiff of legal action they would crumple, cancel an author's book and heave him overboard as excess baggage.

They ended our professional relationship three months after my book had come out (and was selling about fifty copies a week) based on John's threat, deeming me guilty, leaving me no opportunity to defend myself and what I'd accurately written in the book. Worst of all, no notice from John's vaunted lawyers regarding an impending action ever materialized, a blatant sign of lawsuit fraud.

Jack and David fell for the bluff, ignoring the fact that in three places where John had mentioned I'd defamed him, I had actually written positively about him, and in four others, regarding his financial, legal and business activities, every detail I included could be verified in a ten-second Google search.

The one page John told Jack David and David Caron that he found most derogatory of all had nothing to do with him.

He hadn't read the book. I knew he hadn't. It was a perfect con to make two gullible government-subsidized publishers complicit in the fraud by taking his word over mine; all the more hurtful to me because he'd manipulated them into selling me out and ending my book's life with such ease. Rewrite the sections that John identified as ones where I had "lied" about him and replace them with the "truth?" They would insert the new pages in the file and print up corrected books, at my expense? So much for publisher disclaimers . . .

It was a different kind of ending on July 9th, a Tuesday. Nicky checked his texts while making breakfast. There was one from his mother telling him she had noticed on Facebook that his Uncle Peter had died. He googled the obituary:

ILLIDGE, Peter William, August 3, 1955 – July 7, 2019.

Peter died at home, in his apartment, on Sunday, July 7th, aged 63, after a decade long struggle with pulmonary fibrosis. In 2013/14 he had become homeless for some months and at the time of his death was supported by the Ontario Disability Services program.

His fascination with how things work and his talent for photography led Peter to his career in the processing department at Black's Photography during the 1980s and 1990s. As the camera world turned digital, Peter decided to use his trade skills and love of flora to become the go-to handyman and gardener for many families in the Avenue Road and Eglinton West area of North Toronto. Peter's indomitable spirit and positive outlook, against all odds, his work ethic and never-surrender attitude touched many hearts along The Eglinton Way. He will be missed.

I knew the announcement about my younger brother's death had been written by Carolyn and Peter O'Brian, family friends through our parents, who had saved Peter from "the street" and put together a "Peter Committee" to make the last years of his life free from struggle. Peter O. had called me when the committee was getting underway several years earlier to let me know that Pete was thriving as much as a guy in his condition could (he had lung cancer). A memorial service was to be held on Saturday the 20th. I phoned Peter O. to let him know that I would deliver a eulogy.

Four days later, Nicky again making breakfast, a friend of his texted to say he had just heard on *680 Toronto News* that a man named John Illidge had been arrested on Friday morning and charged with running a $1 million dollar Ponzi scheme. *Was he a relative?*

# CHAPTER THIRTY

# THE WOLF AT BAY

## TORONTO STAR

### MAN ARRESTED AFTER INVESTORS LOSE $1 MILLION IN PONZI SCHEME

By Sherina Harris

July 13th, 2019

Toronto police made an arrest Friday after they say a man obtained almost $1 million through a Ponzi scheme.

Between 2009 and 2017, numerous people met a man through social media sites. 'He portrayed himself as an investor for different companies,' police said in a Saturday news release.

People gave him money ranging from $20,000 to $500,000 to invest in companies they were told the man either worked for or owned, police said.

The total amount obtained was $955,980.50, according to police.

Police say the funds were used for money transfers, cash withdrawals, car purchases and car payments, department store purchases, food and personal purchases.

The man provided people with small amounts of money 'portrayed as investment payments over a year or two to make them think they were profiting,' police said. But later attempts to reach the man were unsuccessful.

The investigation began in January 2018.

On Friday, John James Illidge, 66, of no fixed address, was charged with five counts of fraud over $5,000, five counts of theft over $5,000, four counts of laundering proceeds of crime and four counts of pos-

256

sessing property obtained by crime over $5,000.

Anyone with information is asked to contact police or Crime Stoppers anonymously by phone or online. . ."

Apparently he'd been on the run and was holed up in a triplex on Royal York Road in south Etobicoke, West Toronto. Police raided the unit at 5:30 a.m. Friday morning, arrested John and charged him with eighteen counts of fraud, and other Criminal Code offenses (meaning they were indictable and on conviction would result in imprisonment). He appeared in court later that morning and was remanded to the maximum security Toronto South Detention Centre in Mimico, West Toronto.

I obtained the charge sheet for the arrest several days later. Karen Morris, I was pleased to see, was the first plaintiff on the list. All counts were specified as Criminal Code offenses. *Count 1*: defrauded Karen Morris of money with a value exceeding $5,000. *Count 2*: stole from Karen Morris $5,000+. *Count 3*: laundered the above proceeds of crime. *Count 4*: did possess the above stolen money.

The charge count for the other four plaintiffs was the same: fraud, theft, money-laundering the proceeds of crime. Except for Karen Morris, who'd had to wait nine years for this day, the frauds took place between May 2015 and August 2018, when the police investigation began. In my jubilation I sent Karen Morris an email saying I hoped she'd heard the news. I didn't hear back. I didn't expect to.

On Wednesday of the following week the media announced that John's associate Vince Phillips, 74, had been arrested and charged with the same eighteen offences as John.

I wondered about this. Vince was clearly a subordinate, a friend of John's, an accomplice perhaps, but certainly not a partner. In the parlance of predatory fraud he was what is known as *the set-up man*, his job to furnish John with potential investors or, again in fraud parlance, *marks*. Vince could well not even have known that the investment opportunities John was touting were parts of an elaborate Ponzi scheme. Brains weren't required of a set-up man. Unquestioning loyalty was what Vince brought to the operation—as shown by writing off the forged ten-thousand dollar checks as *just a big mix up*. But that would be irrelevant in court: whether he knew it or not, Vince had aided and abetted John's frauds. He was complicit. He could be prosecuted.

But it occurred to me that Vince's arrest might also have been a tactical move on the part of the police. By arresting him on the same charges as John they made him an accomplice. This would scare him into testifying as a prosecution witness, giving the full picture of how the Ponzi scheme operated in return for consideration at plea-bargaining time.

Whether Vince had made bail or not I couldn't find out, but I knew that John hadn't. Still in shock that there had actually been an arrest after nearly thirty years, I called the South Detention Centre on Friday, asked if John Illidge had made bail and was told that John James Illidge was *still there*, two words of relief. I now understood their meaning for crime victims at mention of their perpetrators remaining incarcerated. I could breathe a little easier knowing that John wasn't going anywhere anytime soon.

Nicky and I arrived a few minutes late for my brother Peter's memorial gathering at the funeral home Saturday morning. The speeches had already begun. My sister Judith was talking. The small room packed, my friend Peter O. spotted me standing at the back of the room, came over and shook my hand, glad that I could make it.

Judith finished talking. Peter O. brought me forward during the applause, introduced me, then stepped off to one side beside my ex-wife Jill and my cousin Heather. As I started to speak, Jill and Heather joined hands with my sister Judith, the three of them turning and, chins held haughtily high, made their way through the puzzled guests to the back of the room, walking across the hall and into a smaller room where refreshments were set up on a table—the three of them laughing (I could see them from the podium) at the protest they'd just staged boycotting my eulogy.

Stunned and disgusted, I thought for a second of breaking the confused silence by calling them out for their stunt: telling them to return to the room and explain to the rest of us why they had done the most disrespectful thing of all walking out in protest during a eulogy—ask them why they bothered coming to the memorial in the first place when they knew I'd be speaking?

But I didn't. I talked about Peter being four years younger than me, the baby of the family until our sister Judith came along seven years later. I explained that Peter was what at the time was known as a "blue baby" (born with the cord around his neck, starving the brain of oxygen for a few minutes) and thus would always, according to psychologists, be *slow*.

This proved to be so only in the academic school setting. His marks were always low. He was identified as a "*slow* learner" and was sent to a special school for the *slow*. In those days *slow* was a euphemism for mentally retarded.

Once Peter entered the real world of life he continued to be *slow* (often infuriatingly so). But when he was twelve, one of his teachers announced that he was an autodidact (someone who could teach himself), and by the time he was sixteen he'd taught himself how to learn.

He could talk to anyone on any subject; he could fix, repair, rebuild and revive anything mechanical with an almost mystical ability. He knew current events. He read books, preferably manuals on how to repair things. He had no compunction about talking to people recognized as experts in their fields.

He was never intimidated because he saw so much of life as a learning experience. He loved using his learning to help people, often refusing to take money for work he did unless it was pressed upon him.

He was friendly, gregarious, as positive and well-meaning a person as you could ever hope to meet. He liked and enjoyed people so much and he always expected they would like him back.

I came to think of Peter not so much as *slow* but as someone who simply *preferred to take his time* with life. *Why?* I once asked him. *Because it's less stressful that way, and more to the point, there's only so much time available to us.* Wise words from the master of slow in an increasingly speedy world.

My final point along these lines was that Peter was an *idiot savant*. Among the anecdotes explaining what I meant by the savant part had to do with things such as the incident that occurred when, at the age of nine, he took our broken gas-powered lawnmower apart, put it back together again in less than an hour, pulled the cord and the machine roared to life louder than ever.

As to the idiot part, my final illustration was the story of the two of us driving across Canada, reaching western Vancouver Island on a 92-degrees-in-the-shade day in 1977 twelve days after leaving Toronto. Arriving at the beach at Ucluelet, we jumped out of the hot car, ran down to the water and charged in, Peter shouting as he splashed around: *"Isn't this great? The Atlantic Ocean!!"*

John made five appearances in court for bail hearings over the next six weeks, but as no one showed up to act as surety, the hearings, unsurprisingly, never commenced. Who in their right mind would put up $75,000 to bail out a career fraud, have him living with you for the two or three years until his trial, during which time you were responsible for him twenty-four hours a day, seven days a week? His daughters couldn't. All his friends had abandoned him years ago. And Vince Phillips, the only hope he had to act as surety, was who knows where among the fifteen-hundred other inmates at Toronto South.

As well, with a case this complex, John was going to need a top lawyer who could commit to the formidable workload that would come with defending him on eighteen charges. Costs would run into the hundreds of thousands since each victim's counts comprised a separate court case.

Even if he could have afforded it, John wouldn't have shelled out that kind of money. In the end he always acted as his own lawyer, becoming such a pain with his *delay, delay, delay* tactics that there was still no record of convictions against him; all his cases were in abeyance, in limbo until he could find himself a lawyer who was *just the right fit.*

On September 26th, at John's request, his case was transferred to the mental health court at Old City Hall where, acting as his own lawyer, he asked that all charges against him be dismissed on grounds of severe mental illness. He appeared five more times in mental health court, his request for release on mental health grounds denied on each occasion until on November 4th his case was transferred back to the courthouse on Finch Avenue West where he had originally been booked. Wise to his gambit, the court determined that he was not mentally ill and was fit to stand trial . . .

The months passed. I phoned the jail every few weeks just to hear the clerk say, with firm but understanding reassurance: *Yes, Mr. Illidge, your brother is still here.*

Still in the worst jail in Canada, still suffering through the facility's frequent lockdowns when there was a prisoner incident, a technical issue (it was a fully computerized jail) or a guard shortage, which there often was due to the new provincial direct supervision rules whereby guards mixed in with the general population, one guard to every forty inmates, the stress of such close interaction with murderers and violent offenders very often unmanageable. Lockdown meant prisoners were locked in their cells (two prisoners to an eight by sixteen-foot cell) twenty-three hours a day, for days and sometimes weeks at a time. The atmosphere had been described in a government report as "barbaric." I couldn't see the situation for a manic, obsessive-compulsive, controlling person like John being anything but utterly excruciating every second of every day.

In March 2020, John starting his ninth month in Toronto South, I managed to get in touch with the arresting officer with some questions.

"You're the older brother," he said when I introduced myself. "The writer."

"How did you know that?" I said, taken aback.

"I did my research. Though I'm not going to read *The Bleaks* until after your brother's case is done."

I told him that was nice to hear. That the book I was working on now might be of more interest from a police perspective. "It's been over eight months now, Officer D. I was wondering what the prospects were for a trial sometime soon?"

"Are you kidding? Soon is completely out of the question. It's a very complicated case with multiple counts and five victims. We're probably looking at a trial two years from now, that's if everything runs smoothly, and it never does. Which is why we can't understand why he's in no hurry to be bailed out."

"Who wants to bail out a fraud criminal, Officer D.?"

"There's that."

"I know my brother. He's in for the long haul. Making the justice system earn their money. He has none himself, no friends, no place to live, and he's a bankrupt. In jail he's fed and clothed, and has a warm place to sleep."

"Plus medical attention. He does have some health issues. Blood pressure I think."

Officer D. didn't want to disappoint me but, being realistic, he said there was a possibility that John would do enough pre-trial jail time that in the end he might walk, since he'll be given one-third of a day's credit for each day he's incarcerated.

I said lightly: "Facing life on the street, he might be sorry to leave."

"He wouldn't be the first . . ."

And so, as of April 18, 2020, John James Illidge, 67 now, sits in the Toronto South Detention Centre knocking time off his eventual sentence and, if I know him, dreaming up more schemes for when he's released. *"I'll think of something,"* he said to me once in the early days when his financial situation was perilous. *"I always do."*

Unsurprisingly, the questions I'm most often asked about John are: What made him *go bad* in the first place? Why did he turn to a life of serial fraud? Was there really $100 million hidden somewhere in an offshore bank that he just couldn't get to?

*Who knows?* is the convenient answer I give. How can anyone ever know, really, especially with someone like John whose relationship to the truth ever since he was a boy has always been casual at best? As to the $100 million in an offshore bank somewhere, that's a secret I know John, with his compulsive need to be in control, will take with him to the grave.

The inconvenient answer, the one that I only understand now as I end my story, goes this way:

It's August 3rd, 1959, my brother Peter's fourth birthday. John is six and I am eight. We're at the cottage on Gull Lake in Haliburton walking down Sandy Bay Road to Mrs. Austin's store with my mother. She's going to buy ice cream to have with Peter's birthday cake tonight. We bump into Mrs. Fryer, a neighbour down the road who hasn't been at her cottage until now. We stop so they can talk, Mrs. Fryer smiling, setting one hand on my head and the other on Peter's, ruffling our blond curls. "They're perfect angels, Bev."

John with his brush-cut black hair, a hurt look on his face, cocks his hands on his hips and steps up to her:

"What does that make me then?"

# ACKNOWLEDGEMENTS

. . . Ann and Wayne Tompkins for their unstinting kindness and generosity.

. . . Michael O'Brien for his constant encouragement.

. . . Molly Conners for all her help and agreeing to be in the book.

. . . My children Nicholas, Carson and Hannah for being there during the craziness, and allowing me to include them in the story.

. . . Jeffrey Miller of Irwin Law Publishers for suggesting and supporting the writing of the first draft of the manuscript.

. . . Rebecca Bynum who read a chapter of the book in an online magazine and said that she wanted to publish *RSKY BZNS*.

. . . Kendra Mallock for a brilliant cover that captures the spirit at the heart of the book.

# ABOUT THE AUTHOR

**Paul Illidge** writes investigative nonfiction books on important issues of today in a thriller-fiction style. His belief is that life is moving at such a breathless pace, writing has to keep up or it won't be able to attract and hold people's attention. He started the series with *The Bleaks*, a *Globe & Mail* Best Book of 2014. His *Shakespeare Novels* revolutionized North American high school English teaching and continue to sell around the world. *The Page, the Stage, the Digital Age* predicted a surprise future for 21st century technology. *RSKY BZNS* is his 15th book.

CPSIA information can be obtained
at www.ICGtesting.com
Printed in the USA
LVHW011625220622
721852LV00008B/84